THE ETHICAL PROFESSOR

The purpose of *The Ethical Professor* is to provide a road map to some of the ethical dilemmas that doctoral students and newer faculty members are likely to face as they enter a career in academia (the Academy). Academic career paths appear to be quite standard, transparent, and achievable with dedicated and hard work. Argued in this book, however, is that the road map to a successful academic career is not so easy. There are ethical pitfalls along the way, starting with entry into academia as a new PhD student. These ethical dilemmas remain equally opaque as faculty progress in their careers.

The ethical pitfalls that plague each of the steps along the academic career path are often not visible to doctoral students and young faculty members; nor are they well prepared to spot them. Ethical issues are seldom discussed and little training is provided on how to spot and handle these potential road blocks to a successful career in the academy.

Based on extant research and collective years of academic experience, *The Ethical Professor* seeks to shorten the learning curve around common ethical pitfalls and issues by defining them, sharing research and experiences about them, and offering a discussion framework for continued learning and reflection.

This innovative new volume will be key reading for doctoral students and junior faculty members in social science departments in colleges and universities, as well as managers undertaking an MBA. Due to the increasing complexity of managing academic institutions, more seasoned professors, administrators, and college deans and presidents, will also benefit from the research presented here.

Lorraine Eden is the Gina and Anthony Bahr Professor in Business in the Department of Management at Texas A&M University.

Kathy Lund Dean is the Board of Trustees Distinguished Professor of Leadership and Ethics at Gustavus Adolphus College.

Paul M. Vaaler is the John and Bruce Mooty Chair in Law and Business at the University of Minnesota's Law School and Carlson School of Management.

THE ETHICAL PROFESSOR

A Practical Guide to Research, Teaching, and Professional Life

Lorraine Eden, Kathy Lund Dean, and Paul M. Vaaler

Routledge
Taylor & Francis Group

NEW YORK AND LONDON

First published 2018
by Routledge
711 Third Avenue, New York, NY 10017

and by Routledge
2 Park Square, Milton Park, Abingdon, Oxon OX14 4RN

Routledge is an imprint of the Taylor & Francis Group, an informa business

© 2018 Taylor & Francis

The right of Lorraine Eden, Kathy Lund Dean, and Paul M. Vaaler to be
identified as the authors of this work has been asserted by them in accordance
with sections 77 and 78 of the Copyright, Designs and Patents Act 1988.

Library of Congress Cataloging in Publication Data
Names: Eden, Lorraine, author. | Dean, Kathy Lund, author. | Vaaler, Paul
M., author.
Title: The ethical professor : a practical guide to research, teaching and
professional life / Lorraine Eden, Kathy Lund Dean, and Paul M. Vaaler.
Description: 1 Edition. | New York : Routledge, 2018. | Includes index.
Identifiers: LCCN 2017054432| ISBN 9780815387053 (hardback) | ISBN
9781138485983 (pbk.) | ISBN 9781351049429 (ebook)
Subjects: LCSH: College teaching--Moral and ethical aspects. | College
teachers--Professional ethics. | Social sciences--Study and teaching (Higher)--
Moral and ethical aspects.
Classification: LCC LB2331 .E363 2018 | DDC 174/.9378125--dc23
LC record available at https://lccn.loc.gov/2017054432

ISBN: 978-0-8153-8705-3 (hbk)
ISBN: 978-1-138-48598-3 (pbk)
ISBN: 978-1-351-04942-9 (ebk)

Typeset in Bembo
by Taylor & Francis Books

MIX
Paper from
responsible sources
FSC™ C013985
www.fsc.org

Printed in the United Kingdom
by Henry Ling Limited

This book would not have been possible without our academic communities of colleagues and students. We also dedicate the book to our patient and supportive spouses.

CONTENTS

ILLUSTRATIONS

Figure

Tables

1

INTRODUCTION

You're on Your Way…

You have just landed your dream job – a tenure-track assistant professorship in your top-ranked choice for department and college. Your dissertation is done and defended. You've moved to your new university home; hung up pictures and your diploma on the walls in your new office; prepared and posted your course syllabuses; and are ready for the new semester. Congratulations!

The road ahead to tenure and promotion as an associate professor looks reasonably straightforward. You know that in your new academic home, faculty are judged on their performance on three metrics: research, teaching, and service (often referred to as the "Big Three"). In terms of research, in many departments (e.g., economics, management, or law) that means you need to turn your dissertation into several papers, published preferably in the top journals in your field. Or, your home may be in a department where a book published by a top university press is required (e.g., political science or international affairs). In terms of research, before the tenure clock runs out, you know that you need to have enough top-tier publications that your colleagues and external reviewers will judge your research performance as worthy of tenure and promotion. In terms of teaching, you know you must teach one or more courses each semester and get good (preferably great) student evaluations from your students. Lastly, you need to engage in some service activities both at your institution as well as in your professional association. The service dimension also looks reasonably straightforward.

However… lurking just below the surface of these three performance metrics are a variety of pitfalls – roadblocks, if you prefer to call them that – that can derail your plans for tenure and promotion and your movement up the ladder to career success in the Academy.[1] These roadblocks are mostly invisible and little discussed among your colleagues so it is easy to not see them and make mistakes. What are they? Ethical dilemmas. An ethical dilemma occurs when individuals must make a difficult choice where values, rights, and/or responsibilities are potentially in conflict. Dilemmas are not clear cut – right or wrong – but rather choices between options with differing benefits and costs.

Purpose and Scope

As academics, we are judged annually in performance reviews based on our activities and accomplishments on research, teaching, and service. From the time we are admitted to graduate school as young PhD students through the time when we become senior faculty members in the Academy, we are "programmed" to be assessed regularly in terms of our performance.

Academic career paths appear to be quite standard, transparent, and achievable with dedication and hard work. However, we argue in this book that the road map to a successful academic career is not so easy. We know there are many ethical pitfalls along the academic life cycle. The ethical dilemmas that plague each of the steps along the academic career path are often not visible to doctoral students and young faculty members, nor are they well prepared to spot them. Ethical dilemmas are generally not discussed with or by the thousands of doctoral students and junior faculty in the Academy. Little to no training is provided on how to spot and handle these potential road blocks to a successful academic career. Moreover, these pitfalls can remain equally opaque as faculty progress in their careers to full and senior professors.

Based on extant research, our collective years of academic experience, and our own teaching and writings about ethics, we know that ethical pitfalls in an academic career life are not systematically brought to light during doctoral training, early career experiences, or even as we become more seasoned professionals. The purpose of our book is to highlight some of the most likely ethical pitfalls and suggest ways that doctoral students and junior faculty can prepare for and handle them. We argue that recognizing a decision as an ethical dilemma is the starting point, and that once recognized, there are ways to better handle it. In our book, we hope to shorten the learning curve around what we view as the most common ethical dilemmas by defining them, sharing research and experiences about them, and offering a discussion framework for continued learning and reflection.

The book is organized as follows. This chapter, the introduction, provides a brief history of how we came to write the book, an overview of the main topics, and an explanation of how the book can be used in the classroom and work-shops. The main body of the book is divided into three parts, corresponding to the Big Three performance metrics on which faculty are judged: research, teaching, and service (professional life). The chapters in each part are roughly in chronological order, paralleling the academic life cycle from PhD student through promotion with tenure. Each chapter starts with key insights, follows with the body of the chapter, and ends with discussion questions and additional reading. The book includes multiple short cases and discussion questions that can be used to stimulate discussion in workshops and the classroom. Each of the three main parts also includes an interview with a well-known "thought leader" on ethics. The last chapter in the book, Connecting the Dots, summarizes the themes in each of the three parts (research, teaching, and professional life) and then discusses common themes and key insights across all three parts. The chapter concludes with some thoughts looking to the future for doctoral students and junior faculty in the Academy.

Who Should Read This Book

We view the core audience for this book as doctoral students and junior faculty members in social science departments in colleges and universities in Canada and the United States. Our book was written particularly for this audience.

We believe the book will also be useful for and of interest to three additional groups. First, our book should be useful for doctoral students and junior faculty outside of the social sciences, for example, in liberal arts, the physical sciences, and other professional schools. All of these disciplines are facing increasing pressures from external stakeholders to provide more transparency into what happens inside academia. While the norms and standards differ across the disciplines, the core ideas and philosophies are similar across academia. We share a commitment to high-quality research, teaching, and practice; to academic freedom, diversity, and inclusiveness; and to transparency and accountability.

Second, we believe our book will also be useful for doctoral students and junior faculty in countries outside of Canada and the United States, including both developed and emerging economies. North American academic norms are diffusing to universities and colleges of higher learning around the world. The same pressures to publish in "top-tier" journals (most of which have US-based publishers) face young professors whether they are located in Western Europe or Asia or South America. The same ethical dilemmas in teaching or service are likely to be even stronger in countries where corruption is rife and diversity issues (e.g., gender, race, or color) are viewed as unimportant.

Lastly, while we have aimed our book at doctoral students and untenured faculty, we believe our book is also useful for other faculty groups including non-tenure track lecturers, associate and full professors, administrators, and college deans and presidents. The increasing complexity of managing academic institutions and the proliferation of non-tenure track faculty (now more than 50 percent in many academic institutions) are well-known issues. For these groups, we also offer later career-stage dilemma identification and discussion points.

Who We Are

The three authors of this book are all tenured full professors in US colleges and universities. Lorraine Eden is a professor in the Management Department in the Mays Business School at Texas A&M University, College Station, Texas. Her graduate courses are also cross-listed as courses in the departments of International Affairs and Economics. Kathy Lund Dean is a professor in the Economics and Management Department at Gustavus Adolphus College, St. Peter, Minnesota. Paul Vaaler is a professor in the Carlson School of Management at the University of Minnesota, Minneapolis, Minnesota, where he also holds a cross-appointment in the School of Law. Lorraine began her career as a lecturer in 1971, Kathy as an assistant professor in 1997, and Paul as an assistant professor in 1996, so together as of October 2017 we are now celebrating a total of 87 years as members of the Academy!

We all hold endowed positions and have received many awards and honors over our academic careers. As researchers, we have published multiple books and hundreds of journal articles. Kathy and Lorraine have been editors-in-chief and Paul associate editor at major journals. Our research and teaching interests span a wide variety of areas in business, economics, law, management, and political science. We have held and currently hold a variety of administrative and leadership roles in our universities and various professional societies. We have served as outside commentators, advisors, and consultants to individuals, firms, foundations, government agencies, the media, and international organizations.

What drew us together – and led to this book – is our shared interest in ethics. Kathy holds a chair in ethics at Gustavus Adolphus College and teaches courses in ethics. Lorraine is writing her third code of ethics for the Academy of International Business and teaches workshops on ethics in research. Paul has taught managerial ethics at the University of Minnesota's Carlson School and legal ethics at the University of Minnesota's School of Law. All three of us have many and varied publications on ethics. In addition, for nearly four years (July 2011–February 2015) we were the inaugural writers on ethical issues for the Academy of Management (AOM) blog, "The Ethicist."

Looking Back: From the Academy of Management's "The Ethicist" to This Book

The AOM ethics blog had its genesis in the *New York Times Magazine*'s weekly column "The Ethicist," written by Randy Cohen from 2003 to 2011. Lorraine Eden was addicted to reading Cohen's column, which she saw as offering useful insights into ethical dilemmas that faced individuals in their personal and professional lives.

In 2007, newly appointed as editor-in-chief of the *Journal of International Business Studies* (JIBS), Lorraine had written the first JIBS Code of Ethics. In 2010, she chaired a committee tasked with writing an ethics code for the Academy of International Business; Paul Vaaler was also a member of that committee. As these activities were winding down, Lorraine accepted an invitation from James Davis and Susan Madsen, co-chairs of the AOM's Ethics Education Committee (EEC), to join the EEC.

At the time, the EEC was looking for new ways to communicate with AOM members about ethical issues, and Lorraine saw an opportunity to develop an ethics blog similar to the *New York Times'* "The Ethicist" column. Both the EEC and the AOM leadership endorsed the idea as a "Strategic Doing" initiative. Lorraine invited Kathy Lund Dean and Paul Vaaler to join her as the three co-bloggers and AOM's "The Ethicist" blog went live in July 2011. Lorraine was responsible for the blog and for posts on ethics in research, Kathy for ethics in teaching, and Paul for ethics in professional life.

For each of us, writing "The Ethicist" was a labor of love. It was a 100 percent volunteer activity; we were not paid by nor received any financial support from AOM. For the first two years, the blog was available only to AOM members, but in May 2013, the blog moved to a publicly available website address: ethicist. aom.org. We continued to blog regularly until February 2015 when, after nearly four years of involvement with "The Ethicist," we decided it was time to retire and "pass the baton" to a new group of bloggers.

After stepping down in 2015, we began to think and talk about how to save the content we had written. We knew that our blog posts were more similar to research notes than to a typical blog; for example, our posts were much longer and included references to the academic literature on ethics. A small group of volunteer faculty were invited to read our posts and provide feedback before we finalized them, thus providing a peer-review process and helping to ensure that our posts were of high quality. Because we had consulted regularly throughout the years of working and writing together, our blog posts had a synergy when read together, providing a conceptual flow that we believed could move to book form. We also believed that a book on ethics in academia would fill a hole in the available resources to doctoral students and young faculty members on how to navigate the tricky waters of a successful academic career.

So we selected the best and most useful of our blog posts, rewrote, and updated them as book chapters to reflect the most recent thinking (as of October 2017) on each topic. We also added new chapters to the book to fill missing holes on key topic areas. We arranged the chapters to parallel the stages in a young academic's career from new PhD student through tenure and promotion to associate professor in our universities and colleges. We kept the division of the book into the three parts corresponding to the Big Three performance metrics of research, teaching, and professional life. Although we have jointly written and rewritten each other's chapters several times in writing this book, the careful reader will probably still be able to hear our distinctive "voices" in each of the three core parts to the book.

Unique Features of This Book

First, the book occupies a unique ethics niche in the pantheon of books on life in the Academy by bringing together issues that can be found in disparate ethics works into one volume. There are a variety of books on ethics in research or ethics in teaching, for example, but very few that examine ethical dilemmas involved in all three performance metrics.

Second, we believe strongly in the value of ethics education to equip members of our profession to weather the inevitable ethical challenges they will face. We hope that our readers will find the diversity of our backgrounds and our multi-disciplinary approach to ethics in the Academy together serve to provide readers with experiences they can relate to their own examples and situations.

Third, we have provided, where possible, disguised but detailed accounts of dilemmas our colleagues or students have actually faced, along with the unique feature of "the rest of the story" or how the situation was resolved. Each of us writes from a place of deep understanding of salient and timely topics, and we provide references and other support materials for each chapter.

Perhaps most importantly, our book provides strongly practical advice, helping readers move from reflection to action. Our approaches are fundamentally rooted in behavioral ethics, using research and experience to inform recommendations for action, while drawing on classic models and ways of thinking about ethics to ground the discussion for a broad audience. Although there are a variety of other books within the broad domain of ethics in academic life, we believe our book is unique in its focus on specific, actionable, and common ethical issues that may be experienced at each career life stage in the Academy.

How This Book Can Be Used

The book is designed for active engagement! Individuals from any of the groups we have identified as our potential readers should find our book helpful as a guide to what types of ethical issues might be faced at any stage of their career, and may find examples hit close to home.

An ideal setting for ethics discussions among doctoral students is in a course offered during the first year of a PhD program. Many graduate students arrive with little idea of what their course of study will include, let alone the trajectory of co-curricular work with junior and senior faculty and departmental staff. This book will provide those graduate students with an introduction to various ethical issues that swirl about those first-year curricular and co-curricular routines. Pairing this book with a first-year PhD course offered within a department, or across departments, will start important discussions and awareness early on for graduate students.

Ethical issues related to research are likely to dominate early discussions, with graduate students often occupied with a PhD course typically comprised of dozens of journal articles for review and analysis. But reference to teaching and professional life issues can also find a place in a PhD course – think, for example, how findings in journal articles are translated into MBA and undergraduate course topics, or how journal articles often begin as early-stage research presentations at professional meetings. Today, when PhD courses of study last from four to six years, thoughtful discussion and awareness of ethical issues in the first year will yield multi-year benefits both to the graduate students and the departments of which they are part.

An additional setting in which to use this book with junior faculty is at professional meetings, typically annual meetings of the academic associations that junior faculty and their senior faculty colleagues deem critical to attend and present at regularly. For business school academics, that might be the AOM annual meetings; for social scientists, the Allied Social Sciences Association meetings.

Annual meetings typically offer junior faculty career development workshops, styled as consortia, which are meant to share career experiences and best practices (and a few not-so-great ones) with peers. Senior academics typically comprise the faculty leading these consortia, and they have broad discretion on what to cover over a half or full day. This book fits very well in the pre-consortia reading list. Its inclusion will give consortia attendees a common understanding of ethical issues related to research, teaching, and professional life relevant to their careers right away, in the run-up to tenure and promotion review, and in the immediate aftermath. Discussion questions posed at the end of each chapter can serve as the basis for role-playing simulations involving consortia faculty and attendees. Where annual meetings also offer consortia for graduate students about how to finish their dissertation and go to the academic job market, this book can facilitate a similarly rich learning experience for faculty and attendees. In either setting, this book can provide valuable learning-by-reading and learning-by-doing in consortia settings.

We think this book is also useful as a reference for senior faculty charged with mentoring graduate students and junior faculty in the department or college. Sometimes it is difficult to broach ethical issues at all, let alone explain and work through them in ways that a fourth-year doctoral candidate or first-year assistant professor will find relevant. Think, for example, of how to tell when students in a course are getting "too close" to the assistant professor leading the course. Think, for another example, of when a faculty job offer is sufficiently detailed to merit the doctoral candidate's consideration and timely reply. Our book may help to bridge the gap between mentor experience and articulation for mentees. In the office, over lunch in the university cafeteria, or in a reading group, senior faculty mentors can use this book to identify, describe, and discuss these and other ethical issues with graduate students and junior faculty. Our book may also help to depersonalize the mentor–mentee process in useful ways. Our own experience with ethical issues may not have always been the best experience – we three co-authors will attest to that. Senior faculty can use examples in the book, rather than their own experience, to start a discussion that will help mentees gain a practical understanding of how best to navigate issues we found difficult to navigate years ago.

An Invitation

We invite you to engage with this work, and would be delighted to hear from your experiences with and reactions to anything you read here. As a book, the format is less interactive than as a blog, and some of our favorite moments were getting reader comments on each blog posting and starting a conversation in real time. However, our email is always available and we look forward to your comments, improvements, and examples.

Acknowledgments

No published work is ever the result of the work of the authors; we are all "standing on the shoulders" of many other people who provided help and support along the way. We are grateful for the years-long support and encouragement we have received during this project from many different quarters.

First, our initial vision for and implementation of AOM's "The Ethicist" benefited enormously from advice and help from James Davis and Susan Madsen, Ethics Education Committee Co-Chairs, and Terese Loncar, AOM Associate Executive Director, Programs and Services. Members of the Ethics Education Committee provided helpful comments on many of the blog posts. While blogging, we also harnessed the expertise and critical eyes of many colleagues each time we wrote. Some of the wonderful colleagues who made suggestions to our blog drafts that foundationally improved them included Chi Anyansi-Archibong, Jean Bartunek, Karen Butler-Purry, John Cantwell, Laura Hammons, Benson Honig, Susan Jackson, David Kaplan, Janet Salmons, Anne Tsui, Erik van Raaij, and Sarah Wright.

Early and helpful advice in 2015 on moving this project from blog posts to a book was provided by David Pervin, who at the time was a journals editor at the University of Chicago Press. Early help was also provided from staff and graduate students at Texas A&M. We are grateful to Deanna Johnston and Kevin McSweeney who helped put our initial blog postings together and made suggestions as to how to improve them so they could be read as a coherent whole. We thank Shreya Gandotra for editing the references and Jenner Bate for providing editorial comments on the manuscript. Lastly, we are grateful to Stuart Youngblood (Emeritus, Texas Christian University) for his thorough review comments and encouragement.

Two of the chapters in this book were co-authored as blog postings and we want to thank the co-authors for allowing us to include revised versions of the posts in our book: Chapter 2, "Twenty Questions," was co-authored with Kevin

McSweeney and Chapter 9, "Ethics in Research Scenarios," with James Davis and Susan Madsen. We also want to thank our three "thought leaders," Michael Hitt (Chapter 10), Robert Giacalone (Chapter 20), and Andrew Van de Ven (Chapter 30), for their willingness to share their experiences and knowledge.

Our departments and universities were also important contributors to the success of this manuscript. Lorraine appreciates the help from Texas A&M University, both during her years of writing for "The Ethicist" and through the book process. Kathy appreciated the support from both of the institutions at which she worked while writing for "The Ethicist": Idaho State University (Pocatello, Idaho) and Gustavus Adolphus College (St. Peter, Minnesota). Her department chairman at Idaho State, James P. Jolly, was particularly helpful with allocating time resources for this writing. Paul wants to acknowledge the time and writing resources provided by the University of Minnesota throughout the blog and book's creation.

We also want to thank the Galileo Museum for permitting the use of Lorraine's photograph taken in the museum in 2017 to be used on the book cover, and gratefully acknowledge the artistic help of Stephanie Sale and the design team at Taylor and Francis.

Behind this book are our families, who provided endless cheering and support throughout the process. Lorraine thanks her husband, Chuck Hermann, with whom she regularly discussed and debated the ideas in her blog posts, and who provided support and advice through the book manuscript process. Kathy is grateful for the endless patience of her husband, Dan, and their children, Cooper and Harrison, who contributed to her ability to put the posts in her head onto the written page. Paul is grateful to his wife, Kathy, who always gave him space to get the writing done and then read the earliest drafts with a constructive editor's eye.

David Varley at Routledge championed the book's contribution and shepherded the manuscript through the Routledge publication process with agility, helpful suggestions, and lightning speed! We also thank Miriam Armstrong, Brianna Ascher, Mary Del Plato, Dawn Preston, and Megan Smith for their help in bringing the book into published form.

Note

1 Throughout this book, we refer to universities and colleges of higher education as "the Academy" or "academia"; we refer to ourselves as "professors," "academics," or "faculty."

PART I
Ethics and Research

2

TWENTY QUESTIONS

Ethical Research Dilemmas and PhD Students

> **Key insight:** The PhD timeline, from admission through graduation, is a unique period in a scholar's life. It is a time when students are apprentices, learning from faculty mentors how to become researchers and academics. In the four-to-six years of a typical doctoral program, students engage in all stages of research from problem identification, literature reviews, and theory development, through data collection and analysis, to writing, presenting, and publishing their work. At each stage, doctoral students face ethical research dilemmas, similar to those faced by faculty members, but with unique aspects that come from being doctoral students. This chapter consists of 20 research dilemmas that are meant to facilitate classroom or small group discussions among doctoral students and faculty about research ethics. The scenarios were developed to illustrate the various types of ethical dilemmas that may face doctoral students in their research activities.

An Overview

Faculty in academia, especially in the social sciences and liberal arts, proceed through a fairly standard series of stages in their academic careers.[1] In the first stage, an individual (let us call her "Mary Smith") is admitted to a doctoral program. Typically, Mary already has a master's degree and perhaps some work experience after graduation. Once admitted to a doctoral program, Mary must take a suite of courses, after which she must take comprehensive exams and then write a dissertation. Along the way, Mary will write multiple papers (some co-authored), present her work at conferences and workshops, and may have some of her work published in one or more scholarly journals. Near the end of her doctoral studies,

Mary will go on the job market, looking for a full-time position in a university. Eventually, she receives and accepts an offer and then starts her academic career as an assistant professor, hopefully, in a tenure track position. As a newly minted assistant professor, Mary is then faced with the Big Three metrics against which all faculty are annually evaluated: research, teaching, and service. If Mary is successful at all three metrics, she will apply for and achieve tenure and promotion to associate professor. Mary is then truly launched on a career in the Academy.

The story of Mary Smith looks like a relatively smooth trajectory from acceptance into a doctoral program through tenure and promotion to associate professor. At each stage, there are well-marked and well-understood hurdles to be passed, together with regular assessment of individual performance on research, teaching, and service. However, also along the way, PhD students and young faculty are faced with a variety of decision points where they have to make choices that have ethical ramifications. These ethical pitfalls may offer greater performance (if not caught) or derail their academic careers (if caught).

The purpose of this book is to provide a road map to some of the ethical dilemmas that doctoral students and young faculty members are likely to face as they enter a career in academia (the Academy). To start these discussions, this chapter presents 20 mini-cases of ethical dilemmas that can affect doctoral students and junior faculty as they move along their research trajectory, from the time of admission to graduate studies through graduation and their first years as a new faculty member. The goal of this chapter is to start you thinking about where and how ethical pitfalls can arise, and how best to handle them. In Chapter 3, we explore how and why new entrants to the Academy are more likely to face these ethical pitfalls than senior faculty.

Introduction to the 20 Cases

Each of the cases is deliberately written so that the case may or may not have an ethical dilemma facing the PhD student. By writing the cases in this manner, we hope to encourage discussion on the different topics that face PhD students in their research activities. We recommend the following questions to start the discussion:

- Is there an ethical dilemma here? If yes, what is it and why?
- What are the available options facing the PhD student?
- What ethical course of action do you recommend and why?

Entry/Admissions to the PhD Program

1. Aidan decided to go back to school for his PhD in Management and had talked with the doctoral program director at University X several times by telephone. The program director assured Aidan that he would be able to work with

renowned Professor Macro if Aidan chose to do his doctoral studies at University X. Aidan's research interests aligned perfectly with Professor Macro's research. Aidan was also convinced he would develop excellent research skills working under Professor Macro's direction and might therefore have some publications before graduation. Aidan's official visit to the university as well as his interactions with the program director during the visit went well and further strengthened his views. However, Professor Macro was out of town during Aidan's visit so they did not meet. Nevertheless, the program director assured Aidan that Professor Macro loved to work with doctoral students. Aidan, taking into consideration the professor's reputation in the field and the program director's opinion that Aidan would be able to work with Professor Macro, accepted the offer to attend University X. After Aidan's arrival, however, the situation turned out to be quite different. He discovered that Professor Macro was going on sabbatical leave for a year and that his passion for working with doctoral students had lessened. It became quite evident that the program director had not consulted with Professor Macro about his willingness or ability to work with incoming doctoral students. Aidan feels that he has been misled.

Research Projects

Intellectual Property Rights

2. Nicolas writes a term paper for his PhD seminar and presents it in class. Barbara, another PhD student in the class, is assigned to critique the term paper. Nicolas does not get a very good grade on the term paper and, after the class is over, he decides the term paper needs too much work to bring the paper up to publishable quality so he puts the paper on the "backburner." Barbara, however, really likes this topic and writes her own paper, which she submits to the annual Academy of Management (AOM) conference. Barbara's paper is accepted for presentation at the meetings. Nicolas sees Barbara's paper on the AOM conference program and realizes that her paper is on the same topic as his term paper. He accuses her of stealing his term paper.

Authorship

3. Two PhD students, James and Willem, are office mates. Each of them is working on a single-authored paper and they occasionally discuss their research ideas. They both know it is very important for their job search to have multiple papers on their CVs. James and Willem realize that, if they each added the other as a co-author, they would generate mutual benefits for each other: doubling their chances of a publication and beefing up their resumes when they enter the job market. They agree to go ahead and add each other has a co-author to the other's papers.

4. Xiao is assigned as a research assistant to Professor Micro and spends the semester gathering and analyzing data for one of Professor Micro's projects. Kevin is doing the same thing for Professor Macro. At the end of the semester, Professor Micro invites Xiao to be a co-author on a paper that will be based on their joint research; Professor Macro does not invite Kevin to be a co-author on a paper that will be based on their joint research. Xiao and Kevin discover the different treatment when they get together to discuss their research assignments this semester.

Order of Authors

5. Nadia and Christof are third-year PhD students who will be on the job market next year. Nadia is working on a joint research project with Professor X; Christof is doing the same with Professor Y. One day, Nadia and Christof are discussing their current research projects. Nadia tells Christof how excited she is to receive third authorship on the paper she is working on with Professor X. Christof mentions that he will be the first author on a paper he is working on with Professor Y. Nadia asks Christof how they determined the order of authorship. Christof admits to Nadia that Professor Y did most of the work on the paper, but Christof would be on the job market shortly so Professor Y agreed to give Christof first authorship. Nadia is perplexed. She tells Christof that Professor X, a foreign-born professor from a power-respecting culture, believes that authorship should be determined by seniority. Professor X was therefore unequivocal in assigning authorship based on seniority. Since Nadia had the least seniority on the project, she was automatically the last author regardless of her contribution. Christof informs Nadia that other professors in their department practice the same authorship philosophy as Professor Y, not Professor X.

6. Alain works with Bianca and Carlos, under the direction of Professor X, on a research paper. Alain is in his first year; Bianca and Carlos are both in their fourth year. The terms of authorship are solidified at the beginning of the project as follows (Professor X-Bianca-Carlos-Alain). Alain feels that the authorship agreement was fair and is excited to contribute to a project that has a high likelihood of being published. As the project progresses, Alain finds himself contributing more to the project than either Bianca or Carlos. The paper goes through several rounds of reviews, in which Alain does more work than either Bianca or Carlos. The paper finally gets accepted at a top journal, with the original authorship agreement, despite the incongruence in contributions made by the three PhD students. Alain does not want to upset too many people so he asks Denise, a fellow PhD student, for her opinion on the topic. Denise tells Alain that Professor X tends to give authorship order preference, regardless of actual contribution, to his more senior PhD students who will be entering the job market.

7. Andrew, Barbara, and Cameron are co-researchers on a project. All three are PhD students: Andrew and Cameron are in their second year; Barbara is on the

job market. When they started this project, they agreed that the order of authors would be alphabetical because they each were contributing equally to the project. Now the paper is finished and they are getting ready to submit it to a journal. Barbara approaches Andrew and Cameron to ask if they could change the order of authors so that she can be first author. Barbara argues that she is on the job market and so needs the publication more than they do. Barbara promises to return the favor by being third author on the next two papers coming out of their work together.

Errors and Omissions

8. Justin and Kara are working with Professor X on a joint paper. They are on a tight deadline; submission for the annual AOM meetings is only two weeks away. Justin is tasked to collect some missing data for their empirical work. He is also in the middle of exams and so quickly gathers the data without checking the numbers. Kara discovers that the data are flawed, but realizes that if she brings this to the attention of Professor X they will likely miss the window for submitting the paper to the AOM meetings.

9. Isabella is a research assistant for Professor X on a project that extends work Professor X had already published in a top-tier journal. She is very excited to be included as a co-author on the paper Professor X is writing based on the research they have been doing. When Professor X invites her to read and comment on the first draft of the paper, she realizes that multiple paragraphs in the paper are identical to those in the earlier publication.

Research Presentations

10. Lukas, while in the PhD program at University X, is working on a good paper that he likes very much. He wants to give the paper at a conference where he can get some good feedback prior to submitting it for publication in a journal. Lukas also likes to travel and sees that there are conferences coming up in Vancouver, San Diego, and Miami, places he has not visited and would like to visit. His department has the funds to send PhD students to these conferences. Lukas decides to submit the same paper to all three conferences, and he is delighted when the paper is accepted for presentation at all three venues.

11. Rebecca is the lead author on a paper with two other PhD students Tomas and Jean Luis. Rebecca submits their co-authored paper for presentation at the annual AOM meetings, but does not inform her co-authors, believing that they had a joint understanding that she would submit the paper to the AOM meetings. Jean Luis, as part of his work on three other research teams, had already agreed to submit the three papers to the AOM meetings; Jean Luis, therefore, was in violation of the Rule of Three that limited submissions by any one author to three papers. Jean Luis tells Rebecca that he is violating the Rule of Three. Rebecca suggests that she take Jean Luis' name off their joint AOM submission now.

If the paper is accepted and they do present it at the meetings, they will put Jean Luis' name back on the paper and slide presentation; he can attend the session and present, too. They will tell everyone in the session that Jean Luis is a co-author.

Dissertation Stage

Datasets

12. Kayla has been working for a year, building a dataset for her dissertation. This dataset extends the original dataset provided by her dissertation chair by adding new variables and years. Kayla's dissertation chair has several publications out of the original dataset. Kayla discovers, to her horror, that there is a major error in the variables constructed in the dataset and that the error is large enough to potentially invalidate the papers that her chair has already published. Kayla does not know whether (1) she should fix the error in her own dataset, (2) tell her chair about the problem, and (3) whether to inform the journals where the papers were published that they are fundamentally flawed.

13. Ashley has spent a year developing her dissertation dataset and is very proud of the work she has done. She believes the dataset will enable her to answer several unanswered questions in her field of study. She is getting close to defending her dissertation and her chair has asked for her to share her dataset with him. This particular professor has a reputation for not including PhD students as co-authors on his research projects. Ashley is worried that the professor may use her dataset, without including her as a co-author.

Authorship

14. Jordan's dissertation chair is an internationally famous scholar, traveling so much that she is seldom available to meet with Jordan. As a result, Jordan had basically written his dissertation by himself, with little to no help from his chair. When Jordan submits the dissertation to his chair, she tells Jordan that he must agree to put her name on all publications coming out of his dissertation or she will not sign off on the dissertation.

15. Patrice is working in his office on polishing up his dissertation, which will be defended next week. His chair comes into Patrice's office, very excited, and tells Patrice that she has secured publication of his dissertation with a well-known scholarly press. The only string attached is that the book must have Patrice's chair as a co-author and the chair must be the first author on the book.

Publication

16. Javier's dissertation at a US university is well underway with one main chapter and two supporting chapters. Javier receives an invitation from a former

undergraduate professor in Mexico inviting him to publish a chapter out of his dissertation in the professor's edited book. Javier will have a quick publication on his resume, making him more attractive on the job market. Javier will also have done a favor to his former professor who wrote a strong letter that helped Javier get accepted into this PhD program. Since the book will be published in Spanish, there is little chance that Javier's chapter will be read by non-Spanish-speaking scholars. Therefore, Javier does not think publishing his dissertation chapter in this edited book will create a problem for him submitting the chapter for publication in a scholarly journal afterwards.

17. Karolina's dissertation consists of three papers, which is the norm at her university. While she is writing her dissertation, Karolina and a faculty member submit one of her chapters to a journal and the paper is accepted for publication as a co-authored article before Karolina has defended her dissertation. The chair of Karolina's dissertation committee discovers that one of her dissertation chapters has been co-written with another faculty member, and the chair refuses to accept the chapter as part of her dissertation. Karolina's chair tells her that all three chapters must be sole authored and none published prior to her defense; Karolina must therefore write another chapter.

Post-Dissertation

18. Stefanie's dissertation chair offers Stefanie the opportunity to use the private dataset that he had hand collected for his own research. Stefanie's chair requests, in return for use of the dataset, that he be included as a co-author on all publications by Stefanie that use this dataset. Stefanie and her chair discuss this issue, and she agrees verbally to do this. Stefanie and her chair write several papers together. Ten years later, Stefanie writes and publishes a single-authored paper that uses the original dataset provided by her chair. Stefanie justifies the single-authored paper on the grounds that the theory development is hers and that "enough is enough"; ten years of joint work is long enough to pay for the use of the original dataset. Stefanie's chair is furious, arguing that they had a verbal agreement that all published work coming out of the original dataset should be joint authored.

19. Fletcher and two other PhD students write an empirical paper investigating the impact of a particular set of variables on firm performance. In their paper, a second group of variables are treated as controls in the model. Fletcher graduates and takes a position at another university. Once he is settled in, Fletcher starts a second project with colleagues in his new department. In this paper, the controls from the first paper are now independent variables, and the independent variables from the first paper are now controls. The two projects proceed independently, with only Fletcher aware of both projects. Both papers are submitted about the same time to different journals and, by chance, have a common reviewer. The reviewer tells both journal editors about the other paper and recommends

that both papers should be rejected on the grounds they are too similar to one another.

20. Lorraine is carving her dissertation into papers for submission to journals where she hopes they will be published. She prepares two papers and submits them at about the same time to two journals, making no reference in either submission to the other paper. Both papers use the same dataset and share most of the same variables; however, the theoretical arguments and hypotheses are different. Lorraine is pleased when the first paper receives a positive revise-and-resubmit decision from Journal A, but disappointed when the second paper is rejected after review at Journal B. Lorraine makes minor modifications to the second paper based on the reviewers' comments and submits the revised paper to Journal A, reasoning that the positive success that the first paper has received might be repeated with the second paper.

Note

1 Parts of this chapter are drawn from a blog posting on AOM's "The Ethicist" co-authored with Kevin McSweeney, who at the time was a first-year doctoral student in the Department of Management at Texas A&M University. Please note that all individuals appearing in these cases are fictitious. Any resemblance to real persons, living or dead, or to actual events or incidents is purely coincidental.

3

RESEARCH PITFALLS FOR NEW ENTRANTS TO THE ACADEMY

> **Key insight:** International business scholars argue that firms going abroad are "strangers in a strange land"; they face additional costs arising from liability of foreignness (LOF) when compared with local firms in the host country. Liability of foreignness can be decomposed into three hazards: unfamiliarity, relational, and discriminatory. We argue in this chapter that doctoral students and junior faculty also suffer from the same three hazards. We use insights from the LOF literature to explain how these hazards can create research pitfalls for new entrants to the Academy, and discuss mentoring and ethics training as possible solutions.

New Entrants to the Academy

PhD students at most universities follow a fairly predictable four-to-six-year timeline or life cycle from admission into a graduate studies program through to graduation. Typically, the process involves taking several required courses (with some choice of electives); working as a research and/or teaching assistant for faculty and possibly doing some teaching; writing qualifying examinations; assembling a dissertation committee; and researching, writing, and defending a dissertation.

After graduation with their PhDs in hand, most young scholars will start work as untenured assistant professors in one of our universities or colleges. In their first academic positions, the performance of assistant professors is assessed annually on the Big Three metrics of research, teaching, and service. If the first five to eight years as an assistant professor are judged successful by senior faculty and administrators, tenure and promotion to associate professor follow. At that point, their career is successfully launched and they are no longer considered apprentices in the Academy.

While the PhD process is often satirized (see PhD Comics[1]) and plans and reality often collide,[2] we believe the academic life cycle is a useful framework for understanding the unique research dilemmas that face these students. At each step along the life cycle, new entrants to the Academy engage in research-related activities, which are illustrated in Figure 3.1. Note that research activities start almost from the time of entry into a PhD program. These include class term papers, research assistant work, ad hoc projects with fellow doctoral students, and the largest project of all: the dissertation. Students are encouraged to present their research at a variety of venues (e.g., class presentations, departmental workshops, conferences) and are encouraged to submit their work to multiple publication outlets (e.g., conference proceedings, scholarly journals, book chapters).

After graduating with their PhD in hand, most will take an academic position. At that point, the demands to "publish or perish" become insistent as the "tenure clock" ticks down the five to eight years during which young assistant professors must produce sufficient numbers of publications in sufficiently high enough quality publication outlets to be considered for and achieve tenure and promotion. Each of these stages and activities creates potential ethical pitfalls in research for doctoral students. In this chapter, we develop a theoretical framework for understanding the ethical "pitfalls for the unwary" that face new entrants to the Academy. We develop our framework building on insights from the liability of foreignness literature.

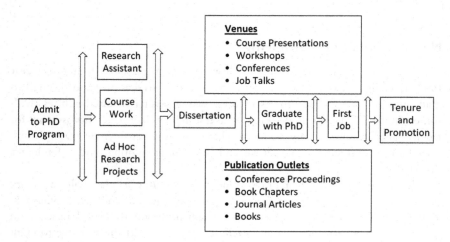

FIGURE 3.1 The life cycle of new entrants to academia.

Liability of Foreignness

International business scholars conceptualize a firm going abroad as suffering from *liability of foreignness* (LOF). The firm is a "stranger in a strange land" in a dual sense: the "land" (the host country and its residents) is strange to the entering firm and the entrant is strange to the land (Eden and Miller, 2004). Liability of foreignness consists primarily of sociocultural costs ("soft" costs) as opposed to the more straightforward economic or activity-based costs ("hard" costs) of operating at a distance (e.g., transportation costs, tariffs, license fees, and so on). As a result, LOF costs are harder to see, to measure, and to cope with than purely economic costs.

In Eden and Miller (2004), LOF costs are decomposed into three different types of hazards: unfamiliarity, relational, and discriminatory hazards. Unfamiliarity hazards arise from lack of knowledge about and inexperience in the host country. Not knowing the rules places the foreign firm at a disadvantage compared to local firms. Relational hazards are the costs involved in managing the foreign firm's buyer–supplier network in the host country; that is, the higher administrative costs of managing the relationships between parties involved in doing business abroad. Discriminatory hazards arise from the foreign firm's relations with host-country stakeholders (e.g., consumers, local government, or the general public). The firm may suffer negative treatment and loss of organizational legitimacy due to consumer ethnocentrism or policies that favor local firms.

Each hazard requires mitigation by the firm if it is to survive and thrive in the host country. Eden and Miller (2004) argue that the hazards differ across countries, industries, and across time, and that the hazards are stronger as institutional distance increases between the home and host countries. Unfamiliarity hazards, for example, may dissipate over time the longer the foreign firm is located in and gathering experiential knowledge about the host country. Discriminatory hazards, on the other hand, may be pervasive and persist over time, especially in countries where the culture is to distrust foreign entrants; taking on a local partner (e.g., an equity joint venture) may help reduce discriminatory treatment. The relational hazards of managing the firm's buyer–supplier network in the host country may also benefit from having a local partner.

New Entrants to the Academy: Insights from Liability of Foreignness

While Eden and Miller (2004) was designed to explore the costs that *firms* face in doing business abroad, we argue in this chapter that their insights can also be applied to *individuals* entering a new institutional environment, in particular, to new entrants to the Academy. We can adapt their insights to individuals as follows.

We argue that new entrants – doctoral students and junior faculty – to the Academy face three kinds of liability of foreignness:

- *Unfamiliarity hazards* that arise from the *liability of newness*, from being new entrants and not knowing the rules of the game. Not knowing the rules of the game in the Academy can lead to mistakes and lower performance.
- *Relational hazards* that arise from the *liability of resource dependence*, of being dependent for resources on one's colleagues and partners; that is, one's organizational network. Resource dependence generates vulnerability, which encourages opportunistic behavior by the powerful taking advantage of the weak.
- *Discriminatory hazards* that arise from the *liability of outsiderness*, from being an outsider – a new entrant to the Academy – and thus not a member of the group. Being an outsider may close doors to opportunities, and encourage stereotyping and discriminatory behaviors.

We further argue that all three types of hazards that face new entrants to the Academy are particularly endemic to research activities. While LOF hazards also affect teaching and service, it is research that offers the greatest pitfalls for the unwary. Research is the primary performance metric on which members of the Academy are judged, starting with papers and examinations all the way through to citation counts to scholarly books and articles published in top-tier journals. Research is the strongest and most visible of the three metrics (research, teaching, and service) for assessing performance and thus the most likely to suffer from LOF hazards.

Looking first at doctoral students, it is clear that they suffer from a *liability of newness*, which leads to *unfamiliarity hazards*. Doctoral students are unfamiliar with the rules of the publication game and can therefore easily make mistakes or be guided in the wrong direction. Moreover, PhD students are typically young and enthusiastic, more inclined to say yes without thinking about the consequences.

When students are admitted to a doctoral program, the subjects that PhD students must study in their classes are likely new to them, and the language in scholarly journal articles difficult to follow. Their first papers are likely to be derivative – that is, repetitious of what they have been reading and learning. They may unwittingly engage in plagiarism, without knowing or recognizing the consequences.

Moreover, PhD students typically have had little to no research experience and therefore look to faculty members to train them in the research process. Research activities are seldom done alone in academia. Graduate students typically work in close collaboration with faculty members and other graduate students. Still, working together is not necessarily the same as on-the-job training. Azuma (1997, 4) provides a nice analogy. He argues that graduate school is like an apprenticeship. Each student has his/her own project and the supervisors (faculty members) may not be very helpful. He argues that:

> It's like training clock designers by locking students inside a clock factory with some working clocks and lots of clock parts and machines for building

clocks. However, the instructions are at best incomplete and even the masters themselves don't know exactly how to build next year's models.

Second, PhD students are at a power disadvantage relative to faculty members, which opens them to *relational hazards*. As apprentices, they seek instruction and guidance from their professors and mentors. Doctoral students are dependent on faculty for resources (knowledge, networks, access to classes and grants, letters of reference) at every stage of the PhD life cycle from admission through coursework, research projects, dissertation, and post-graduation. This power disadvantage leaves doctoral students open to relational hazards whereby the students are exploited by unscrupulous or self-aggrandizing faculty members. Faced with unethical behavior by a senior professor or administration, few PhD students are willing to be whistle blowers. For example, twice as many graduate students as faculty (53 versus 26 percent) said they could not report a faculty member for ethical violations without expecting retaliation (Swazey, Anderson, and Louis, 1993).

Third, PhD students are outsiders to the academic profession, seeking admission to – and status within – the academic community; thus, doctoral students face *discriminatory hazards*. As outsiders, they want to belong, to be accepted, and to gain the respect of their peers and colleagues as they move through the apprenticeship process from entrance to graduation. Faculty members have tenure and security; PhD students can be dropped from their doctoral program at several points along the dissertation process if faculty should judge their performance insufficient.

Moreover, the combination of resource dependence (relational hazards) and outsiderness (discriminatory hazards) can be a powerful one, particularly for minorities. Doctoral students may be more affected by discriminatory behaviors based on their race, color, or gender because of their resource dependence on faculty and administrators. Recent research, for example, found that faculty in US universities were more responsive to requests for mentoring from white male students than from white female students or students who were black, Hispanic, Indian, or Chinese, and that this discrimination was particularly strong in higher-paying disciplines (e.g., business schools) and private institutions (Milkman, Akinola, and Chugh, 2015). Thus, discriminatory hazards can positively interact, raising the liability of foreignness for doctoral students who are minorities within the Academy.

LOF hazards are also likely to be much higher for foreign students who have gone abroad to study in another country. The percentage of foreign-born students is typically highest in doctoral programs in the United States, with great variation across programs in the percentages of US versus foreign students. Often, these students come from countries where the institutional distance between the home country (typically where their undergraduate training occurred) and the host country (where their graduate training is done) can be very high. Eden and Miller (2004) argue that the greater the institutional distance, the higher the liability of foreignness. Thus, issues of language, miscommunication, cultural and ethical differences are likely to play a much greater role in generating ethical pitfalls for foreign graduate students.

We argue that liability of foreignness problems continue after PhD students start their first academic job. In their first job, young assistant professors face unfamiliarity hazards due to liability of newness, relational hazards due to resource dependence, and discriminatory hazards from liability of outsiderness. The problems may even become even more intense for new hires due to the pressure to publish in order to achieve tenure and stay in the Academy. The tenure clock is constantly ticking for non-tenured faculty. Moreover, new hires are in a disadvantaged power position and vulnerable to exploitation because they are dependent on senior faculty for mentoring, research, and teaching experience and career advancement. The multiple overlapping relationships with senior faculty may make junior faculty reluctant to assert themselves in authorship for fear of impact on their other roles.

PhD students and young assistant professors are under a lot of pressure to perform. Examples include competition with classmates, pressure to come up with "original and novel" contributions, and frequent assessments of performance. Pressures to perform can lead to shortcuts, and shortcuts can lead to unacceptable and unethical practices.

The 20 mini-cases presented in Chapter 2 are designed to provide examples of the ethical dilemmas that may confront PhD students and young faculty in the research domain. So what can we do as senior scholars and mentors to help guide the new entrants to the Academy to a successful landing with tenure and promotion to associate professor?

Mitigating Liability of Foreignness in the Academy

Given the high likelihood that doctoral students and junior faculty are going to be faced with a variety of ethical dilemmas, starting from the time of entry through the ten or more years it is likely to take to achieve tenure and promotion to associate professor, what can we do to help these young apprentices in the Academy navigate through the various ethical pitfalls they are likely to face?

Mentoring

The liability of foreignness literature may be helpful here by providing insights into ways that we can help doctoral students and junior faculty deal with the pitfalls that arise from being a "stranger in a strange land." Eden and Miller (2004), for example, argue that taking on a local partner can help reduce unfamiliarity, relational, and discriminatory hazards.

The equivalent to a local partner for PhD students and junior faculty is to find a mentor or mentors who can provide advice and counsel about navigating successfully within the Academy. Mentoring networks are prevalent in most disciplines (see for example, McBride et al., 2017 on mentoring networks in nursing). Mentoring approaches can vary from the typical one-on-one pairing of a senior faculty member with a new entrant to junior faculty creating their own peer-mentoring networks (Agosto et al., 2016). Mentoring relationships may be particularly helpful for minority students, but harder relationships to build successfully. Brunsma, Embrick, and Shin (2017), for example, find that good mentoring is an important indicator of graduate student success, but that most universities do not do a good job of mentoring graduate students of color.

In terms of the research dimension, we recommend that when doctoral students are assigned to faculty as research assistants, faculty need to recognize that they must also play a mentoring role in addition to training the student in how to gather and manage data. Students need help learning the rules of the game and faculty are best situated to provide that education. Having a weekly doctoral seminar guided by a senior scholar and devoted to deconstructing the research process – including ethical issues – is an important way also to provide mentoring opportunities. Departmental heads can help by instituting a formal mentoring program for new entrants, both doctoral students and junior faculty, particularly during their first year at the institution when unfamiliarity hazards are at their highest.

Ethics Training

Another way to help new entrants to the Academy handle the LOF hazards they are going to face, particularly in the research dimension, is to provide them with ethics training. This applies to PhD students and to new faculty hires. Providing this training on an ex ante basis can help new entrants make ethical decisions and encourage the "better angels of their nature."

However, PhD students and junior faculty typically receive little to no training on ethics. Even when ethics training is federally mandated, universities often do not comply (National Science Foundation, 2017). Our examination of codes of ethics in our professional organizations found little to no references to PhD students in the codes (see Chapter 6, "Slicing and Dicing: Ex Post Approaches"). Moreover, codes of ethics once written often disappear, never to be heard from again. For example, Hofmann, Myhe, and Holm (2013) surveyed PhD students in Norway and found little awareness of departmental policies on research ethics. Graduate students tend to rely on their advisors, rather than on university ethics resources, for advice on research ethics (Mole, 2012).

A few professional associations provide ethics training as part of the professional development workshops (PDWs) at their annual conferences. The Ethics Education Committee within the AOM, for example, provides ethics training at the AOM divisional doctoral PDWs, albeit typically for only for 30–60 minutes (Madsen and Davis, 2009). Most professional associations, however, do not have pre-conference PDWs so their PhD students receive no ethics training. AOM also has an Adjudication Committee, recognizing that an ethics code without an enforcement mechanism is a toothless code.

Reading material, websites, and videos (e.g., AOM research ethics videos) are other ways to provide ethics training. The Committee on Professional Ethics website (publicationethics.org) in particular has excellent training materials in research ethics. The references attached to this chapter provide a list of articles, books, websites, and resources that deal specifically with ethics and PhD students. These, too, can be helpful.

Ethical dilemmas, when viewed through the lens of the academic life cycle, suggest we need to devote more work to ethics training at the beginning of the life cycle. Much of the inspiration for this book comes from our desire to provide ex ante materials to help new entrants avoid the pitfalls for the unwary.

Discussion questions

1. Are you aware of examples where PhD students or junior faculty made ethical mistakes that were due to one or more of the three hazards identified in this chapter: unfamiliarity, relational, and discriminatory hazards?
2. Are there policies in place at your university or college to help provide new entrants to the Academy with ethics training?
3. Does your department provide any ethics training to its PhD students and new faculty hires?
4. Are there formal mentoring relationships at your university, either for doctoral students or for junior faculty?
5. Does your professional association offer PDWs before the regular conference? Is there a PDW specifically for PhD students? Is there a PDW specifically for junior faculty? Is ethics training part of those PDWs?
6. Does your professional association have an Ethics Education Committee? If yes, what are its tasks and what does it provide in terms of ethics training for PhD students and new faculty hires?
7. Does your professional association have a Code of Ethics? If yes, is there anything in the code that is specific to PhD students and new faculty hires?

Notes

1 http://phdcomics.com/comics/archive/phd050599s.gif
2 http://blog.devicerandom.org/wp-content/uploads/2011/02/phd082803s.gif

References

Agosto, Vonzell, Zorka Karanxha, Ann Unterreiner, Deirdre Cobb-Roberts, Talia Esnard, Ke Wu, and Makini Beck. 2016. "Running Bamboo: A Mentoring Network of

Women Intending to Thrive in Academia." *NASPA Journal about Women in Higher Education*, 9. 1: 74–89. DOI: 10.1080/19407882. 2015.1124785

Azuma, Ronald T. 1997. "'So long and Thanks for the Ph.D.!' a.k.a. 'Everything I Wanted to Know about C.S. Graduate School at the Beginning but Didn't Learn until Later.' The 4th Guide in the Hitchhiker's Guide Trilogy (and if that doesn't make sense, you obviously have not read Douglas Adams)." Revised in 1997 and 2014. Accessed February 19, 2017. www.cs.unc.edu/~azuma/hitch4.html

Bartlett, Tom. 2010. "Document Sheds Light on Investigation at Harvard." *Chronicle of Higher Education*, August 19. Accessed January 8, 2017. www.chronicle.com/article/Document-Sheds-Light-on/123988

Baruch College PhD Students of Marketing. "Fostering an Ethical Research Community as Doctoral Students: Building Our Own Professional Standards of Ethics." Accessed February 19, 2017. www.ejcr.org/Baruch_Students.pdf

Boskovic, Milos, J. Djokovic, I. Grubor, B. Jakovljevic, M. Jurisevic, D. Ljubisic, M. Mijajlovic et al. 2013. "PhD Students' Awareness of Research Misconduct." *Journal of Empirical Research on Human Subject Ethics: An International Journal*, 8. 2 (April): 163–164.

Brunsma, David L., David G. Embrick, and Jean H. Shin. 2016. "Graduate Students of Color: Race, Racism, and Mentoring in the White Waters of Academia." *Sociology of Race and Ethnicity*, 3. 1: 1–13.

Council of Graduate Schools. 2012. "Research and Scholarly Integrity in Graduate Education: A Comprehensive Approach." Project for Scholarly Integrity (September 1). Accessed February 19, 2017. www.cgsnet.org/project-scholarly-integrity

Eden, Lorraine and Stewart R. Miller. 2004. "Distance Matters: Liability of Foreignness, Institutional Distance and Ownership Strategy." In M.A. Hitt & J.L.C. Cheng (eds), *The Evolving Theory of the Multinational Firm: Advances in International Management*. Volume 16. Amsterdam: Elsevier.

Hofmann, Bjorn, Anne Ingeborg Myhe, and Soren Holm. 2013. "Scientific Dishonesty: A Nationwide Survey of Doctoral Students in Norway." *BMC Medical Ethics, 14*. 3.

Grover, Varun. 2001. "10 Mistakes Doctoral Students Make in Managing Their Program." *Decision Line* (May): 11–13.

Grover, Varun. 2007. "Successfully Navigating the Stages of Doctoral Study." *International Journal of Doctoral Studies*, 2. Accessed February 19, 2017. www.ijds.org/Volume2/IJDSv2p009-021Grover21.pdf

Madsen, Susan R. and James Davis. 2009. "Ethics in Publishing (11 Workshops) Academy of Management (Doctoral Consortium Workshops)." Chicago. January. Accessed February 19, 2017. http://works.bepress.com/susan_madsen/109

McBridge, Angela Barron, Jacquelyn Campbell, Nancy Fugate Woods, and Spero M. Manson. 2017. "Building a Mentoring Network." *Nursing Outlook*, 65: 305–314.

Mitchell, Theresa and Jude Carroll. 2008. "Academic and Research Misconduct in the PhD: Issues for Students and Supervisors." *Nurse Education Today*, 28: 218–226.

Mole, Beth. 2012. "How to Train Graduate Students in Research Ethics: Lessons from 6 Universities." *Chronicle of Higher Education*, August 14. Accessed February 19, 2017. http://chronicle.com/article/How-to-Train-Graduate-Students/133623/

Milkman, K.L., M. Akinola, and D. Chugh. 2015. "What Happens Before? A Field Experiment Exploring How Pay and Representation Differentially Shape Bias on the Pathway into Organizations." *Journal of Applied Psychology*, 100. 6 (November): 1678–1712.

National Science Foundation. 2017. "OIG Review of Institutions' Implementation of NSF's Responsible Conduct of Research Requirements." Office of Inspector General. OIG Tracking No. RP120300006.July 25.

Oberlander, Sarah E. and Robert J. Spencer. 2006. "Graduate Students and the Culture of Authorship." *Ethics and Behavior*, 16. 3: 217–232.

Oddi, Lorys F. and A. Samuel Oddi. 2000. "Student-Faculty Joint Authorship: Ethical and Legal Concerns." *Journal of Professional Nursing*, 16. 4, 219–227.

Pawlik, Timothy. 2009. "Clinical Case: Suspected Ethical Misconduct in Research." *Virtual Mentor: American Medical Association Journal of Ethics*, 11. 4, 287–290.

Pope, Kenneth S. 2008. "Developing and Practicing Ethics." In J. Prinstein and M. Patterson (eds), *The Portable Mentor: Expert Guide to a Successful Career in Psychology*. Amsterdam: Kluwer. www.kspope.com/ethics/ethical.php

Schniederjans, Marc. 2007. "A Proposed Ph.D. Student Bill of Rights." *International Journal of Doctoral Studies*, 2: 1–8.

Schrag, Brian (ed.). 1997–2002. "Graduate Research Ethics: Cases and Commentaries. Online Ethics Center for Engineering 3/11/2007." National Academy of Engineering www.onlineethics.org/Topics/RespResearch/ResCases/gradres.aspx

Swazey, Judith, Melissa Anderson, and Karen Louis. 1993. "Ethical Problems in Academic Research: A Survey of Doctoral Candidates and Faculty Raises Important Issues about the Ethical Environment of Graduate Education and Research." *American Scientist*. Accessed February 19, 2017. www.americanscientist.org/issues/pub/ethical-problems-in-academic-research/1

Thibodeau, Ryan. 2009. "Academic Integrity in the Mentoring Relationship: A Sampling of Relevant Issues." In Tyra Twomey, Ken Sagendorf, and Holly White (eds), *Pedagogy, Not Policing: Positive Approaches to Academic Integrity at the University*. Clemson, SC: Clemson University. Accessed February 19, 2017. http://graduateschool.syr.edu/programs/graduate-school-press/pedagogy-not-policing-toc/#page=81

Willyard, Cassandra. 2011. "Should You Blow the Whistle? What to Do When You Suspect Your Advisor or Research Supervisor of Ethical Misconduct." *American Psychological Association*, 42. 7: 74.

4

SCIENTISTS BEHAVING BADLY

Insights from the Fraud Triangle

> **Key insight:** Defining unethical behaviors such as plagiarism, multiple submissions, and fabricating data. Exploring how the fraud triangle can provide useful insights into the pressures that lead scholars to engage in research fraud.

Two of the co-authors of this book, Lorraine Eden and Kathy Lund Dean, have been editors-in-chief of scholarly journals. All three of us have played a variety of other editorial roles over many years, including guest editing special issues, departmental/area editor handling submissions in a particular area, and consulting editor on special topics or areas.

As a result, each of us fairly regularly has an email exchange with faculty who know of our editorial experience and ask for advice. A recent example appears in Box 4.1.

Box 4.1
From: xxx
To: Journal Editor X
Subject: ethical question

Dear Journal Editor X, I have an important ethical question to ask you: I have received the same article from two different journals to review. One journal wants me to send them a regular referee form evaluating the quality of the article and the other wants me to write a commentary on the piece. Should I inform the editors that the manuscript has been submitted to two journals simultaneously? Thanks, xxx

– –Original Message – –

From: Journal Editor X
To: xxx
Subject: Re: ethical question

Dear xxx, I would inform the editors of both journals, attach the other paper, and not do either review. I'll send you tomorrow my editorial on journal ethics.

– –Original Message – –

From: xxx
To: Journal Editor X
Subject: Re: ethical question

Thanks for the editorial on the ethics of scientific writing. I found it very useful myself, especially the section on redundancy (self-plagiarism). I was not aware that it would be an issue! Below you will find the reaction of one of the editors. Rather disappointing I think. I would have sent the author a rejection. Best, xxx

From: xxx
To: EDITOR
Subject: FW: request to review...

Dear EDITOR, Thank you for your kind invitation to write a commentary on paper... for your journal. I was very surprised when I got your email yesterday as I had just finished reviewing the SAME article for another journal. I asked a couple of senior scholars on the usual procedure for this kind of problem, and they advised me to let you and the other editor know the article had been simultaneously submitted to two venues. I am curious to know how this will play out, so please keep me abreast of the journal's decision regarding this article. Sincerely, xxx

– –Original Message – –

From: EDITOR
To: xxx
Subject: RE: request to review...

Dear xxx, Thank you so much for this message. This is not acceptable at our journal. I am going to contact the author and I will let you know. As far as I know, the author is currently revising the paper for our journal based on suggestions of two reviewers. If he/she withdraws the submission of the paper from the other journal it would not be a problem here. Sincerely, EDITOR

We believe that most if not all university and college professors would see the email exchange in Box 4.1 as unethical behavior by the author. Sending the same or substantially the same paper for review at and possible publication in two different journals is unacceptable behavior at most social science journals. At least one of the journals was unaware that this was happening, based on one editor's response, and probably both were unaware. Why would an author engage in this activity? We argue that insights from the fraud triangle can help explain why and when scientists are likely to behave badly.

Fraudulent behavior involves "intentional deception, lying, deceitful pretenses, cunning, willing misrepresentation of material fact, and deliberate trickery intended to gain an unfair and dishonest advantage" (Chui, 2010, 8). Fraud involves deliberate intent – lying – either by (1) concealing relevant facts that the individual is under an obligation to disclose or by (2) distorting relevant facts. Building on this definition, we define research fraud as *a deliberate intent by an author to conceal or to distort facts relevant to the research process, all the way from the original research idea through to publication.*

Individuals are more likely to commit fraud when three conditions or pressures, which we now call the "fraud triangle," occur together: opportunity, incentive, and rationalization (Cressey, 1953). "[I]nformation asymmetries, uncertainty, or ambiguity combined with absent or lax monitoring and enforcement mechanisms" create the first corner of the fraud triangle, opportunity, according to Stuebs and Wilkinson (2010, 127). Second, the individual must have an incentive (financial, social, or otherwise) to commit fraud. Third, the individual must rationalize the act as consistent with his or her code of ethics. To rationalize fraud, the individual may view his or her actions as compliant (fitting within existing norms or rules) or as strategically non-compliant (modifying or stretching the interpretation of the rules or norms to include the action). There is a large literature providing empirical support to the fraud triangle at both the individual and organizational levels (e.g., Hogan et al., 2008).

Let us apply the fraud triangle to the example above where a reviewer is sent the same paper by two journals. Eden (2010) and Schminke (2009) provide other examples of scientists behaving badly where the fraud triangle could also be applied.

Opportunity, the first corner of the research fraud triangle, comes from informational hazards, weak monitoring, and poor enforcement mechanisms. Clearly, information asymmetries characterize the journal submission process. Individuals voluntarily submit papers to journals for possible publication, and journal editors rely either wholly or primarily on authors to disclose relevant information about their manuscripts.

Monitoring mechanisms are typically weak. Most journals now have a "check the box" mechanism whereby authors must state that their submission is new and not under review elsewhere. Some journals, such as the *Journal of International Business Studies*, have an elaborate Code of Ethics, and authors are required to "check the box" that they have read and abided by the code.[1] However, editors normally cannot verify author statements and, given the huge number of submissions, may not have the time or ability for due diligence. Detection depends on serendipity or accident, as in the case above where the same individual was asked to review both manuscripts. (Monitoring mechanisms may be improving, however, as many journals now run submitted manuscripts through cross-checking programs, such as iThenticate, that highlight overlaps with already published research.)

Lastly, weak enforcement also creates opportunity. As the case above demonstrates, many journal editors may not punish authors for misbehavior. When detection and punishment are both low, authors may make a rational benefit–cost calculation and decide to engage in research fraud.

Our search for the phrase "publish or perish" generated 415,000 results in Google in February 2017; clearly, the *incentive* to engage in research fraud is well known inside and outside of academia. Publication pressures can occur at any stage of a faculty member's career, whether searching for the first or a new job, seeking tenure and/or promotion, or merit salary increases. One might expect that pre-tenured faculty face the strongest pressures to publish and therefore might be most expected to engage in research fraud; however, Schminke (2009) found otherwise based on his interviews with 16 journal editors. He found that most ethical violations were not caused by "junior scholars running ethical yellow lights because of pressures imposed by tenure time lines" (588). Thus, pressures to publish occur across one's academic career, not only for junior faculty.

Moreover, financial rewards can involve more than simple merit pay increases. Some universities now pay a faculty member $US 10,000 or even $20,000 for a top-tier journal publication, providing a strong incentive to engage in research fraud, particularly where opportunity, the first corner of the fraud triangle, is also strong.

The third corner of the research fraud triangle is *rationalization*. In order to commit research fraud, the scholar must be able to rationalize the action as consistent with his/her code of ethics. Either the individual sees the action as fitting within existing norms or rules, or they can be bent to encompass the activity. Simple egoism (what benefits me most?) can also be a rationalizing factor.

As a starter, authors may simply be unaware of publication norms and rules; for example, PhD students or junior scholars may not be familiar with existing rules and procedures at major scholarly journals. Authors may "check the box" that they have read and abided by the journal's ethics code without actually having done so. How many times have you installed an updated version of a software program where you had to check the box that you had read the terms and conditions, and you checked the box – but didn't read the 30+ pages of terms and conditions?

In the case of research fraud above, where the author sends the same paper through the review process at two journals, the author may have also rationalized the behavior on the grounds that the reviewing process of satisfying the demands of two or three reviewers plus an editor, through two or three rounds of review, would result in two sufficiently different papers by the end of the process. Thus, the ends (two separate publications) justified the means (sending the same paper to two journals).

Moreover, individuals may be conditioned by their colleagues and peers that it is OK because "everyone is doing it." If authors believe or see other scholars also engaged in strategic non-compliance with ethical norms and rules – particularly where the behavior is not caught and may even be rewarded – it is easier to rationalize engaging in research fraud.

Cressey (1953) argued that all three corners of the fraud triangle had to occur simultaneously for individuals to engage in fraudulent behavior. Similarly, we argue that when opportunity, incentive, and rationalization combine to create strong pressures to engage in research fraud, we will find scientists behaving badly.

Discussion questions

1. What do you see as research fraud?
2. Please share examples from your own experience – as an author, reviewer, and/or editor – of pressures affecting research fraud.
3. Is the research fraud triangle a useful framework for explaining pressures for scientists to behave badly?
4. Can you provide other examples of the three pressures (opportunity, incentive, and rationalization) in addition to the ones we have outlined above?
5. Some authors argue the appropriate framework for understanding fraud is a diamond rather than a triangle, adding capability as a fourth pressure (Wolfe and Hermanson 2004). Capability considers personal traits and abilities (e.g., intelligence, experience, creativity, ability to lie, and cope with stress) that make it more or less easy for individuals or organizations to successfully commit fraud. Can capability apply to research fraud also?

Note

1 www.palgrave-journals.com/jibs/jibs_ethics_code.html

References and Additional Reading

Chui, Lawrence. 2010. "An Experimental Examination of the Effects of Fraud Specialist and Audit Mindsets on Fraud Risk Assessments and on the Development of Fraud-Related Problem Representations." Unpublished doctoral dissertation, University of North Texas.

Cressey, Donald R. 1953. *Other People's Money: A Study in the Social Psychology of Embezzlement.* Glencoe, IL: Free Press.

Eden, Lorraine. 2010. "Letter from the Editor-in-Chief: Scientists Behaving Badly." *Journal of International Business Studies*, 41. 4: 561–566.

Hogan, Chris E., Zabihollah Rezaee, Richard A. Riley, and Uma K. Velury. 2008. "Financial Statement Fraud: Insights from the Academic Literature." *Auditing: A Journal of Practice and Theory*, 27. 2: 231–252.

Schminke, Marshall. 2009. "Editor's Comments: The Better Angels of Our Nature – Ethics and Integrity in the Publishing Process." *Academy of Management Review*, 34. 4: 586–591.

Stuebs, Marty and Bret Wilkinson. 2010. "Ethics and the Tax Profession: Restoring the Public Interest Focus." *Accounting and the Public Interest*, 10: 13–35.

Wolfe, David T. and Dana R. Hermanson. 2004. "The Fraud Diamond: Considering the Four Elements of Fraud." *CPA Journal* (December): 38–42.

5

SLICING AND DICING
Ex Ante Approaches

> Key insight: Research projects are often huge undertakings that lead to more than one publication. How do authors determine whether the papers coming out of one project are sufficiently different from one another to be considered new papers? We argue that scholars slice and dice at their peril; people get caught and the consequences are long-lasting. We provide some ex ante methods to determine whether a paper is sufficiently new.

Case Example

Example 1

Two co-authors have a major project underway and want to maximize the number of publications from the project. They recognize that journal editors frown on "slicing and dicing" and want to make sure that the papers are sufficiently different so they really *are* different papers. However, the co-authors don't know what makes one paper *sufficiently different* from another. Is it the dataset? The hypotheses? The empirical findings? They search for information on what makes one paper sufficiently different from another and cannot find a definitive answer.

Example 2

A new assistant professor is carving up his dissertation into journal articles. He sends the first article, which has the major theoretical and empirical contributions of the dissertation, to the *Academy of Management Journal* (AMJ). The second article, which looks at two moderators of the main effects in the first paper, is sent to the *Journal of International Business Studies* (JIBS). Both papers use the same dataset and variables, with the exception that the moderator variables in the JIBS submission are treated as control variables in the AMJ submission. The hypotheses in the JIBS submission include some of the same hypotheses that appear in the AMJ submission, with the addition of new ones for the moderator effects. The AMJ submission goes in first; the JIBS submission follows a month later. In the JIBS submission, the author makes no mention of the prior submission to AMJ, either in the letter to the editor or in the body of the paper. Nor does the author tell AMJ that a second submission to JIBS is planned. The author reasons that he does not need to mention either submission to the other journal because neither submission has been published and, even if both papers should eventually be accepted for publication, they will be so changed during the reviewing process that the likelihood of duplicate material is low.

Example 3

Two years earlier, a professor published an article in the *American Journal of Political Science* (AJPS). She has now refined her thinking and has a follow-up article building on the first one, but still using the same dataset. Can she also submit the follow-up paper to AJPS?

Example 4

Three co-authors submitted a paper to the *American Economic Review* (AER), which was rejected after the first round of review. The co-authors spent a year significantly revising the paper based on the reviewers' and editor's feedback. The co-authors believed that the revised paper was sufficiently different that they could submit the revised paper to AER as a "new submission." In their cover letter to the journal, they make no mention of the previously rejected submission.

The Problem

All four of the above examples are slightly disguised real-world examples with which we are familiar, either from our own research, our terms as editors on various journals, and/or from discussions with other journal editors. We suspect you can add examples to those listed above.

All four examples involve what we refer to as the potential for "slicing and dicing" and what the Committee on Publication Ethics (COPE)[1] calls "salami publishing" or "redundancy"; that is, the excessive cutting up of a research project into multiple papers where each paper overlaps significantly with other papers from the same project. Examples 1 and 2 involve situations where the papers come simultaneously out of the same project. Example 3 (closely related papers follow one another in sequence) and Example 4 (the authors revise a previously rejected paper and send the revised paper to the same journal) involve sequential slicing and dicing.

The core issue in all of these cases is determining *when a paper is really or sufficiently new*. How do we know when it is OK to publish two or more papers out of one project? Where do we cross the line from being OK to engaging in slicing and dicing?

We all know how heavy the publish-or-perish pressures are, especially for junior faculty.[2] An author's desire to segment his or her big research project into multiple, stand-alone papers aimed at different journals is therefore not surprising. The key issue is where to draw the line between two papers that are "siblings" (with the same intellectual parents but different children) and those that are "clones." In this chapter, we address ex ante approaches to handling the ethical dilemma of slicing and dicing. In Chapter 6, we look at ex post approaches as recommended by COPE.

Ex Ante Approaches

We see four possible ex ante approaches for handling the slicing-and-dicing problem.

Craft Different Papers at Project Inception

Kirkman and Chen (2011: 437) provide our first ex ante approach. When authors are starting out at the beginning of a project, it is easier if they "intentionally craft and design... separate papers from the inception of the project." By starting at the beginning, authors have a roadmap that helps keep the papers separate. The papers can, for example, be aimed at different audiences, start with different research questions and theoretical approaches, and/or use different datasets.

Follow the Journal's Instructions

What if "the horse is out of the barn" and you didn't craft separate papers from the beginning? What can you do? Our advice is to first turn to what the journal editors say on this topic. Editors want innovative, thought-provoking, original articles published in their journals. They know about the pressures to engage in slicing and dicing, and that authors may check the box that an article is "original" even if it comes out of a big research project. Most journals therefore have an explicit policy defining originality and asking authors to confirm at the time of submission that their paper is original.

Journals usually require authors to "check the box" that their manuscript (1) is original, (2) is not published or under review at another journal, and (3) will not be submitted to another journal during the review process. In addition, the submission requirements ask authors to check the box to confirm that their manuscripts have not previously been submitted to the journal for review. Some journals go beyond this list to define what they see as an original manuscript; the JIBS Code of Ethics for Authors, for example, devotes several paragraphs to what the editors see as original and what the journal considers to be self-plagiarism or redundancy.[3]

In Example 1 (carving out papers from a project) and Example 2 (carving up a dissertation into papers), the authors should therefore look to the journals for definitions of originality, both to the Instructions to Authors and to the Code of Ethics (if the journal has one).

Example 3 (sequential papers) and Example 4 (revised and submitted to the same journal after rejection) are slightly different problems. Journals do provide instructions that are helpful for these situations. Michele Kacmar's 2009 AMJ "From the Editors" letter, "An Ethical Quiz," specifically addresses these cases in her *Scenario 2: Data Reuse*. Kacmar (2009, 432) explains that AMJ requires authors to answer two questions, quoted here:

> Has another manuscript from this same database ever been previously submitted to AMJ? If yes, please note this in your cover letter, explain how this paper differs from the earlier one, and attach a copy of the previous manuscript.
>
> Has another manuscript from this same database been accepted by or previously published at AMJ or at another journal? If yes, please note this in your cover letter, explain how this paper differs from the previous one, and attach a copy of the accepted or published manuscript.

The first question addresses papers that have been previously submitted to AMJ (Example 4); the second addresses articles previously published in AMJ (Example 3). In a situation where the author says "yes" to either question, AMJ requires the author to add an explanation to the cover letter at the time of submission and attach the other manuscript.

JIBS also has an FAQ posted that discourages resubmissions when a manuscript has been rejected after review, except in special circumstances that are outlined in the FAQ.[4] The JIBS Code of Ethics for Authors does not specifically address Example 3 (sequential publications), but we believe the case would fall within the section on Self-Plagiarism.[5]

Do an Originality Analysis

Both AMJ and JIBS, interestingly, do allow a bit of wiggle room for exceptions from what might be called the "no second kick at the can" rule, deterring authors from making sequential slice-and-dice submissions to the same journal. It is this wiggle room – as mapped out by AMJ and JIBS – that we see as really helpful to authors in determining as to when carving up a project into papers moves from OK into the unacceptable realm of slicing and dicing.

The JIBS FAQ would allow the authors in Example 4 to make a new submission if "the revised manuscript becomes a new manuscript through significant revision in terms of theory development, empirical work and discussion, and also uses a substantially different dataset."[6] The FAQ adds that "the addition of one or two new variables to an old dataset does not make a new dataset."

Example 4 was also directly addressed in a 2009 AMJ "From the Editors" letter by (at the time) Editor-in-Chief Duane Ireland. His editorial, "When Is a 'New' Paper Really New?," specifically lists three criteria that must be met for a previously rejected manuscript to be considered a new submission to AMJ: "The new manuscript must (1) address modified or new research questions, (2) use new theoretical arguments, and (3) use additional or new data to test the proposed relationships. Satisfying or meeting one or two of the three criteria is not sufficient" (Ireland, 2009, 10) So, if the authors in Examples 3 and 4 were to meet all three criteria, it would be OK for them to make a new submission to AMJ.

These two editorial policy statements suggest a useful way for authors to determine when a paper that is part of a project is sufficiently new to be separately published. If the authors create an originality matrix comparing the two papers in terms of their component parts, it should be clear both to authors and to the journal editors whether there is sufficient differentiation to justify separation of the papers. The statements by the two journals suggest that AMJ would require differentiation in three areas: research questions, theoretical arguments, and dataset. To this list, JIBS would add empirical tests and discussion. Kirkman and Chen (2011) develop a similar matrix, which they call a *uniqueness analysis*, based on five components: research questions, theories used, constructs/variables, and theoretical implications and managerial implications. Kirkman and Chen provide two helpful tables, using their own published papers, to show how authors can compare manuscripts in terms of originality.

Based on these three sets of criteria for originality identified by Ireland, Kirkman, and Chen, and the JIBS FAQ, we recommend that authors set up a matrix where the columns are papers and the rows are criteria used to judge originality (see Table 5.1).

To make the comparison even sharper, we argue that it is important not only to fill in the table cells, but also to examine *differences* and *similarities or overlap* between the two papers. Table 5.1 therefore also has two columns at the end where the author must assess overlap and differences.[7]

Completing Table 5.1, of course, forces the author to stand back and be ruthlessly honest about both papers – not an easy task. Authors must use a self-critical eye or the exercise is pointless. Once the exercise has been completed, the author should look hard at the answers, particularly the last two columns on overlaps and differences. These columns may well suggest ways that the two papers could be further revised so as to make them even more separate. Is Table 5.1 sufficient to determine originality? Probably not for empirical papers. To do this rigorously and thoroughly, we must go further and delve into the issue of what makes two datasets different. To do this we recommend adding Table 5.2, an "original data" matrix (see Box 5.1).

TABLE 5.1 An originality matrix (part 1).

	Paper 1	Paper 2	Overlap	Difference
Research question(s)				
Theoretical arguments				
Dataset				
Constructs/variables used				
Empirical tests				
Discussion: theoretical implications				
Discussion: managerial implications				

TABLE 5.2 JAP original data appendix (originality matrix part 2).

Variables in the complete dataset	MS 1 (status)	MS 2 (status)	MS 3 (status)
Variable 1			
Variable 2			
X			
X			
Variable N			

BOX 5.1

Instructions: Authors should edit accordingly to describe what has been done and what is planned. Use as many columns as necessary. Provide any additional information necessary to clarify the unique contribution of each manuscript. Please note the status of each manuscript connected to the data collection: under review, in press, published, current ms, planned (anything else). The data reported in this manuscript have been previously published and/or were collected as part of a larger data collection (add when). Findings from the data collection have been reported in separate manuscripts. MS 1 (status) focuses on variables _____; MS 2 (status) focuses on variables _____. MS 3 (status) focuses on variables _____. Attach additional columns for more manuscripts as needed. Table 5.2 displays where each data variable appears in each study, as well as the current status of each study.

Journal of Applied Psychology (JAP) has a long-standing policy of publishing *original data*. JAP requires authors to inform the editorial team, either in their cover letter or in the methods section, if their dataset has or will be used in other journal submissions not only to JAP but to other journals. If an author says "yes," JAP sends the author a separate form to complete.

Based on the completed Table 5.2, together with any accompanying documentation (e.g., other manuscripts), the JAP editors can more easily and accurately determine whether or not to accept the manuscript as a new submission.

We therefore view a completed originality matrix as consisting of carefully and honestly prepared Tables 5.1 and 5.2. A completed originality matrix can help with all four of the above examples, whether starting a project and trying to determine the optimal number and content of the papers (Example 1), carving up a dissertation (Example 2), or the sequential issues discussed in Examples 3 and 4. By completing both tables, authors can determine whether two papers are sufficiently different that they can ethically be submitted to the same or different journals and published separately.

Transparency Matters

In addition to determining originality, there is an additional ethical issue involved in slicing and dicing: *transparency*. What should the author tell the journal editors at the time of submission? We recommend that authors "spill the beans." Transparency is the best policy. Go for full disclosure, as Schminke (2009) argued. Submitting a cover letter with the completed originality matrix and the relevant papers to the journal editors accomplishes full transparency.

Kirkman and Chen (2011, 442) are also strong advocates for full transparency. They recognize that transparency jeopardizes the double-blind review process, but argue that transparency matters more, given that the "ultimate goal of science is to *build* and *advance* our knowledge base," which requires a clear assessment of the unique contributions of each paper. We recognize the problem (see Chapter 8 on "double-blind review"), but also agree with their assessment and have argued so elsewhere (Eden, 2010). Transparency – especially in the case of possible slicing and dicing – matters. Journal editors should be provided with full information by authors, and then the decision on whether to share the originality matrix and papers with the journal's reviewers (and thus violate one side of the double-blind review) should be left up to the journal editors.

Recap

We argue that there are established criteria for determining whether two papers from the same research project are sufficiently different to be considered that both can be treated as new papers. Authors should use these criteria to determine whether a paper is original. We summarize the implications for our four Examples as:

- Example 1 (carving up a project into papers): Best to do this at the beginning, not the end, of a project. Authors should deconstruct their papers using the originality matrix (Tables 5.1 and 5.2) and share these results with journal editors of the different papers at the time of submission.
- Example 2 (main effect paper followed by moderator paper): The case, as described, would not pass the originality matrix test; moreover, there is a lack of transparency. The author should revise both papers, using the originality matrix, until they are sufficiently different to be treated as separate. He should provide both the matrix and papers to both journals.
- Example 3 (second paper that grew out of the first one): The answer is this depends on how different the two papers are from one another. Again, an originality matrix is needed and all information should be supplied to the journal if the author decides to go forward with submission.
- Example 4 (once rejected after review, can I revise and make a new submission?): The answer is probably not, except in exceptional circumstances. These circumstances require an assessment that the two papers were sufficiently different, based on a completed originality matrix, and submission of the matrix and papers to the journal editors.

Discussion Questions

1. Do you think that "slicing and dicing" (or "salami publishing") is a problem?
2. Have you been faced with situations such as the ones described here? How did you or you and your co-authors handle them?
3. What criteria would you use to determine when a manuscript is new?
4. Is the policy advocated here (an originality matrix plus transparency) too onerous a burden to place on authors?
5. What advice do you give to your doctoral students and junior faculty about managing a big research project like a dissertation through to publication?

Notes

1 http://publicationethics.org/
2 See also Chapter 4, "Scientists Behaving Badly: Insights from the Fraud Triangle."
3 www.palgrave-journals.com/jibs/jibs_ethics_code.html
4 www.palgrave-journals.com/jibs/faq.html#resubmit
5 www.palgrave-journals.com/jibs/jibs_ethics_code.html
6 www.palgrave-journals.com/jibs/faq.html#resubmit
7 When Lorraine Eden was JIBS editor-in-chief, she occasionally asked authors to complete a version of Table 5.1 in cases that appeared to possibly involve slicing and dicing.

The authors and Lorraine then engaged in a dialogue, based on the matrix, to determine whether the new submission was sufficiently new. These dialogues led to the JIBS FAQ.

References and Additional Reading

Eden, Lorraine. 2010. "Letter from the Editor-in-Chief: Scientists Behaving Badly." *Journal of International Business Studies*, 41. 4(May):561–566.

Ireland, R. Duane. 2009. "From the Editors: When Is a 'New' Paper Really New? *Academy of Management Journal*, 52. 1: 9–10.

Kacmar, K. Michele. 2009. "From the Editors: An Ethical Quiz." *Academy of Management Journal*, 52. 3:432–434

Kirkman, Brad and Gilead Chen. 2011. "Maximizing Your Data or Data Slicing? Recommendations for Managing Multiple Submissions from the Same Dataset." *Management and Organization Review*, 7. 3, 433–446.

Schminke, Marshall. 2009. "Editor's Comments: The Better Angels of Our Nature – Ethics and Integrity in the Publishing Process." *Academy of Management Review*, 34. 4: 586–591.

6

SLICING AND DICING

Ex Post Approaches

Key insight: In Chapter 5, we discussed an important issue facing researchers: How do authors determine whether the papers coming out of one project are sufficiently different from one another so that they can be considered to be new papers? We looked at ex ante methods that authors could use to determine whether a paper was sufficiently new. In this chapter, we follow up with ex post methods for determining novelty; that is, once the paper has been written and submitted for review, how can reviewers and editors be assured of its originality?

Introduction

Let us start by saying that we are not against working in teams and developing multiple papers from a big research project that are then published in different journals. In fact, we are all very much in favor of team-based research projects, and have been actively doing that for some years now with various co-authors. Clearly, we want scholars to gain the advantages of economies of scale, scope, and learning that come from developing big projects that lead to multiple publications. Working in teams offers the advantages we typically associate with strategic alliances: The ability to bring together and leverage complementary resources, the creation of routines and capabilities that generate efficiencies and synergies, and the opportunity for greater flexibility and speed, among other advantages.

Big projects with two or more co-researchers are now common, perhaps even dominant, in terms of how we do research now within the Academy, at least based on our observation of authorship in our scholarly journals where the norm now appears to be two, three, and even four or five co-authors. The October

2016 issue of the *Academy of Management Journal*, for example, has 15 articles; only two are single authored. The December 2016 issue of *International Studies Quarterly* has 17 articles, five of which are single authored. The February 2017 issue of the *American Economic Review* has 12 articles and only two are single authored.

When a team of researchers work together for several years, each new paper builds off the previous ones as the authors develop a deeper understanding of their research area, see more nuances, and find more puzzles to solve. As that building and expansion occur, basic ideas are likely to be repeated across the papers and may look repetitious to an outsider – and to the authors themselves.

Chapter 5 addressed the issue of how authors themselves can determine the "bright line" between "sufficiently new" and "excessive overlap." We recommended that authors do an originality analysis (see Tables 5.1 and 5.2) to compare papers, and that authors share this analysis with journal editors at the time of submission. The originality analysis would then help the editor (and reviewers if the editor chooses to share the information) determine the degree of novelty. Our general advice was: Be transparent. Assuming an author has been transparent, it is up to the reviewers and editors to assess the extent of overlap and unique contribution.

However, what if the authors are not transparent and do not provide this information at the time of submission? How can a journal editor and the paper's reviewers separate acceptable overlap from "slicing and dicing"? More generally, how can editors and reviewers identify instances of scholarly dishonesty, and what should they do if they find such evidence?

Case Example

Perhaps you have read Honig and Bedi (2012), "The Fox in the Hen House." The authors examined the 279 papers presented at the 2009 Academy of Management (AOM) meetings, in the International Management division, for evidence of plagiarism. They used regression analysis to test hypotheses about possible antecedents to plagiarism (for example, gender, degrees from non-English-speaking countries, junior/untenured faculty, authors located in emerging ("non-core") economies). The software program Turnitin.com was used to determine the amount of plagiarized material in each paper.[1]

The results were startling: One quarter of the presented papers (71 of the 279 papers) showed some evidence of plagiarism, and 13.6 percent had an average of 5 percent or more of the text plagiarized (approximately 1,000 words). For authors from "core/developed" countries (North America, Europe, Australia, and New Zealand) the percentages were low, but still higher than most faculty might have expected: 21 percent of papers showed some evidence of plagiarism and a quarter of those had more than 5 percent of the text plagiarized. The highest offenders appear to have been papers by an author or co-author located in a non-core (emerging or developing) country. Over 40 percent of the papers written by scholars in "non-core" countries showed some evidence of plagiarism; half of those had more than 5 percent of the text plagiarized (Honig and Bedi, 2012, 113). Education in a non-core rather than a core country was also a differentiating factor (27 percent non-core vs 21 percent core); however, neither gender (male versus female) nor rank (untenured/junior versus tenured/senior) appeared to matter (Honig and Bedi, 2012, 116).

While one might argue that authors are typically less careful on conference submissions than they are on submissions to scholarly journals, the plagiarism issue clearly matters for both. Moreover, the plagiarism estimates of Honig and Bedi are underreports because the authors deliberately excluded self-plagiarism, stating that "If authors used sections from their own previous work or cited the primary source, then it was not considered plagiarism" (112). If the authors had taken "slicing and dicing" into account, we suspect that the percentages – across the board – would have been much higher.

Ex Post Approaches 1: Software Solutions

If plagiarism is a real problem, and it apparently is, what should we do, as a community of scholars, about scholarly dishonesty? Honig and Bedi conclude that "Institutional norms that many of us take for granted are clearly and brazenly being disregarded"; they call for AOM to "implement more rigorous standards in order to reduce plagiarism and to ensure high-quality and original scholarship" (2012, p. 119).

Jean Bartunek, in her introduction to Honig and Bedi (2012), noted that, starting in spring 2012, all journals published by AOM would use the software program CrossCheck to detect plagiarism in submissions.[2] The move to use CrossCheck since then has been rapidly spreading through the journals, with publishers deciding whether only conditionally accepted manuscripts or all manuscripts should go through the CrossCheck process. Obviously putting all papers through CrossCheck substantially increases the financial cost.

However, regardless of the financial cost, submitting papers to some form of software such as Turnitin.com, iThenticate, or CrossCheck is now a necessary part of the journal review procedure. We may not like this nor like the psychosocial (lack of trust) message that it sends to prospective authors, but given the huge numbers of papers now being submitted to our journals and the evidence in Hong and Bedi (2012), plagiarism-checking software was inevitable. As of 2017, more than 500 publishers now use Crossref Similarity Check powered by iThenticate to test journal submissions for plagiarism.[3]

In addition to software options such as CrossCheck, scholarly journals benefit from membership in national and international organizations that are devoted to improving ethics in professional associations and scholarly publishing. Through their memberships, journals and publishers can signal their commitment to scholarly and professional ethics, learn and adopt best practices, and bring the weight and voice of their professional associations to bear on these issues. One of the best known of these associations is the Committee on Publication Ethics (COPE), which we discuss below.[4]

Ex Post Approaches 2: COPE to the Rescue

The Committee on Publication Ethics is a non-governmental organization that was set up by a group of journal editors to share best practices for handling ethical violations.[5] Over time, COPE has developed a whole set of procedures that it recommends editors follow when faced with problems such as plagiarism and self-plagiarism. Nearly 11,500 universities, journals, and publishers are now COPE members as of February 2017.[6]

As an example of how COPE could be helpful, the Committee has a whole section on "salami publishing" (which we call "slicing and dicing"; see Chapter 5). The key issues identified by COPE are (1) the degree of overlap between the two publications and (2) whether the author sought to hide the overlap.

COPE provides a variety of flowcharts to help editors determine best practice in identifying and handling cases of suspected misconduct.[7] For example, flowchart 1 deals with a suspected redundant publication in a submitted manuscript; flowchart 2 with the same issue in a published article. In both flowcharts, the key issue is whether there is major or minor overlap/redundancy between the two papers. Major redundancy is defined as both papers having the "same dataset with identical findings and/or evidence that authors have sought to hide redundancy, e.g. by changing title, author order or not referring to previous papers." Minor overlap is defined as "salami publishing with some element of redundancy or legitimate re-analysis (e.g. sub-group/extended follow-up/discussion aimed at different audience)." Note that evidence of appearing to hide the overlap can raise the level from minor to major redundancy.

Some examples of actual cases submitted to COPE may be helpful here in distinguishing between major and minor redundancy (search the COPE website for other examples):

- Salami publication:[8] Four papers were completed by the same research team, with each paper referencing the prior publications. The fourth paper in the series was rejected on the grounds that there was significant overlap between the new paper and the earlier publications. COPE recommended, first, distinguishing between salami and redundant publication; arguing that if there were two thirds of overlap between the two papers, this was a redundant publication. COPE defines a salami publication as covering "the same population, methods, and question." Second, if the two papers asked related questions, they should be published as one paper; if the two papers asked separate questions, they could be separate publications. Splitting up papers by outcomes was not legitimate.

- Duplicate publication or salami publication?[9] A paper submitted to a journal is discovered by a reviewer to have been already published in another journal. When the editor contacts the author, he responds that the two papers are different. COPE's advice was to focus on the overlap between the two papers, determining whether the overlap was major (two thirds would make it a duplicate publication) or minor (a salami publication) and then follow COPE's rules for one or the other event.
- Duplicate submission:[10] Two papers based on the same research project on pathogens in school children were submitted to different journals. One analyzed the data by socioeconomic class; the other by school attended. A substantial portion of the texts were the same in the two manuscripts, especially in the data description and research methods. COPE recommended determining whether this was a duplicate or salami publication.

We have much to learn from other associations and journals that have faced the same or similar issues to the ones identified in Honig and Bedi (2012). In addition, we have much to offer to other associations and journals by being at the table and exercising voice. We believe that AOM, with its Code of Ethics and well-developed ethical policies and procedures, can help shape international best practice in the research ethics arena.

Ex Post Approaches 3: Education

A third ex post method to handle scholarly dishonesty is to create a library of resources for sharing key reports among authors, editors, and reviewers. CODEX (Centre for Research Ethics and Bioethics) in Uppsala, Sweden, for example, now maintains a very useful website with rules and guidelines for research that includes multiple links to resources on research ethics.[11] The CODEX page includes the 2009 (a, b, c) reports by the Organisation for Economic Co-operation and Development (OECD). Bringing guides to best practices together in one location on a website creates worldwide value, by making these reports widely and quickly available to scholars.

Individual professional associations are already gathering together resources on academic dishonesty. For example, the AOM now maintains an ethics page at ethics.aom.org with links to articles on ethics in research published in AOM journals, the Ethics Education Video Series, and "The Ethicist" blog posts, among other resources.

Ultimately, while software programs like CrossCheck and iThenticate and organizations like COPE can help journal editors and reviewers find and evaluate possible cases of scholarly misconduct, the "rubber meets the road" through student and faculty education. This is where our professional associations and journals can and do already play an important role, through activities such as:

1.   Providing ethical training of PhD students and junior faculty in Professional Development Workshops at annual meetings.
2.   Organizing panels and roundtables on ethics at annual meetings and elsewhere.
3.   Creating publicly available videos on ethics in research.
4.   Writing and publishing on ethics.

We conclude by reporting on how our major professional associations in the social sciences are currently dealing with ethical issues, in terms of professional codes of ethics, as of February 2017. Lorraine Eden is currently working with the Academy of International Business (AIB) Executive Board and Headquarters to develop a Code of Ethics, which will (assuming the code is adopted) apply to all AIB members in terms of their AIB activities. In preparing the draft AIB Code of Ethics, she looked at websites for the major professional associations in the social sciences to determine whether or not they have a Code of Ethics for their members. Her results are reported in Table 6.1. As you can see from the table, most of our associations now do have a code of ethics for their members.

Discussion Questions

1.   What is your response to the Honig and Bedi article?
2.   If you are a journal editor, have you been faced with situations similar to those described here? How did you handle them? Do you agree with the COPE templates? Is your journal a member of COPE?
3.   As a reviewer, what would you do if you were presented with evidence of two overlapping papers? Should you inform the editors?
4.   Is your professional association and its journals a member of COPE?

Notes

1   www.turnitin.com/. A brief aside: Lorraine Eden requires her undergraduate and graduate (masters and PhD) students to turn their papers into Turnitin.com before they are submitted to her. The students can submit as often as they like, and in this manner, they can learn what is and is not plagiarism. She accepts the papers only after they have received a "green" rating from Turnitin.com. Her cases of plagiarism have basically disappeared since she started this practice some years ago, and she highly recommends it to other instructors.
2   www.crossref.org/crosscheck/index.html
3   www.ithenticate.com/products/crosscheck
4   Lorraine gives away her bias here by noting that the *Journal of International Business Studies* joined COPE (as did all the Palgrave journals) at the beginning of her term as editor-in-chief.
5   http://publicationethics.org/
6   http://publicationethics.org/members
7   http://publicationethics.org/resources/flowcharts
8   http://publicationethics.org/case/salami-publication

TABLE 6.1 Codes of ethics in social science professional organizations

Organization	Department	College	Website	Code of ethics	COE webpage
American Accounting Association	Accounting	Business	http://aaahq.org/	no?	X
American Bar Association	Law	Social sciences	http://americanbar.org	yes	www.americanbar.org/groups/professional_responsibility/committees_commissions/ethicsandprofessionalresponsibility.html
American Economic Association	Economics	Social sciences	www.aeaweb.org/	no	no
American Finance Association	Finance	Business	www.afajof.org/view/index.html	yes	www.afajof.org/details/news/9947561/AFA-Code-of-Professional-Conduct-and-Ethics.html
American Institute of CPAs	Accounting	Business	www.aicpa.org/Pages/default.aspx	yes	www.aicpa.org/RESEARCH/STANDARDS/CODEOFCONDUCT/Pages/default.aspx
American Marketing Association	Marketing	Business	www.ama.org/Pages/default.aspx	yes	www.ama.org/AboutAMA/Pages/Statement-of-Ethics.aspx
Academy of Management	Management	Business	http://aom.org/	yes	http://aom.org/About-AOM/Code-of-Ethics.aspx?terms=code%20of%20ethics
American Psychological Association	Psychology	Social sciences	www.apa.org/	yes	www.apa.org/ethics/index.aspx
American Political Science Association	Political science	Social sciences	www.apsanet.org/	yes	www.apsanet.org/RESOURCES/For-Faculty/Ethics

Organization	Department	College	Website	Code of ethics	COE webpage
American Sociological Association	Sociology	Social sciences	www.asanet.org/	yes	www.asanet.org/membership/code-ethics
American Statistical Association	Statistics	Sciences	www.amstat.org/	yes	www.amstat.org/ASA/Your-Career/Ethical-Guidelines-for-Statistical-Practice.aspx
European International Business Academy	International business	Business	www.eiba.org/r/default.asp?iId=GFDGHJ	no	no
Institution of Operations Research and the Management Sciences	Management information sciences	Business	www.informs.org/	yes	www.certifiedanalytics.org/ethics.php
International Studies Association	International studies	Social sciences	www.isanet.org/	no	International ethics section but no COE

9 http://publicationethics.org/case/conflict-interest-duplicate-publication
10 http://publicationethics.org/case/duplicate-submission
11 http://www.codex.vr.se/en/etik6.shtml

References and Additional Reading

Bartunek, Jean. 2012. "Introduction: Plagiarism in Submissions to the AOM Conference." *Academy of Management Learning and Education*, 11. 1: 99–100.

Honig, Benson and Akanksha Bedi. 2012. "The Fox in the Hen House: A Critical Examination of Plagiarism among Members of the Academy of Management." *Academy of Management Learning and Education*, 11. 1: 101–123.

Honig, Benson, Joseph Lampel, Donald Siegel, and Paul Drnevich. 2014. "Ethics in the Production and Dissemination of Management Research: Institutional Failure or Individual Fallibility?" *Journal of Management Studies*, 51. 1: 118–142.

Kirkman, Brad and Gilad Chen. 2011. "Maximizing Your Data or Data Slicing? Recommendations for Managing Multiple Submissions from the Same Dataset." *Management and Organization Review*, 7:3: 433–446.

OECD Global Science Forum. 2009a. *Best Practices for Ensuring Scientific Integrity and Preventing Research Misconduct*. Paris: OECD. Accessed February 18, 2017. www.oecd.org/dataoecd/37/17/40188303.pdf

OECD Global Science Forum. 2009b. *Facilitating International Research Misconduct Investigations. Final Report of the Co-ordinating Committee*. Paris: OECD. Accessed February 18, 2017. www.oecd.org/dataoecd/29/4/42713295.pdf

OECD Global Science Forum. 2009c. *Practical Guide for Investigating Research Misconduct Allegations in International Collaborative Research Projects*. Paris: OECD. Accessed February 18, 2017. www.oecd.org/dataoecd/42/34/42770261.pdf

7

RETRACTION

Mistake or Misconduct?

Key insight: Seeing a journal article with the word "RETRACTION" stamped in diagonal watermark across its front page is probably a shock to most social science scholars. Not only is the percentage of articles withdrawn from publication across all disciplines very small, the number of retracted articles in the social sciences is small relative to those in, for example, biomedical journals. Why are articles retracted? In this chapter, we discuss the various categories of article retraction, look at retraction in the context of business and management journals, provide examples of retraction categories, and end with questions for discussion.

Introduction

Are you familiar with the names of these individuals: Joachim Boldt, Ulrich Lichtenthaler, Naoki Mori, and Diederik Stapel? Probably not – unless you work in the same research area as they do. They have been incredibly prolific scholars, with many more publications than most other researchers. Unfortunately, their publication records have been too good to be true and many of their publications have now been withdrawn – retracted – by the journals. Because their number of retracted articles is so large, these individuals have been identified as "repeat offenders" and some (Stapel, for example) have even become household names (Bhattacharjee, 2013).

Retraction Watch, with the support of the MacArthur Foundation, maintains an "unofficial leaderboard" tabulating the 30 worst offenders in terms of their number of retracted articles.[1] They come from all disciples. At the top of the list, as of February 18, 2017, are two anesthesiology researchers, Yoshitake Fujii

(183 retracted articles) and Joachim Boldt (94 retractions). Third on the list is Diederik Stapel, a social psychologist, with 58 retracted articles. A former accounting professor, James Hunton, is 8th on the list with 37 retracted articles. Ulrich Lichtenthaler, a management professor, is 28th on the list with 16 retractions, including one at the *Academy of Management Journal*.

Where do article retractions appear? If you said "in biomedical journals," you would be right, but that is only partly correct. Retracted articles appear in journals from all disciplines across the board; and they can be found in our own management and business journals, including *Strategic Management Journal, Journal of Management Studies, Organization Science, Research Policy*, and (even!) the *Journal of Business Ethics*.

In this chapter, we explore categories of article retractions and provide examples, look at retractions in business and management journals, and suggest a reading list for those interested in this topic for teaching and/or research purposes.

First, it is important to separate "corrections" and "expressions of concern" from retractions (International Committee of Medical Journal Editors, 2013). *Corrections* can occur in the form of typos or non-consequential mathematical mistakes; the normal process is to publish the correction and link it to the original article. *Expressions of concern* are typically published by journals when they are not sure of the conduct or integrity of the work. A "repeat offender" (an author who has had multiple papers retracted) may lead other journals to question his/her other publications and to publish an expression of concern as a warning to readers. For example, after Shigeaki Kato (a former endocrinology researcher at the University of Tokyo) had five articles retracted, an expression of concern was issued by *Molecular and Cellular Biology* about five other of his papers that were published in that journal (Retraction Watch, 2013). An expression of concern can be used to indicate that the journal editors have started an investigation into a particular article. Since the time from initiation to completion of a retraction can take years, such a statement can be an "early warning signal" to readers that a particular article may be seriously flawed (Jasny, 2011).

Retraction, on the other hand, is the withdrawal of a previously published article from a journal. This is "science's ultimate post-publication punishment: retraction, the official declaration that a paper is so flawed that it must be withdrawn from the literature" (Van Noorden, 2011b, 26). Retractions are very rare; most scholars who work in this area estimate retractions are only 0.02 percent of published papers, that is, 2 in 10,000 (Van Noorden, 2011b, 27). A low percentage, however, may represent the proverbial "tip of the iceberg" since Van Noorden notes that prior surveys suggest "1–2% of scientists admit to having fabricated, falsified or modified data or results at least once."

Retractions are a huge amount of work for journal editors and publishers. Typically, the decision to retract an article is taken after extensive consultation among the journal editor(s), publisher, and the author(s). Because the issues are so sensitive and involve potential damage to author reputation, employment, and income, investigations tend to take place in secret. The average time to retract a published article is estimated as two years, longer when a senior scholar is involved (Chen et al., 2013, 239). Normally, but not always, the journal publishes a formal retraction statement explaining the reason or reasons for withdrawal, and the article appears with a large "retracted" watermark across the front page or entire article.

Why Are Journal Articles Retracted – Mistake or Misconduct?

The key reasons why a journal article is so flawed that it must be withdrawn from publication boil down to two: author misconduct or mistakes. A small percentage of retraction cases involve publisher errors, but by far the most common are author related. For example, Grieneisen and Zhang (2012: 6) found only 9 percent of retracted articles where the reason for retraction was given as "publisher error."

In Table 7.1, we categorize the main types of article retractions. Our list is a compilation and interpretation of lists proposed and used by other authors. We separate author from publisher errors, and then separate the author category into three main types: research misconduct, distrust of data or interpretations, and publishing misconduct.

A key dispute among researchers who study retractions is what percentage of author errors are due to misconduct (deliberate intention to deceive) versus mistakes (inadvertent, unintended errors). There are at least two issues here: (1) imputing motives from actions, and (2) defining what is and is not a fraudulent action.

First, motives are, of course, difficult to identify from actions. Box 1 in Table 7.1 makes it clear how difficult it is to separate mistakes from misconduct because of our inability to distinguish action from motive. We would probably identify "mistakes" as including 1.b.i and possibly other parts of 1.b in Box 1; whereas "misconduct" would most likely include all of 1.a, parts of 1.b, and all of 1.c. Others might put more of these actions into the mistake category.

As an example, suppose the reader or journal editor can see an author error (for example, duplicate paragraphs in two publications), but cannot tell what motivated the author's action. Honest error or deliberate fraud? Most authors, when faced by an editor questioning them about the duplication, will argue they made an honest mistake and no intentional fraud was involved. Moreover, editors are also reluctant to attach motive to action – at least in print – fearing possible retribution such as being sued for defamation of character by the author. As a result, retraction statements tend to be "safe summaries" of "the facts" without much detail, in order to avoid implying anything about the author or author's motivations for their actions.

Second, there have been several attempts in the literature to separate mistakes from misconduct. Below, we review recent empirical work on this topic.

TABLE 7.1 Categories of article retraction.

1. Author error		
	a. Research misconduct	
		i. Data fraud (data falsification, fabrication, or manipulation, intentionally biased research design, data used without permission)
		ii. Inaccurate or misleading reporting of results
		iii. Other research misconduct (failure to obtain legally required oversight such as institutional board approval, ethical problems with research)
	b. Distrust data or interpretations	
		i. Honest error (incorrect data; calculation errors)
		ii. Findings cannot be replicated
		iii. Published data or interpretations no longer considered valid or reliable by some or all the authors (e.g. unexplained data irreproducibility, experimental artifacts discovered post-publication)
	c. Publishing misconduct	
		i. Plagiarism from the works of others
		ii. Redundant publication (duplicate publications, self-plagiarism, failure to disclose or acknowledge original publications)
		iii. Authorship issues (failure to consult or inform listed authors, excluding authors who contributed substantially to the work)
		iv. Vague copyright issues or legal concerns
2. Publisher error		
	a. Accidental duplicate publication	
	b. Accidental publication of version without final author corrections	
	c. Published in wrong journal or wrong issue	
3. Other and unspecified reasons		

Source: Authors' integration and revision of retraction categories identified in Fang, Steen, and Casadevall (2012, figure 1), Grieneisen and Zhang (2012, table 2) and Wager and Williams (2011, table 1).

Steen (2011) hypothesized that inadvertent error papers should be randomly distributed throughout the literature; whereas deliberately fraudulent papers would be quite different: non-random, clustered, targeting particular journals, with larger numbers of co-author teams. He separated the 788 English-language papers that had been retracted from the PubMed database between 2000 and 2010 into three categories: fraud (197), research error (545), and unknown (46). Research fraud was defined so as to only include data fabrication or falsification; plagiarized and self-plagiarized papers, for example, were classified as research error. As a result, the research fraud category was defined quite narrowly. Looking at the data, Steen found clear evidence of deliberate fraud, concluding that "papers retracted because of data fabrication or falsification represent a calculated effort to deceive" and that "such behavior is neither naïve, feckless nor inadvertent" (113). More than 50 percent of the fraudulent papers had a first author who had written other fraudulent papers; whereas less than 20 percent of the erroneous papers had a first author who was a repeat offender.

In Fang, Steen, and Casadevall (2012), misconduct is defined so as to include fraud, suspected fraud, duplicate publication (self-plagiarism), and plagiarism. The "error" category, in this paper, is therefore much smaller and more likely closer to the definition of mistakes, when compared to Steen (2011). The authors found that about three quarters of the 2,047 retracted papers indexed in PubMed since 1973 were due to misconduct, while less than one quarter were due to error. Their percentages, however, are based on all retracted articles, including those where no reason was given for the retraction. In Table 7.2, we recalculate the percentage distribution using the smaller denominator of articles where reasons for retraction were provided.

A broad statistical analysis of retracted articles, by Grieneisen and Zhang (2012), analyzes a database of 4,232 retracted articles in the PubMed and Web of Science (WoS) databases between 1928 and 2011. By including WoS journals, this paper branches out of the biomedical literature to include the social and physical sciences. The addition of WoS articles is very useful because the authors can capture retractions across a much wider array of disciplines, and can also perform subgroup analysis comparing WoS with PubMed journals. The

TABLE 7.2 Retracted articles in PubMed, 1977–2011.

Articles by type*	Number	Distribution (category as % of articles with reasons)
All articles	2,047	
Articles with provided reasons	1,865	
• Fraud (fabrication/falsification)	697	37.4
• Suspected fraud	192	10.3
• Plagiarism	200	10.7
• Duplicate publication	290	15.5
• Error	437	23.4
• Other	108	5.8
No reason given	182	

* Articles can be classified in more than one category

Source: Authors' calculations using data in Fang, Steen, and Casadevall (2012, table 2).

TABLE 7.3 Retracted articles in PubMed and Web of Science, 1980–2010.

Articles by Type*	Number	Distribution (category as % of articles with reasons)
All articles	4,232	
Articles with provided reasons	3,631	
• Fraudulent/fabricated data	602	16.6
• Distrust data or interpretations	915	25.2
• Other research misconduct	123	3.4
• Plagiarism	796	21.9
• Duplicate publication	562	15.5
• Authorship issues	271	7.5
• Unspecified "copyright issues"	44	1.2
• Other publishing misconduct	100	2.8
• Publisher error	328	9.0
No reason given	601	

*Articles can be classified in more than one category.

Source: Author's calculations based on data in Grieneisen and Zhang (2012, figure 3).

article also differentiates between author and publisher errors, and breaks the reasons for retraction into nine categories. See Table 7.3 for a summary of their results.

It is interesting to compare Table 7.2 (based on Fang, Steen, and Casadevall's data) and Table 7.3 (based on Grieneisen and Zhang's data). While there are differences in the way the authors grouped the data (see the discussion posted on Retraction Watch, 2013), perhaps the most important difference between the two studies is that Table 7.2 includes retractions in WoS journals and Table 7.1 does not. The percentage of retractions for plagiarism is twice as high in the dataset that includes WoS journals (21.9% versus 10.7%); whereas the duplicate publication percentages are the same (15.5%). The percentage for fraudulent/fabricated data, on the other hand, is half as large (16.6% versus 37.4%). This suggests that biomed journals may be more likely to be plagued by author research problems (data fraud); whereas other journals may see more author publication problems (plagiarism and duplicate publications).

The Grieneisen and Zhang (2012, 1) article also highlights the role played by *repeat offenders* – authors with more than one article retraction – noting that "15 individuals account for more than half of all retractions due to alleged research misconduct." Some authors have so many retractions that they can completely skew total retraction numbers for a particular discipline, university, and country; see table 4 in Grieneisen and Zhang (2012) and Retraction Watch's leaderboard.[2]

In addition to the phenomenon of repeat offenders, some researchers have argued that the profession is shifting in ways that encourage greater probability of fraudulent behavior. Honig et al. (2013), for example, argue that academia is tilting toward treating research as an entrepreneurial activity where authors are more likely to attempt to "game" the system. They argue this is due to the pressures and rewards involved in today's publish-or-perish environment, for example, where tenure and promotion depend on the number of top-tier publications one has in hand.

Steen (2011) provides supportive empirical evidence, finding that research fraudsters are more likely to target top-tier journals. With the publication-to-submission ratio in our top journals well below 10 percent, these authors suggest that scholars will be more likely to cut ethical corners in order to increase their chances of successful publication, especially in top-ranking journals. The rise in self-plagiarism, "slicing and dicing into the smallest publishable unit," coercive citation, and manipulation of data and results are not surprising in this environment. Similar points are made in, for example, Elliott, Marquis, and Neal (2013). When coupled with large financial rewards and/or release time from teaching for high-publishing faculty, the incentives for research misconduct can be significant, as witnessed in several Asian universities (Ching, 2013; Economist, 2013b), Lorraine Eden's *Journal of International Business Studies* (JIBS) editorial (Eden, 2010) and in Chapter 4, "Scientists Behaving Badly: Insights from the Fraud Triangle."

It is also important to point out that research misconduct carries with it a variety of direct and indirect costs. The old adage that "one bad apple spoils the bunch" exemplifies the worry that research misconduct taints and devalues all research, creating a "market for lemons" (Cottrell, 2013). Retractions are also frequently referred to as the "tip of the iceberg," which promotes the view that research is tainted and, similar to littering, may encourage others to engage in misconduct on the grounds that "everyone does it."

An article by Chen et al. (2013) focuses on the costs that retracted articles pose to other scholars and research in general by examining how retracted articles are cited in subsequently published research. Their visuals make it abundantly clear that high-profile retracted articles that are tightly networked into a research area can cause enormous damage to the whole area. Moreover, the damage done to co-authors and to PhD students writing dissertations built on fraudulent or fabricated data provided by their chair can be career threatening; see, for example, the Diederik Stapel case where data fraud occurred in at least 55 papers, many with co-authors, and ten PhD dissertations under his supervision (Bhattacharjee, 2013; "Flawed Science," 2012).

Retractions in Business and Management Journals

If Honig et al. (2013) and Steen (2011) are correct, top-tier journals in the social sciences are likely to be inundated with submissions that now carry a higher likelihood of having research fraud attached. This suggests our journal editors and reviewers need to develop and practice better "trust, but verify" procedures in order to protect research integrity.

Let us illustrate the problem by looking at retraction rates in business and management journals, which are the journals we know best. Karabag and Berggren (2012) used four databases (Business Source Premier, Emerald, Science Direct, and JSTOR) to scan for retracted articles in economics and management, finding a total of 31 articles in management journals (see their table 1) and an even lower number (six) in economics journals (see their table 2). Of the 31 management journal retractions, eight were publications involving Ulrich Lichtenthaler (who now has 12 retractions according to Retraction Watch). Once repeat offenders are removed, the number of retracted articles falls considerably.

Karabag and Berggren are puzzled by the low number of retracted articles and provide some possible explanations. A key reason they give is that the business and management journals do not have an explicit code of ethics in place to handle either plagiarism or research dishonesty. It is true that most of our business and management journals have been "late to the table" at adopting explicit "rules of the game." Perhaps this is because the large publishers (e.g., Wiley, Elsevier) have set up ethics codes to which all of their journals are expected to subscribe. The adoption of software to catch plagiarism and self-plagiarism, such as CrossCheck, is also fairly recent.

However, as a former editor-in-chief of JIBS, Lorraine Eden was distressed to discover that Karabag and Berggren were unaware that JIBS since July 2007 has had an explicit Code of Ethics for authors, editors, and reviewers, and has been a member of COPE, the Committee on Publication Ethics (www.cope.org).

The JIBS Code of Ethics was developed with the explicit goal of NOT having to make ex post journal retractions. The argument for doing so was straightforward. By setting up clear ex ante rules of the game with formal dispute-settlement procedures, JIBS hoped to deter and catch research fraud *before* the papers were published in JIBS. Wide publicity through JIBS editorials, ethics workshops for doctoral students and junior faculty, and JIBS paper development workshops were also used (and continue with the current editorial team) to disseminate best ethical practice. In terms of enforcing these norms and practices, Lorraine's editorial team did have a number of difficult cases that covered many of the types of author error identified in Table 7.1 (primarily plagiarism, self-plagiarism, and authorship issues). However, these were handled almost exclusively at the pre-publication stage. Give us ex ante over ex post rules any day!

Reliance on software programs like CrossCheck and iAuthenticate alone, however, is unlikely to be enough. They do not help with non-publishing-related forms of research misconduct such as data manipulation or fabrication. Even with plagiarism and self-plagiarism cases, as one journal editor reminded us, software is a "rather unsatisfactory first step in a longer process." It may help with the most egregious cases, but comes at a high cost and not only in terms of time needed for already busy editors.

The policies in place at JIBS have now been followed by most business and management journals. The subsequent isomorphic behavior, however, varies considerably. The response by some journals can be quite weak (for example, a journal's publisher has joined COPE so the journal puts a COPE membership stamp on its home page, but does little else to disseminate or enforce ethical norms and practices). Others may take a strong stand with the journal introducing its own code of ethics, which is widely communicated to editors, authors, and reviewers.

There will also be differences between norms and practices since it requires much more effort (and involves more risk) to actually enforce ethical norms than to create and publish them. Reviewers and readers must be prepared to be whistle blowers, identifying suspected cases of author error (both mistakes and misconduct). Journal editors and publishers must have dispute-settlement procedures in place – and be willing to follow them through – even up to the point whereby the journal may actually have to identify a published article as belonging in the 0.02 percent of articles that have been retracted from publication. Indeed, at least one paper (Marusic, Katavic, and Marusic, 2007) has attempted to categorize journals' responsibility for addressing and enforcing research ethics by doing a SWOT (strength, weakness, opportunity, threat) analysis! The 2012 report on the Stapel case, "Flawed Science" (2012), provides a good sense of the work involved.

Examples of Retraction Statements

It may be helpful to understand retraction categories if we share some examples. The statements below are lightly paraphrased versions of the original published statements attached to a number of retracted articles. The original articles are referenced in brackets. We have paraphrased the statements in order to generalize them by taking out the author, journal, and article specifics. YVIP stands for "year, volume, issue, pages." All of these retraction statements are examples of author error.

  1   Data Fraud (Trampe, Stapel, and Siero, *Journal of Consumer Research*, 2011)
      It has come to our attention that TITLE by AUTHOR, which appeared in JOURNAL (YVIP), contained fraudulent data that had been manipulated and at times fabricated by the author. This has been determined by a joint investigation by the Universities of XXX. We are therefore informing our readers that this article has been retracted. We apologize for any problems that the publication of this article may have caused.

2 Data Fabrication (Marx and Stapel, *European Journal of Social Psychology*, 2012)

The following article from JOURNAL (AUTHOR 1, AUTHOR 2, TITLE, JOURNAL, YVIP) has been retracted by agreement between AUTHOR 1, the journal Editor-in-Chief and the publisher. The retraction has been agreed following the results of an investigation into the work of AUTHOR 2. The Committee has determined that this article contained data that was fabricated by AUTHOR 2. His co-author, AUTHOR 1, was unaware of his actions, and not in any way involved.

3 Statistical Errors (Lichtenthaler, *Strategic Management Journal*, 2012)

The following article (AUTHOR, TITLE, JOURNAL, YVIP) has been retracted by agreement between the authors, editors and publisher. The article is retracted at the authors' request due to material technical errors which have rendered many of the article's conclusions incorrect. The first author takes responsibility for these statistical errors.

4 Statistical Errors and Duplication (Lichtenthaler, *Journal of Business Venturing*, 2008)

This article (AUTHOR, TITLE, JOURNAL, YVIP) has been retracted at the request of the Editor-in-Chief and the author. The author contacted the Editor-in-Chief about statistical irregularities in this article in DATE. The Editor-in-Chief thoroughly investigated this article and other preceding papers from the same database. On this basis, the Editor-in-Chief made the decision to retract the paper. The grounds for retraction are an error in statistical analyses, an omitted variable bias, and a "new" measure that was not "new" because it was already used in AUTHOR, TITLE, JOURNAL, YVIP. These errors undermined the review process and are too substantial for a corrigendum. Please see our publisher's policy on Article Withdrawal.

5 Statistical Errors (Ernst, Lichtenthaler, and Carsten, *Journal of Management Studies*, 2011)

The following article from JOURNAL (AUTHOR 1, AUTHOR 2, AUTHOR 3, TITLE, JOURNAL, YVIP) has been retracted by agreement between the authors, the journal's editors and the publisher. The article is retracted due to errors in the reported empirical results, which form part of the basis for the conclusions drawn by the authors in the study. While the second author did not collect the data, he takes the responsibility for these technical errors.

6 Cannot Reproduce Results (Lee et al., *Science*, 2013)

As a result of additional experiments, we wish to retract our paper (AUTHOR, TITLE, JOURNAL, YVIP). Specifically, we have not been able to consistently reproduce the results shown in Figure X. We have also discovered critical errors in Figures Y and Z. Although we recognize that some parts of this paper may remain valid, we note that key parts of the paper depend on the results of these figures. For these reasons, we retract the main conclusion of the paper.

7   Self-Plagiarism (Salam, *Journal of Business Ethics*, 2009)

The Editors and publisher regret to report that the paper published by AUTHOR as TITLE in JOURNAL (YVIP) is nearly identical to that published earlier by SAME AUTHOR as TITLE in JOURNAL (YVIP). This is a serious violation of publication ethics which according to our Policy on Publishing Integrity warrants a retraction notice to be published in the journal and a ban from publishing in any of the journal's publications for an initial period of X years.

8   Authorship Errors (Lunsford, *Analytical Letters*, 2011)

We, the editor and publisher of JOURNAL, are retracting the following article (AUTHOR, ARTICLE, JOURNAL, YVIP). The author's institution has conducted an investigation into the authorship of this article, and established that the claim of sole authorship is not justified. This constitutes a breach of warranties made by the author with respect to authorship. We note we received, peer-reviewed, accepted and published the article in good faith based on these warranties, and censure this action. The retracted article will remain online to maintain the scholarly record, but it will be digitally watermarked on each page as RETRACTED.

9   Duplication and Statistical Errors (Lichtenthaler, *Research Policy*, 2010)

The article (AUTHOR, TITLE, JOURNAL, YVIP) has been retracted at the request of the Editors-in-Chief. After discussions with the author about concerns raised by readers concerning papers he published earlier in JOURNALS in YEARS, the Editors have decided that the current article should be retracted. There are two main grounds for this retraction. (1) The author failed to disclose (through specific citations, or through a mention in the Acknowledgements section, or in a covering letter to the Editor) the existence of other closely related papers by the same author. In the absence of this information, the referees and editors involved in handling the paper were misled as to the level of originality of the paper. If they had been aware of these parallel papers, they would almost certainly have concluded that each of the two papers in question did not represent a sufficiently substantial and original contribution to knowledge in its own right to merit publication in a leading journal. (2) In this paper and other closely related papers, the author has been inconsistent in his treatment of the variables. In particular, variables treated as important in one paper are disregarded in a parallel paper, and vice versa… This raises severe doubts as to the validity and robustness of the conclusions. If the referees and editors involved in handling the paper had been aware of this (i.e. if their attention had been drawn to the other closely related papers and they had spotted this inconsistency), they would undoubtedly have rejected the paper on methodological grounds.

10 Duplication and Statistical Errors (Lichtenthaler, Ernst, and Hogel, *Organization Science*, 2010)

This article (AUTHOR, TITLE, JOURNAL, YVIP) is being retracted after an assessment that the work violates our publication standards in two important respects. First, the citation to highly related prior work by the first two authors is quite incomplete. As a result, it was not possible to assess the novelty of the work. In addition, there is reason to believe that key results in the paper would not hold if variables included in this related work had been incorporated into the analysis.

11 Plagiarism (Rosoi, *Applied Economic Letters*, 2012)

The following article has been retracted from publication in JOURNAL (AUTHOR 1, TITLE, JOURNAL, YVIP). This article substantially reproduced the content of the following paper (AUTHORS 2, 3, 4, TITLE, JOURNAL, YVIP). The Editors and publisher note that submission of a paper to JOURNAL will be taken to imply that it represents original work, not previously published, and that it is not being considered elsewhere for publication.

12 Plagiarism (Geh, *Journal of Business Ethics*, 2012)

The editors and publisher regret to report that the paper published by AUTHOR as TITLE in JOURNAL (YVIP) includes several passages (about X percent) that duplicated passages published earlier by AUTHOR B in TITLE (JOURNAL, YVIP). This is a violation of publication ethics, which according to our Policy on Publishing Integrity warrants a retraction of the article and a notice to this effect to be published in the journal.

Discussion Questions

1. Have you ever read two articles (either both published or one published and the other in the publication process) and realized there was substantial overlap that looked to you like plagiarism/self-plagiarism? If so, what did you do about it and what happened?

2. As a reviewer or editor, have you ever been faced with a manuscript submission with what appears to be an example of research misconduct? How did you handle it?

3. Why do you think the number of retracted articles in our business and management journals is (apparently) so low? Is an entrepreneurial culture for research partly to blame, as argued by Honig et al. (2013)? Is it the lack of ethics codes and plagiarism software, as argued by Karabag and Berggren (2012)?

4. Should journals have their own formal Code of Ethics or is membership in COPE sufficient to deter research misconduct?

5. What are your views on plagiarism-detection software like CrossCheck? Should it be used on all journal submissions?
6. If a case of research misconduct appears after publication, who should be responsible for deciding whether misconduct occurred? Should it be up to the journal? What role should the home university/ies of the author(s) play? The journal publisher?
7. Should examples of research misconduct be treated differently from author error, in particular, should the term "retraction" be used for author error?
8. How should journals treat article retractions? Should they provide detailed descriptions that explain why the retraction happened, or simply list the retraction?
9. Which of the retraction statements do you find most/least helpful and why?
10. How should journals treat repeat offenders? Should they be banned from publishing in our journals for a fixed time period, and if so, how long?

Notes

1 http://retractionwatch.com/the-retraction-watch-leaderboard/
2 http://retractionwatch.com/the-retraction-watch-leaderboard/

References and Additional Reading

We attach below a short bibliography of the pieces we found most useful on journal retractions. The website Retraction Watch run by Adam Marcus and Ivan Oransky is also highly recommended (http://retractionwatch.wordpress.com). The process for finding retracted articles is particularly well described in Chen et al. (2013) and Grieneisen and Zhang (2012).

Bhattacharjee, Yudhijit. 2013. "The Mind of a Con Man." *New York Times*, April 26.
Chen, Chaomei, Zhigang Hu, Jared Milbank, and Timothy Schultz. 2013. "A Visual Analytic study of Retracted Articles in Scientific Literature." *Journal of the American Society for Information Science and Technology*, 64. 2: 234–253.
Ching, Naomi. 2013. "Fame Is Fortune in Sino-Science." *Nautilus: Science Connected*, 5. http://nautil.us/issue/5/fame/fame-is-fortune-in-sino_science
Colquitt, Jason A. 2012. "From the Editors: Plagiarism Policies and Screening at AMJ." *Academy of Management Journal*, 55. 4: 749–751.
Colquitt, Jason A. 2013. "From the Editors: Data Overlap Policies at AMJ." *Academy of Management Journal*, 56. 2: 331–333.
Corbyn, Zoe. 2012. "Misconduct Is the Main Cause of Life-Sciences Retractions." *Nature*, 490 (October). www.nature.com/news/misconduct-is-the-main-cause-of-life-sciences-retractions-1.11507
Cottrell, Richard C. 2013. "Scientific Integrity and the Market for Lemons." *Research Ethics*, 10. 1: 1–12.
Economist. 2013a. "How Science Goes Wrong: Problems with Scientific Research." October 19.
Economist. 2013b. "Looks Good on Paper: Scientific Research." September 28.

Eden, Lorraine. 2010. "Letter from the Editor-in-Chief: Scientists Behaving Badly." *Journal of International Business Studies*, 41: 561–566. www.palgrave-journals.com/jibs/journal/v41/n4/pdf/jibs20109a.pdf

Eden, Lorraine. 2011. "Scientists Behaving Badly: Insights from the Fraud Triangle." *Ethicist*. July 27. http://ethicist.aom.org/2011/07/scientists-behaving-badly-insights-from-the-fraud-triangle/

Elliott, T.L., Marquis, L.M., and Neal, C.S. 2013. "Business Ethics Perspectives: Faculty Plagiarism and Fraud." *Journal of Business Ethics*, 112. 1: 91–98.

Fang, Ferric C. and Arturo Casadevall. 2011. "Editorial: Retracted Science and the Retraction Index." *Infection and Immunity*, 79. 10: 3855–3859.

Fang, Ferric C., R. Grant Steen, and Arturo Casadevall. 2012. "Misconduct Accounts for the Majority of Retracted Scientific Publications." *PNAS*, 109. 42: 17028–17033.

"Flawed Science: The Fraudulent Research Practices of Social Psychologist Diederik Stapel." 2012. Report of the Levelt Committee, Noort Committee and Drenth Committee, Universities of Tilburg, Amsterdam and Groningen. November 28. www.commissielevelt.nl/wpcontent/uploads_per_blog/commissielevelt/2013/01/finalreportLevelt1.pdf

Grieneisen, Michael L. and Minghua Zhang. 2012. "A Comprehensive Study of Retracted Articles from the Scholarly Literature." *PLoS ONE*, 7. 10: e44118. doi:10.1371/journal.pone.0044118

Honig, Benson, Joseph Lampel, Donald Siegel, and Paul Drnevich. 2013. "Ethics in the Production and Dissemination of Management Research: Institutional Failure or Individual Fallibility?" *Journal of Management Studies*. doi:10.1111/joms.12056

International Committee of Medical Journal Editors. 2013. "Recommendations for the Conduct, Reporting, Editing, and Publication of Scholarly Work in Medical Journals: Publishing and Editorial Issues Related to Publication in Medical Journals: Corrections, Retractions and 'Expressions of Concern.'" www.icmje.org/publishing_2corrections.html

Jasny, Barbara R. 2011. "The Science Retraction Experience." *Science*. http://publicationethics.org/files/u661/Jasny_Science%20presentation_final.pdf

Karabag, Solmaz F. and Christian Berggren. 2012. "Retraction, Dishonesty and Plagiarism: Analysis of a Crucial Issue for Academic Publishing and the Inadequate Responses from Leading Journals in Economics and Management Disciplines." *Journal of Applied Economics and Business Research*, 2. 3: 172–183.

Martin, Ben R. 2013. "Editorial: Whither Research Integrity? Plagiarism, Self-Plagiarism and Coercive Citation in an Age of Research Assessment." *Research Policy*, 42: 1005–1014.

Marusic, Ana, Vedran Katavik, and Matko Marusic. 2007. "Role of Editors and Journals in Detecting and Preventing Scientific Misconduct: Strengths, Weaknesses, Opportunities and Threats." *Med Law*, 26: 545–566.

National Academy of Sciences, National Academy of Engineering, and Institute of Medicine of the National Academies. 2009. *On Being a Scientist*. Third Edition. Washington, DC. National Academies Press. www.nap.edu/download.php?record_id=12192

Retraction Watch. 2013. "Five Kato Papers Subject to an Expression of Concern, Plus, a Statute of Limitations on Correcting the Literature?" May 30.

Steen, R. Grant. 2011. "Retractions in the Scientific Literature: Do Authors Deliberately Commit Research Fraud?" *Journal of Medical Ethics*, 37: 113–117.

Van Noorden, Richard. 2011a. "The Reasons for Retraction." *Nature Newsblog*. October 6. http://blogs.nature.com/news/2011/10/the_reasons_for_retraction.html

Van Noorden, Richard. 2011b. "The Trouble with Retractions." *Nature*, 478 (October 6): 26–28.

Wager, Elizabeth and Peter Williams. 2011. "Why and How Do Journals Retract Articles? An Analysis of Medline Retractions 1988–2008." *Journal of Medical Ethics*, 37: 567–570.

Wager, Elizabeth, Virginia Barbour, Steven Yentis, and Sabine Kleinert. 2009. "Retractions: Guidance from the Committee on Publication Ethics (COPE)." http://publicationethics. org/files/u661/Retractions_COPE_gline_final_3_Sept_09__2_.pdf

Williams, Peter, and Elizabeth Wager. 2013. "Exploring Why and How Journal Editors Retract Articles: Findings from a Qualitative Study." *Science and Engineering Ethics*, 19: 1–11.

8

DOUBLE-BLIND REVIEW IN THE AGE OF GOOGLE AND POWERPOINT

> **Key insight:** Double-blind peer review is one of the Academy's most cherished principles. Its purpose is to ensure that our scholarly journals make decisions to accept or reject manuscripts based solely on the quality, fit, and contribution of the paper. Double-blind review, however, has costs as well as benefits, and may be more fiction than fact in today's world of Google and PowerPoint.

Introduction

In 2008, more than 1.3 million articles were published in peer-reviewed journals (*Sense about Science*, 2009). Using one's peers to review manuscripts for possible publication goes back to the 1660s and has been adopted by most scholarly journals since the late 1940s (Mulligan, Hall, and Raphael, 2013). In the social sciences and humanities, double-blind peer review (DBR) is the norm. DBR requires that authors and reviewers be anonymous to each other throughout the reviewing process. DBR means that, as an author, I do not know who is reviewing my paper, and, as a reviewer, I do not know who authored the paper.

In a few social science disciplines, notably economics, single-blind peer review (SBR) is common.[1] For faculty in most social science departments, however, DBR applies to almost if not all of the scholarly journals where we and our colleagues publish. So, are we following the DBR norm? See the examples below.

Case Examples

Example 1

Martha was sitting in a job talk where the candidate for a position in her department was reviewing his research activities. The activities were nicely organized into "papers published," "papers under review," and "in progress." What caught Martha's attention was the list of journals attached to the "under review" category. The job candidate had listed author names, paper title, journal where the paper was under review, and the stage in the reviewing process (first round, revise, and resubmit, etc.). He then proceeded to briefly discuss each of the papers – even though there was a fairly high probability that one or more of his reviewers was sitting in the room.

Example 2

Thomas was on a departmental search committee, reading job candidate applications and their curriculum vitae (CVs). Thomas was also writing a couple of tenure and promotion letters for candidates up for tenure and promotion at their universities. In both situations, almost all the CVs listed "work in progress" and provided full details of authors, paper titles, names of journals, and stage in the reviewing process.

Example 3

Frank updated and posted his resume on his university's website. As a faculty member teaching undergraduate courses, Frank was required to post his CV so it could be read by faculty and students. On his CV, Frank listed all of his research in progress, including identifying where his articles were currently under review and the journals where he planned to send the papers on which he was currently working.

Example 4

Olivia was on an awards committee for one of her professional associations. All the nominees for this particular award had to supply their CVs, and all of the CVs listed the names of journals where the authors currently had papers under review.

Is there an ethical issue here? What about DBR?

The Benefits of Double-Blind Review

An editorial in *Nature* (2008a) reported that a 2008 survey by the Publishing Research Consortium of 3,000 academics in the sciences and humanities found that 71 percent of the respondents had "confidence in the double-blind review process" and 56 percent preferred it to other forms of review (e.g., SBR where the author is known but the reviewers are not).

In 2008, *Sense about Science* (2009) surveyed more than 4,000 academics and found that over three quarters of the respondents favored DBR. The reasons cited by the respondents were that DBR is "the most effective form of peer review because it eliminates bias, encourages forthright opinion and allows the reviewer to focus on the quality of the manuscript."

"The purpose of double-blind reviewing is to focus the evaluation process on the quality of the submission by reducing human biases with respect to the authors' reputation, gender, and institution, by not revealing those details" (McKinley, 2008). McKinley reviewed several studies that found DBR did reduce bias and improve the quality editorial process outcomes. The *Nature* (2008a) editorial agreed that DBR reduced the bias against female authors; however, a subsequent editorial, *Nature* (2008b), retracted that statement, noting the DBR studies on gender bias also had mixed results.

Much of the debate on DBR over the past ten years has focused on the issue of gender and/or race. The references to this chapter include several of these studies. Budden et al. (2008), for example, examined publications in the journal *Behavioral Ecology* before and after its adoption of DBR. The authors found a significant increase in female first-authored papers after the adoption of DBR and recommended that scholarly journals should move to adopt DBR. Not only gender and ethnicity matter. Okike et al. (2016), for example, found that reviewers were more likely to accept papers when a prestigious name or institution was visible on the manuscript (SBR) than not (DBR). Thus, the Matthew Effect (Merton, 1968) is also more prominent with SBR.

Problems with Double-Blind Review

DBR is not without its problems, however. We provide some examples. First, the Nature (2008a) editorial noted that reviewers, on average, can identify at least one of the authors on about 40 percent of journal submissions. Hill and Provost (2003), for example, found that self-citations were able to identify authors 40–45 percent of the time. Moreover, reviewers can easily Google the title of a manuscript and often discover the full paper or a conference abstract paper on the internet. This suggests the reviewing process may not be as "double-blind" as we think.

Second, Chen (2011) provides another criticism, arguing that authors can use various unethical strategies to "game" the reviewing system. For example, by sending papers out for review before journal submission, authors may be able to assess which individuals are likely to provide negative reviews. Listing the names of negative reviewers in the paper's acknowledgments section might persuade the journal editor to not select them as reviewers on the grounds that this would violate DBR. Authors might even acknowledge names of individuals known to be hard reviewers, without sending them the paper or receiving comments, deliberately and unethically hoping to influence reviewer selection by a journal editor.

Third, there are some advantages that come with SBR. If reviewers know the identity of authors, the questions asked by reviewers can be more pointed. For example, if a team of authors already has two papers published on the same topic with the same database, the reviewers would be more likely to know this and therefore better able to judge the novelty of the current journal submission. At present, if authors do not fully report their prior research (whether to preserve DBR or for the gaming reasons cited by Chen, 2011), reviewers may be more likely to overestimate novelty and more inclined towards a positive review. Eden (2010) refers to this ethical dilemma as the "failure to cross-reference."

Lastly, email discussions with other scholars have raised additional concerns. Suppose we wanted to get serious as authors about maintaining the sanctity of DBR. Suppose authors did not include information on where their papers were in the reviewing process, either on their CVs or in conference presentations or job talks. The forced lack of disclosure might be particularly harsh treatment for fresh PhD graduates and junior faculty who need to show their work-in-progress to recruiters. Moreover, discussing our work-in-progress with colleagues is what we do as scholars; it's a normal part of the creativity process. Also, given the long lag time between journal submission and publication (often years), it is not surprising that authors present their work at conferences during the reviewing process. Even at most academic conferences the rule is that: "Submitted papers must not have been previously presented, scheduled for presentation, published, or accepted for publication. If a paper is under review, it must not appear in print before the conference." These practical concerns suggest that asking authors to "not disclose" information about their papers under review would not only inconvenience the authors, but also damage our professional and educational activities.

Editorial Policy Options

So, the jury is out: DBR has both benefits and costs. It is not surprising therefore to find that journals vary in terms of their policy choices. The range of policy options can range from no peer review (the editor decides) to the full DBR process.

Some journals have moved from one form of review to the other so, clearly, their editors and publishers must have weighed the pros and cons and made a decision. What rationalizations did they give for the switch?

First, some journals that have switched have chosen to "ride two horses." *Nature* is a recent example. The *Nature* journals have historically practiced SBR (*Nature*, 2008a). The reason given in the 2008 editorial for using SBR was that: "*Nature*'s policies over the years have generally moved towards greater transparency. Coupling that with the lack of evidence that double-anonymity is beneficial makes this journal resistant to adopting it as the default refereeing policy any time soon." Starting in March 2015, however, all *Nature* journals began to offer a DBR option (*Nature*, 2015). The reason for the change, according to the article, was the popularity of DBR among researchers. The *Nature* article cited Mulligan et al. (2013)'s study showing that 76 percent of researchers saw DBR as an "effective peer-review system" compared with 20 percent for open review and 45 percent for SBR. The article also mentioned editors' concerns with involuntary gender biases.

Second, some journals have moved from DBR to SBR. In July 2011, the American Economic Association replaced DBR with SBR for all of its journals including the prestigious *American Economic Review*. The reason given by the Association for shifting to SBR was:

> Easy access to search engines increasingly limits the effectiveness of the double-blind process in maintaining author anonymity. Double-blind refereeing also increases administrative costs of the journals and makes it harder for referees to identify an author's potential conflicts of interest arising, for example, from consulting.[2]

Commenting in the *Chronicle of Higher Education* article on the Association's policy shift, Jonathan Katz, co-editor of the journal *Political Analysis*, made the memorable quip that "in the age of Google, double-blind has become a fiction" (Jaschik, 2011).

Our own view on the choice between SBR and DBR is clear. When Lorraine was editor-in-chief of the *Journal of International Business Studies* (JIBS), she developed a Code of Ethics that was strongly in favor of DBR. The code had a separate section on DBR, and mentioned DBR several times. JIBS does occasionally publish SBR articles, and these are formally identified in the journal as single-blind reviewed. Authors, editors, and reviewers are told they must "ensure the confidentiality of the double-blind review process." Authors are told they must explicitly cite their own earlier work and ideas, but "avoid self-citation that might violate the double-blind review process." In addition, during the manuscript submission process, authors are requested to "check the box" that their papers will not be posted on the internet while under journal review so as to lessen the likelihood of Katz's quip about fact becoming fiction.

Having said this, there was nothing in the JIBS Code of Ethics that restricted authors from "spilling the beans" to other individuals at conferences, job talks, or in their CVs about the status of their papers under review at the journal. Nowhere were there admonitions to authors to not include the particulars of their work-in-progress and under review articles in their CVs, PowerPoint presentations, and so on.

Going beyond Journal Codes of Ethics

Regularly at conferences, workshops, and job talks, we see individuals as authors violating the DBR process – including ourselves. Looking at other journal and professional codes of ethics, we find that the same problems exist (see, for example, Chapter 6, "Slicing and Dicing: Ex Post Approaches").

McKinley (2015) has blogged about this problem and made some useful suggestions for improving the effectiveness of DBR outside of the regular journal reviewing process, including external review committees and conference submissions. Still, where are the codes of ethics that restrict authors from "tooting their own horn" in ways that can indirectly affect the publication process? If we are serious about DBR, should we not also make changes to the ways we write and circulate our CVs, give presentations at job talks, and talk about our research projects?

In the age of Google and PowerPoint, DBR may not be a fiction but is, at best, a fig leaf.

Discussion Questions

1. As an *author*, if you have a paper under review at a journal that enforces DBR, is it OK for you to provide the information about the status of your paper on your CV or in PowerPoint presentations at conferences, job talks, and the like?
2. As a *reviewer*, how often has an author "spilled the beans" to you about the status of his/her paper in the reviewing process at a journal, and you realized that you were one of the reviewers? If that happened to you, what did you do afterwards? Did you tell the journal editor that you now knew the author? What did the editor decide?
3. As a *journal editor*, what is your position on DBR? If your journal enforces a DBR process, what advice as the journal editor do you give authors and reviewers in terms of self-monitoring so that they maintain the DBR process? What is your view on authors including full information on the status of their papers in CVs, job talks, and the like? Should authors take "under review at X" and "second R&R at Y" off their CVs, conference presentations, and job talks?
4. As a *teacher*, what do you tell your PhD students? Should or should they not include full information on papers under review, on their websites, CVs, job applications, and in job talks and conference presentations?
5. As a *member of your major professional association*, what is your position on DBR for your association? Should it shift from DBR to SBR? Should it move to an approach where authors self-monitor and do not share information about their papers under review? Or, like *Goldilocks and the Three Bears*, is the status quo "middle-sized bowl" just right?[3]

Notes

1 www.aeaweb.org/journals/pol/about-pol/editorial-policy
2 https://organizationsandmarkets.com/2011/05/26/aea-drops-double-blind-reviewing/
3 http://en.wikipedia.org/wiki/The_Story_of_the_Three_Bears

References and Additional Reading

Alam, M., N.A. Kim, J. Havey, A. Rademaker, D. Ratner, B. Tregre, D.P. West, and W. P.ColemanIII. 2011. "Blinded vs Unblinded Peer Review of Manuscripts Submitted to a Dermatology Journal." *British Journal of Dermatology*, 165. 3: 563–567.

Budden, Amber E., Tom Tregenza, Lonnie W. Aarssen, Julia Koricheva, Roosa Leimu, and Christopher J. Lortie. 2008. "Double-Blind Review Favours Increased Representation of Female Authors." *Trends in Ecology and Evolution*, 23. 1: 4–6.

Chen, Xiao-Ping. 2011. "Author Ethical Dilemmas in the Research Publication Process." *Management and Organization Review*, 7. 3: 423–432.

Eden, Lorraine. 2010. "Letter from the Editor-in-Chief: Scientists Behaving Badly." *Journal of International Business Studies*, 41. 4: 561–566.

Fisher, Martin, Standford B. Friedman, and Barbara Strauss. 1994. "The Effects of Blinding on Acceptance of Research Papers by Peer Review." *Journal of the American Medical Association*, 272. 2: 143–146.

Garvalov, Boyan K. 2016. "Who Stands to Win from Double-Blind Peer Review?" *Advances in Regenerative Biology*, 2. 1. Accessed February 19, 2017.http://dx.doi.org/10.3402/arb.v2.26879

Hill, Shawndra and Foster Provost. 2003. "The Myth of the Double-Blind Review? Author Identification Using Only Citations." *SIGKDD Explorations*, 5. 2: 179–184.

Jaschik, Scott. 2011. "Rejecting Double Blind." *Inside Higher Ed*, May 31. Accessed February 19, 2017. www.insidehighered.com/news/2011/05/31/american_economic_association_abandons_double_blind_journal_reviewing

McKinley, Kathryn S. 2008. "Editorial: Improving Publication Quality by Reducing Bias with Double-Blind Reviewing and Author Responses." *ACM SIGPLAN Notices*, 43. 8: 5–9.

McKinley, Kathryn S. 2015. "More on Improving Reviewing Quality with Double-Blind Reviewing, External Review Committees, Author Response, and in Person Program Committee Meetings." Accessed February 19, 2017. www.cs.utexas.edu/users/mckinley/notes/blind-revised-2015.html

Merton, Robert K. 1968. "The Matthew Effect in Science." *Science*, 159. 3610: 56–63.

Mulligan, Adrian, Louise Hall, and Ellen Raphael. 2013. "Peer Review in a Changing World: An International Study Measuring the Attitudes of Researchers." *Journal of the American Society for Information Science and Technology*, 64. 1: 132–161.

Nature. 2008a. "Working Double-Blind: Should There Be Author Anonymity in Peer Review?" February 7. Accessed February 19, 2017. www.nature.com/nature/journal/v451/n7179/full/451605b.html

Nature. 2008b. "Working Double-Blind [Corrected]." June 5. Accessed February 19, 2017. http://blogs.nature.com/peer-to-peer/2008/02/working_doubleblind.html

Nature. 2015. "Nature Journals Offer Double-Blind Review." February 19: 274. Accessed February 19, 2017. www.nature.com/news/nature-journals-offer-double-blind-review-1.16931

Okike, Kanu, Keven T. Hug, Mininder S. Kocher, and Seth S. Leopold. 2016. "Single-Blind vs Double-Blind Peer Review in the Setting of Author Prestige." *Journal of the American Medical Association*, 361. 12: 1315–1316.

Sense about Science. 2009. "Peer Review Survey, 2009: Full Report." Accessed February 19, 2017. http://senseaboutscience.org/activities/peer-review-survey-2009/

Snodgrass, R.T. 2006. "Single- versus Double-Blind Reviewing: An Analysis of the Literature." *ACM SIGMOD Record*, 35. 3: 8–21.

van Rooyen, Susan, Fiona Godlee, Stephen Evans, Richard Smith, and Nick Black. 1998. "Effect of Blinding and Unmasking on the Quality of Peer Review." *Journal of the American Medical Association*, 280. 3: 234–237.

Ware, Mark and Mike Monkman. 2008. "Peer Review in Scholarly Journals: Perspective of the Scholarly Community: An International Study." Publishing Research Consortium, January. Accessed February 19, 2017. http://publishingresearchconsortium.com/index. php/prc-documents/prc-research-projects/36-peer-review-full-prc-report-final/file

9

ETHICS IN RESEARCH SCENARIOS

What Would You Do?

Key insight: In 2008, James Davis and Susan Madsen (former co-chairs of the Academy of Management's Ethics Education Committee) developed four "ethics in research" scenarios, which they taught in doctoral consortia at several Academy of Management annual meetings. This chapter introduces and outlines the four Davis-Madsen scenarios. A short, annotated list of internet resources on teaching research ethics follows.

What Are Ethical Scenarios?

Are you confident that you and your colleagues – and your PhD students – can handle the typical ethical dilemmas that affect scholarly research and publishing? Ethical issues vary widely and can affect a variety of decisions including, for example:

- Whether to include an author and how to decide the order of authors.
- Whether chairs should co-author research coming out of their PhD students' dissertations.
- Who owns a dataset developed by two or more authors.
- Whether it is OK to "slice and dice" projects into multiple papers, and if so how to do this appropriately.
- How to avoid plagiarism and self-plagiarism concerns in one's own work, and what to do if you find evidence that someone else appears to have done this.

Rather than deal with ethical violations after the fact, *pre-training in ethical scenarios* can help faculty and PhD students become more aware of possible ethical complications, think through ethical dilemmas before they occur, and point out where to turn for extra support.

When Jim Davis and Susan Madsen were co-chairs of the Academy of Management (AOM)'s Ethics Education Committee they developed several ethics scenarios, which they taught to multiple doctoral consortia at AOM annual meetings starting in 2008. Each scenario was a little example of one or more ethical dilemmas, and was designed to motivate discussions about ethical issues in the research process. The goal of the ethics training was to raise the consciousness of the participants, stimulate dialogue, and serve as an introduction to online ethics resources.

At the annual AOM meeting, Jim and Susan, usually with a journal editor, would visit each doctoral consortia. Copies of the scenarios were distributed to the participants. Each table of participants was asked to focus on one of the scenarios, and debate among themselves how they believed the situation should be approached from an ethics standpoint. The small-group discussions were then opened up to the full group, with individuals from each table presenting their views and the journal editor and discussion leaders also commenting on the scenario.

Below, Jim Davis and Susan Madsen share some comments on their experiences with this project; their scenarios follow. We follow with a short list of recommended internet-based resources that can be used as, or to provide background reading for, ethics in research pre-training should you decide to develop additional scenarios for use at your institution.

The Davis-Madsen Ethical Scenarios

James Davis, Utah State University, james.h.davis@usu.edu

Susan Madsen, Utah Valley University, madsensu@uvu.edu

The ethics scenario topics were developed after a pre-conference symposium held at the national AOM meetings in 2007. At that symposium a panel of journal editors described ethical violations in publications they had experienced. Audience members, consisting of doctoral students and faculty of all ranks and backgrounds, described the ethical problems they had experienced and the professional dilemmas that resulted. We were surprised by the breadth and complexity of the ethical violations, and also by the confusion about what the participants could and should do. We left that symposium convinced that those stories should not end with that symposium, that they needed to be shared with the Academy.

The cases capture the ethical issues discussed in the 2007 AOM symposium. While the stories were real, the identity of those involved was protected. The cases were designed to stimulate discussion. As described above, the cases were presented in one-hour training sessions at 12 divisional doctoral consortia the year following the symposium. The emotional and passionate discussions that took place during the training were amazing. Both the consortia faculty and students engaged in heated discussions about the ethical issues in the cases. Surprisingly, in some of the consortia the faculty and/or students claimed that there were no ethical violations in a particular case, despite the fact that the cases were grounded solidly upon the AOM Code of Ethics!

To provide further evidence that the ethical violations described in the cases were indeed violations, we made a series of videos, in our role as co-chairs of the AOM Ethics Education Committee; these Ethics in Research videos can be found on the AOM website and also on YouTube. The videos show AOM officers, thought leaders, and journal editors discussing the ethical issues found in the cases. We have found that the cases open up lively discussion and that the videos bring closure by making the ethical codes associated with the cases absolutely clear.

We strongly encourage faculty to review the cases and the videos. Ignorance of ethical standards is a poor defense of ethical violations in the AOM. Our profession is grounded upon the highest academic ideals and ethics. It is essential that those entering the scholarly profession understand the code of ethics they must abide. We have found that the cases and videos are ways of learning and teaching the AOM Code of Ethics.

Below are the four scenarios we developed in 2007 and have used at various AOM meetings since then. We welcome your comments and hope they stimulate discussion among your colleagues.

Scenario 1: The Data Sleuth

Professor Data has been a very productive scholar; he has been publishing in major journals for many years. Because of his productivity, he is now known as one of the thought leaders in your field of study. You have recently begun to work with Professor Data and discovered that he has an interesting approach to research. He typically begins by gathering and analyzing data (which may include using a student data set) to "see if the data have anything to say." You have found that Professor Data often manipulates the data and changes the dependent variable to ensure a statistically significant result and increase the probability of a major publication.

1. Have you seen this type of research before?
2. Is Professor Data's approach to scholarship ethical? Why/why not?
3. Is there anything you could/should do?

Scenario 2: Too Much of a Good Thing? Multiplying Your Productivity

Professor Re Peat's resume is long and impressive. She had an endless list of conference presentations and publications. Upon closer examination you realize that much of the research seems to be quite similar. One day you met Professor Re Peat and commented on her impressive body of work. She said that she never writes anything that doesn't get as much ink and attention as possible. Among other things she said that she may change the name of some of her papers to get them into conferences. She also said that she spends so much time gathering data she finds that she can be more productive by using the same data and theory on multiple studies.

1.   Can one plagiarize oneself?
2.   How often can data be used ethically?
3.   Can the same paper be submitted for publication and for a conference?

Scenario 3: It's Good to Be the King: Authorship Dilemmas

Three PhD students (Chi, Square, and Pearson) were chatting one evening about their frustrations during their doctoral work. Chi said that she had written a final paper for a doctoral course taught by her advisor. She had asked him if the paper was worthy of submitting to a conference. Her advisor advised that it was worth submitting and suggested the insertion of a few references. He then requested that he be listed as co-author on that paper. Square stated, "That's nothing! Let me tell you about my advisor's request." He then explained that he had just finished writing his dissertation with some wonderful support from his advisor, Ms. Mean. She had recently insisted on being first author on all publications coming out of the dissertation research. Pearson trumped all three by saying that her advisor said that he owned the data and all intellectual property coming from the dissertation because he consented to supervise the research.

1.   How is authorship resulting from your dissertation determined?
2.   Who owns the intellectual property and data from your dissertation?

Scenario 4: Creative Problem Solving in Scholarly Research: Desperately Seeking Significance

You are on the horns of a dilemma. You have been working on your research for some time and have nothing but disappointing results. Your work pushes the theoretical boundaries of internal and external strategic alliances in ways that advance knowledge in extraordinary ways. Your problem lies with your inconclusive, mixed, and just plain bad empirical results. When you wrote the theory you argued that performance using two particular, theory-driven metrics would be influenced by the characteristics of alliances you developed. One afternoon, out of frustration, you found that when you manipulated one of the variables by making it a dichotomous rather than continuous variable you could get the results you desired. You also found that by restricting the range of the other variable you could also get better results (more than just removing outliers and the relationship is not curvilinear) that might increase the chances of producing a major publication.

1. Do you believe you should move forward with these changes? Is there an ethical problem?
2. When does data analysis become data snooping?
3. How should you proceed with your research?

References and Additional Reading

Banja, John. "Ethical Dilemmas in Scientific Research and Professional Integrity." Atlanta Clinical and Translational Science Institute, Emory University. Multiple short cases on research ethics, where each case is followed by an expert opinion on how to resolve the issue. The cases are intended to be used for teaching purposes. Accessed February 19, 2017. www.actsi.org/discovery/ethics-center.html

Committee on Publication Ethics. A forum for editors and publishers to discuss publication ethics. The resources and cases are helpful for authors and reviewers, not only editors and publishers. The cases, for example, include discussions on gift and ghost authorship, data fabrication, author mistakes, overlapping publications, multiple submissions, etc. http://publicationethics.org/

Management and Organizational Review. All ten articles in the "Editors' Forum: Research and Publishing Ethics," *Management and Organization Review*, published in English and Chinese (November 2011, 7. 3: 389–518) are downloadable from Wiley at http://onli nelibrary.wiley.com/doi/10.1111/more.2011.7.issue-3/issuetoc

Office of Research Integrity, US Department of Health and Human Services. This federal government website provides not only federal policies and regulations, but also training resources on what is and how to handle research misconduct,[1] case summaries involving research misconduct (these make for sobering reading), and free forensic tools[2] (e.g., for detecting plagiarism). http://ori.hhs.gov/

"Resources for Teaching Research Ethics." Poynter Center for the Study of Ethics and American Institutions, Indiana University, Bloomington. https://provost.indiana.edu/ poynter-center/

Stern, Judy E. and Deni Elliott. 1997. *The Ethics of Scientific Research: A Guidebook for Course Development.* Hanover and London: University Press of New England. Useful monograph about teaching research ethics by two professors at Dartmouth who taught an ethics in research course. www.dartmouth.edu/~ethics/archives/Stern_Elliott.pdf

1 http://ori.hhs.gov/case_summary
2 https://ori.hhs.gov/forensic-tools

10

THOUGHT LEADER

Michael A. Hitt on Ethics in Research

Key insight: How do influential thought leaders in the social sciences think about and practice research ethics? Professor Michael A. Hitt is one of the world's most respected and prolific management scholars. In this chapter, Professor Hitt and Lorraine Eden discuss the ethics of research based on his many years of working in collaborative groups and with PhD students.

Thought Leaders

Thought leaders, according to Nichols (2012), are "experts in their field, whether through extensive experience or academic research." The term "thought leader"[1] was originally used to identify invited guests who were interviewed about their opinions. We now use the term more broadly to encompass individuals who – by their thoughts, words, and actions – can lead, mobilize, and inspire others in the same profession.

Nichols (2012) argues that thought leaders have certain traits that make these individuals stand out in their professions:

- Active sharers: They actively share their research, theories, and ideas, and are comfortable with people questioning them and their work.
- Outgoing: They like people; that is, they enjoy networking and interacting with people, they freely share their ideas and engage with others.
- Confident: They are confident in their work and intelligence.
- Write: They like to write and use writing as a primary form of communication.
- Conversations: Thought leaders are often the subject of other people's conversations; people care about what thought leaders think, say, and do.

Michael A. Hitt: A Brief Introduction

At the time of this interview (September 2012), Michael (Mike) A. Hitt was a distinguished professor and holder of the Joe B. Foster Chair in Business Leadership at Texas A&M University. He is a former editor of the *Academy of Management Journal* and founder and former co-editor of the *Strategic Entrepreneurship Journal*. He is a fellow and former president of both the Academy of Management and the Strategic Management Society. A 2012 *Academy of Management Perspectives* article by Aguinis et al., "Scholarly Impact Revised," ranked Mike Hitt 15th in terms of number of citations and 9th in terms of Google pages among the 384 high-impact management scholars included in the study. In terms of overall impact, Mike Hitt tied for first place with James G. March (Stanford, emeritus) among the 384 high-impact scholars. Calling Michael A. Hitt a *highly influential thought leader* is therefore a fitting designation.

Question: What are some of the challenges of managing a team of authors involved in a multi-paper project?

Managing a multi-person team engaged in a multi-paper project presents several challenges, including who does what, how work is shared, handling differences in ideas.

I have had very few projects collapse (that is, not come to fruition in terms of publication). The reason is being committed to seeing it through (not wanting to let go of a project that I see as having value). When I perceive a project to have value and I have an ownership stake in it, I will push it to fruition. In the rare cases where that hasn't worked, I did not have ownership and so could not push the project forward and had to leave it to the individual who was lead on the project.

Every author on a research project should have a role to play and should add value to the project. I have seldom had a co-author drop off a project, but have occasionally added co-authors when they added value.

One case where an author might be added is the situation in which the research project requires access to a unique database that a faculty member has invested time, energy, and possibly financial resources developing. In this case, the faculty member's investment has value and I would expect that individual to be included on the project as a quid pro quo for providing the data. In many such cases, these colleagues add value in other ways as well.

Question: Do multi-author multi-paper research projects generate any different types of ethical dilemmas compared with single-author and/or single-paper projects?

I think we are all more aware of ethical violations now than in the past. Several examples have been in the newspapers and more has been written on this problem in our journals (editorials). There is also much more pressure on junior faculty to publish and we must be sensitive to these pressures.

Where a team of researchers is involved in a project, more often than not one researcher will handle the analytical work. If the other co-authors do not examine the data nor examine the analyses, there is always the possibility of errors, most often simply by mistake or occasionally they may be deliberate in order to obtain "better" results. I trust my co-authors to be professionals and believe that almost all of them share my professional ethics. Still, if there was a concern, asking to see the models and results of the analyses (e.g., regression results) is one way to check for errors. Looking carefully at the descriptive statistics can also be very useful.

Another way to do this is for the team of researchers to divide up the work among themselves, and for each lead author on a particular stage of the project to have one or more back-up individuals to double check the work. So, for example, if one person is primarily handling the data analysis, another one or two members of the team could also look over the data and analyses to provide additional checks.

Other ethical violations such as self-plagiarism and "slicing and dicing" (maximizing the number of papers out of a research project) have also received a lot of recent attention in the journals. I worry that perhaps too much attention is paid to these issues. First, in terms of self-plagiarism, it is time consuming to rewrite the methods section when much of the methods section applies to two or more papers. I worry that the journal editors are becoming oversensitive about these issues.

Where two papers share the same dataset, I do believe the papers need to "stand alone" on their own merits and are normally submitted to different journals. The only caveat here might be where the two papers should be merged into one; for example, one paper had the main analysis and the second a moderator analysis. Even though the paper would be longer, integrating them into one paper would make the paper stronger. I recognize that junior scholars often want to separate their research project (or their dissertation) into multiple papers, but they must take care not to weaken the papers' contributions. These cases may lead to several publications in lower-tier journals rather than a single publication in a top-tier journal. Even though many institutions count "numbers" rather than "quality" of publications, I believe it is in the author's best interests to focus on the long term and go for the strongest paper, even if that means fewer publications.

When two papers are submitted to different journals, I believe the authors should be transparent, and explain to the journal editors how and why the two papers are distinct from one another. However, I do worry that sometimes there is oversensitivity about this concern, leading to extra caution by journal editors.

Question: Can the order of authors on a paper be an ethical issue?

The order of authors may not always be an ethical issue, but it can be one. My informal rule – which has worked for me – is the following. I believe the first author on a paper should be the one who had the original idea and largely directs the project. Second, that person should also take the lead on writing the paper, and/or the lead on key parts of the paper such as the theory development. Certainly, all co-authors should take an active part in the project and paper development thereby adding value.

There are some exceptions to my general rule. For example, when a senior scholar has an idea for a paper, s/he might ask a junior scholar to take the lead on the project (and become the lead author), for a variety of reasons, and if the junior scholar accepts the responsibility, s/he would move into first-author position.

Another example is the following. If a senior author is working with one or more PhD students and is concerned that the PhD student(s) would not receive full credit for the paper if the senior author's name is listed first on the paper. In that case, I have occasionally decided to drop back in terms of author order so my co-authors would have more prominence.

Another exception is when there are two co-authors working on multiple papers on which they are both equal partners and they decide to reverse the order of authorship on every other paper (so, for example, on paper 1 the order could be alphabetical, on paper 2 in reverse alphabetical order, paper 3 would be alphabetical, etc.).

A problem arises when the original order of authors on a paper does not reflect relative contributions to a paper, for example, when the lead author on the first draft of the paper no longer is directing the project nor leading the development of the paper. Even though this presents a problem, I would probably only move to address it by confronting the lead author if I felt that another co-author deserved more recognition. In that case, I would speak directly to the first author about the order of authorship and explain my concern about another co-author not receiving appropriate recognition for his/her contribution.

Question: What about managing the sequencing of projects?

How to handle the scheduling and management of multiple projects is a challenge. I nearly always move R&Rs (revise-and-resubmits) to the top of the queue. R&Rs are both a blessing and a curse. They are closer to the end of the publication process, but need to be attended to quickly and require careful attention. Second, deadlines will move a project up in the queue, for example, if a special issue has an upcoming submission deadline.

Question: What are some of the ethical dilemmas involved as a senior professor chairing PhD dissertations and subsequent publications out of that dissertation?

I believe the PhD student who designed and conducted the research and wrote the dissertation is the owner of the dissertation. As such, s/he should always be first author on any paper that is published out of the dissertation. If a PhD student were to ask me to be the lead author on a paper out of his/her dissertation, I would refuse (and I have refused).

When I agree to chair a dissertation, I tell the students that it is their dissertation. I am generally willing to be involved, but will not impose my name on any papers coming out of the dissertation. If the student wants my help with a paper, I will agree to co-author but not as the first author.

However, I do recognize that some professors ask to be co-author on at least one paper coming out of the dissertation because of the workload involved in chairing a dissertation. I do not have a problem with that – although it is not my practice – as long as this issue is discussed between the student and the faculty member in advance of the dissertation. In my opinion, this should not be a condition imposed by the chair after the dissertation process has started or has been completed.

I do not want my own research program to depend on PhD students. I have my own research agenda and want to pursue that. I am pleased to help PhD students, but their dissertations should be based on their own research agendas. I do recognize that some faculty members have their research agendas directed by their students' dissertations, but I have chosen not to do that.

I want to add two caveats to my comments on dissertation chairs being co-authors on one or more papers coming out of the dissertation.

The first caveat is the case where the faculty member has developed a unique and proprietary dataset and makes that dataset available to a PhD student for his/her dissertation. In this case, I would normally expect to be included in papers coming out of the dissertation. I would discuss this in advance with the student so that we both had a clear understanding. The key here is to be transparent; that there is an open discussion between the faculty member and student about what the expectations are.

Normally, however, I believe a PhD student should develop his/her own dataset and I encourage that. Creating the dataset gives the student independence which can be important for a student's career development. Still, there may be cases in which using a dissertation chair's dataset makes sense.

The second caveat is the situation when an author includes another author's name on a paper without telling him or her; for example, the dissertation author including the chair's name without asking them in advance. This could happen either in terms of submission of papers to conferences or in terms of an actual publication. In both cases, I would be very unhappy about my name being included without my consent and would so inform the author. Doing so can create problems for the author, for example, causing him/her to violate the "rule of three" that limits authors to three appearances on a conference program.

It seems to me that the key here is transparency; to be upfront with one's co-authors and in supervisor–PhD student relationships.

Question: Do you have any last piece of advice for junior scholars?

My last piece of advice is that authors should look to the long term. Make sure the data are accurate. No games with the data or the analysis should be played. Do quality research. Authors should feel good enough about their work that they can easily defend what they have done to their peers. I recognize that the pressures to publish are very high, but the costs of engaging in inappropriate actions are even higher. I believe that if you do good research that fits with your personal values – and look to the long term – you will realize positive returns.

Discussion Questions

Below are the questions that Lorraine Eden used to jump start her conversation with Mike Hitt on ethics in research. The questions are included here in case other scholars would like to use these questions to jump start their own conversations with faculty or PhD students.

1. Order of authors on a paper – who goes first and why? When should the order change?
2. If someone only provides data to a project... how do you deal with authorship? With authorship order?
3. What do you recommend in the following situation? A colleague provides data to a project, but he won't share the data with the rest of the team. Instead, the data provider performs all the methods and shares the results with the team.
4. Bringing on a new author or dropping one off on a paper/project. What is a "sufficient enough" contribution to include someone as an author on a paper? What is too little? For example, a colleague is struggling with moving on to another project without a co-author because the co-author "only" did the lit review for that particular paper, and the (lit review co-author) is insisting he is included on another paper.
5. Who "owns" the dataset on a project? Can one author impose restrictions on another author (or a dissertation chair on a student) in terms of subsequently using the dataset on another project without the first author?
6. Do all members of the team have to do everything or can the project be compartmentalized and divvied up among the team so that one person does all the empirical work, one writes the paper, etc.?
7. With your co-authors, how do you manage the moral dilemma of working on new manuscripts, rejected papers, and revised and resubmits? How do you convey your approach to co-authors? Does your approach depend on the journal for the R&R or do you have a universalistic approach?
8. Can you think of situations in which you removed your name as an author... even for a revise and resubmit? Without identifying co-authors, what were the conditions underlying the decision?

9. During the dissertation, what are the expectations for the chair in terms of helping a student develop the dissertation? How about other members? For other committee members, what are your thoughts on authorship of papers stemming from a dissertation?

10. The role of a dissertation supervisor as an author on papers that come directly out of the dissertation. More generally, the power dynamic between supervisor/student or senior/junior faculty.

11. How do you manage the R&R process in groups? That often seems so difficult to manage and allocate equitably. I would think that more issues arise in the remaking rather than the making of research.

12. Do you have any thoughts on reviewer behavior? Given the critical role that reviewers play in our profession, this seems like an important topic.

13. What would you consider to be unethical behaviors? Could you comment on those you have seen in others, or experienced yourself, rather than just 'objective' no-no's? For example: quid pro quo sexual harassment is unethical and we know that. Are there dicey situations particular to the two overall topics you have direct knowledge of, and can perhaps even offer examples/scenarios and what happened/resolution?

Note

1 http://en.wikipedia.org/wiki/Thought_leader

References and Additional Reading

Aguinis, Herman, Isabel Suarez-Gonzalez, Gustavo Lannelongue, and Harry Joo. 2012. "Scholarly Impact Revisited." *Academy of Management Journal* (May): 105–132.

Nichols, Jim. 2012. "Are You Cut Out to Be a Thought Leader?" *Forbes*. September 29. www.forbes.com/sites/jimnichols/2012/09/27/are-you-cut-out-to-be-a-thought-leader/

PART II
Ethics and Teaching

11

BEYOND COURSE CONTENT
Ethical Dilemmas in Teaching

Key insight: Despite differences in course content across disciplinary fields, there are common teaching dilemmas that most academics face at one time or another. This chapter shares examples of basic ethical dilemmas embedded in the process of teaching itself, and organizes the remaining teaching ethics chapters.

Teaching Dilemmas

What do the following have in common?

- Grading student work fairly and consistently.
- Taking into account for final grades some 'outlier' student life experience or individual student need, such as a mid-semester baby birth or care of a sick family member.
- Discovering that a student has disclosed private or inappropriate information to others in an online discussion.
- Considering extreme consequences of students' earning failing grades, such as with international students being deported or being subjected to significant family shame.

You guessed it – all of these issues represent some kind of ethical judgment that we routinely have to make as instructors. There is a distinction we want to make at this point that will set the stage for this section of the book.

There has been enormous energy around "teaching ethics" as a disciplinary arena. Teaching ethics involves ethical content instruction, and can be manifested as a stand-alone ethics course or integrated into multiple courses within under-graduate or graduate curricula. Distinctively, although not mutually exclusively, is "ethics in teaching." This is a process- and judgment-oriented topic and spans any course or format within any disciplinary school. Ethics in teaching is relevant to any instructional environment – what are we communicating with respect to ethics when we teach *per se*? Do the teaching methods, student management practices, student information management practices, and course management policies we employ treat students ethically? It is in this latter domain, "ethics in teaching," that we'd like to continue our conversation for this section. "Ethical dilemmas in teaching" includes topics such as the nuances of cheating and academic honesty, pedagogical caring, letters of recommendation for marginally performing students, the vagaries of student evaluations of teaching, and impli-cations of social media relationships between faculty and students, among others. Teaching is, at its heart, an ethical endeavor and we invite your engagement with the following chapters that highlight many different aspects of ethics in teaching.

Patricia Keith-Spiegel and colleagues noted that, "members of a profession who undertake an open and constructive examination of their own behaviors are less likely to fail in their obligations to meet the needs and expectations of their students, their institutions, and ultimately, the profession itself" (2002, xii). If we are habitually 15 minutes late to begin class, or treat a student problem dis-missively, or post inappropriately to an online chat, we are signaling a norm of behavior that no ethics or professionalism policy on a syllabus can counteract. Instructors need to be present to the breadth of responsibilities that simply *teaching* requires.

Discussions about ethics in teaching can involve almost any subject where harm may occur and where responsibility in judgment must occur. There are, for example, potential perils in the affect associated with experiential learning as well as reflections on the dissonance created when students are presented with unwelcome ideology. Field observation offers invaluable insights, but may also come with correlative negative impacts on students' subsequent evaluations of 'others,' including incarcerated youth or mental health patients (e.g., Meisel, 2008). There are ethical issues surrounding our use of deeply embedded and accepted pedagogies. They've been around so long, we rarely reconsider them in new light.

While college learning should involve exposure to new and potentially dis-ruptive ideas, some scholars (e.g., Trelstad, 2008) ask us to be present to our assumptions that a liberal learning environment is always a good thing. Some students may simply not be ready to integrate ideas that directly challenge their core belief systems, and therefore challenge their very identity. Classroom activities and discussions themselves can be identity-threatening experiences that may do harm before any good (Lund Dean and Jolly, 2012). It becomes an ethical con-sideration when we present our ideology as 'good' information when students will likely encounter such ideas as hostile to their personal sense of self. That conversation is itself becoming much more complex as students push back against being challenged in values-disrupting ways, a trend that is well documented and that involves significant changes to the student–professor relationship (Bruni, 2016; Lukianoff and Haidt, 2015; Chory and Offstein, 2017).

Issues surrounding ethics in teaching are ubiquitous, and may be encountered both in and out of the classroom. While many disciplines and their professional associations proffer ethics statements, what about ethics in action, and in real time? That's where this book section comes in!

Let us offer you a couple of scenarios to consider – what would you do if you encountered these issues? What are the ethical issue(s) in each case?

"The Tough Exam Giver"

You are a professor in management at Large State University and are well respected for your teaching rigor. Your exams routinely engender between 30 and 50 percent failure rate and your reputation as a difficult instructor is well established. One of the key reasons you administer such difficult exams is to encourage weaker performing students to drop out of your course early, letting better performing students have more attention.

Susanne passed your first exam by only a few points, and has now failed your second exam. She must pass your class to graduate, which she is planning on doing next semester. She has come to your office to discuss her performance with you, and to seek advice. She tells you that, due to financial strains in her family, if she does not graduate on time, she will likely not finish college at all. What do you advise her to do?

"Too Much of a Good Thing"

Students have come to greatly appreciate your classroom style, which is discussion-based rather than lecture-based. Students are encouraged to verbally participate in and are rewarded for adding thoughtful comments to the discussion. You have no plans to change your teaching to a lecturing style.

Kyle is a very bright, energetic student in your class who frequently does outside reading on course topics. As such he feels compelled to respond to every question you pose, and he raises his hand for every discussion opportunity. While he does usually add something interesting to the conversation, he also has a tendency to lecture his classmates, and go off on tangents that monopolize class time. You do not want to quell his engagement, but you're noticing very negative body language from his peers. You also received specific comments about Kyle's endless talking on the mid-term course evaluation you administer, asking you to get other opinions during discussions. How do you handle Kyle?

Discussion Questions

1.   How would you handle Susanne's and Kyle's dilemmas? Why?
2.   Have you ever had real experiences along these lines? What happened? How do you feel now about it?
3.   Within your discussion group, are there common dilemmas that may be unique to your teaching or institutional context? How might rules of thumb for handling them appropriately be developed?
4.   What do we owe students with respect to teaching practice, in your opinion?

References and Additional Reading

Bruni, Frank. 2016. "College Turmoil, Signs of a Changed Relationship with Students." *New York Times*, June 22. www.nytimes.com/2016/06/23/education/in-college-turm oil-signs-of-a-changed-relationship-with-students.html?hp&action=click&pgtype=Hom epage&clickSource=story-heading&module=mini-moth&region=top-stories-below& WT.nav=top-stories-below&_r=0

Chory, Rebecca M. and Evan H. Offstein. 2017. "Your Professor Will Know You as a Person." *Journal of Management Education*, 41. 1: 9–38.

Keith-Spiegel, Patricia, Bernard E.Whitely, Jr., Deborah W. Balogh, David Perkins, and Arno F. Wittig. 2002. *The Ethics of Teaching: A Casebook*. Mahwah, NJ: Lawrence Erlbaum.

Lukianoff, Greg and Jonathan Haidt. 2015. "September: The Coddling of the American Mind." *Atlantic Monthly*. www.theatlantic.com/magazine/archive/2015/09/the-cod dling-of-the-american-mind/399356/

Lund Dean, Kathy and James P. Jolly. 2012. "Student Identity, Disengagement, and Learning." *Academy of Management Learning and Education*, 11. 2: 228–243.

Meisel, Joshua S. 2008. "The Ethics of Observing: Confronting the Harm of Experiential Learning." *Teaching Sociology*, 36. 3: 196–210.

Trelstad, Marit. 2008. "The Ethics of Effective Teaching: Challenges from the Religious Right and Critical Pedagogy." *Teaching Theology and Religion*, 11. 4: 191–202.

12

TEACHING AND ETHICS

A Critical Incident

Key insight: Sometimes an unexpected student event or interaction reveals larger issues in the way we handle ethics in teaching. In this chapter, a student's 'confession' about cheating paves the way for a discussion about morals, impression management, and the motivations students might have for being honest.

Kathy had the most interesting event occur recently – one that she had never encountered before. One of her strategy students came to her office the morning after they had all handed in an assignment – a case analysis practicing basic tools such as Five Forces and SWOT. "Scott" (not his real name) told her to remove the back page of his analysis because he had largely filled it in during the class discussion, and as such it should not be evaluated as homework completed. Scott said, "I had to come see you. I fretted [he actually used that word] about it all night." She had already graded the assignment, and had no idea he had not filled it all out as homework.

It is not often that Kathy is at a loss for a response. After a long moment she stood up, shook his hand, and genuinely thanked him for being transparent about how his work had been completed. Once he had left her office, there were a variety of aspects about that exchange that gave her pause, and she asked him if she could write about this situation as a mini-case example for the academic community.

First off, she wondered what had compelled him to come and admit what he had done. Certainly, his personal moral compass may have been tweaked and it became for him a relatively simple situation: it was wrong, and he had to both admit it and face any consequences pursuant to his actions. All of the authors of

this book share a paradigm that students come in wanting to do the right thing...
but that doesn't always happen. He's one of only a handful of students we have
had over the years to proactively admit something fishy had occurred with his
work. What else might be going on?

Although our course policies always include our institution's academic honesty
policy or honor code as the expected norm, well, we all probably have some kind
of policy statement to that effect and it's not been shown to be terribly effective
at deterring dishonest student behavior. Given the magnitude and scope of academic dishonesty, any moral suasion of having academic honesty policies should
be carefully put into perspective (Teixeira and Rocha, 2010). We think our students,
particularly juniors, seniors, and MBAs, encounter the policy language mindlessly
and automatically, as described by Ellen Langer's (1993) work.

Maybe it is because Kathy knew Scott from a prior class, and their iterative
relationship was meaningful to him. It's harder to be dishonest to someone with
whom we have a respectful relationship, and Kathy both liked and trusted Scott,
something that came through in their interactions. Perhaps finding ways to see
students more than once in our programs, more than in a semester's course, could
be a way of fostering their commitment to behaving honestly.

Maybe it is because the assignment was only worth 50 points in a course that
has about 1,000 total points. What may have happened if this assignment were
worth 20 or 25 percent, as some assignments are? Admitting guilt on a small
assignment may be easier to stomach if there were a penalty, but, we also know
from the literature that smaller transgressions are easier to justify than large ones.

On the not-so-rosy side of the coin, Scott could be thinking down the road,
and hoping to manage Kathy's impression of him so she will write a winning
letter of recommendation for him or serve as a job reference for him. Maybe he is
thinking of graduate school, in which we all teach, so he's working it for later on.
Maybe he knows the research that has indicated that even if we catch him, the
probability that faculty will report him further up to administration is very much
in his favor (McCabe, Treviño, and Butterfield, 2001). All of those are possible,
but Scott seemed genuine to Kathy and it also seems unlikely that he has duped
her this effectively for this long without her "B.S. radar" going off. So perhaps
another conclusion was necessary.

In discussing this situation, it has struck us since that time that we have been
unwilling to accept that it was indeed Scott's personal moral orientation that led
him to Kathy's office. In every organization in which we have ever worked we
have found that the situation dramatically affects how ethically folks behave, and
we are thus devotees of the interactionist ethical decision-making model, first put
forth in a seminal paper by Treviño in 1986 (Treviño, 1986). We have a hard
time with 'pure' moral intent and behavior, given so many incentives to not
behave well and so little probability of being caught.

And of incentives: the last musing we want to offer is considering how else to
reward him. Kathy's thanks were sincere, and we have to think he realized that.

Given that we know peers' behavior is the most influential consideration in how we'll behave, how can we alert other students to Scott's decision to tell Kathy? Our go-to norm of publicly praising is wholly inappropriate here – "Hey everyone, guess what Scott did?" Kathy did not penalize him on the assignment, and perhaps that is the best reinforcement. But it still seems like a golden moment, and we wonder still how we could have leveraged it as an ethics-in-action teaching opportunity.

Discussion Questions

1. If the assignment had been worth much more, do you believe Scott would have come forward? Why or why not?
2. As you consider your course policies, have you unwittingly created incentives for unethical behavior? What might they be, and how might you change them?
3. Do student honor codes work, in your opinion or experience? What have you encountered with honor codes?
4. What might have been ways to applaud Scott's behavior so his classmates knew, without compromising him? What options for celebrating his decision to come forward did we miss?

References and Additional Reading

Langer, E.J. 1993. "A Mindful Education." *Educational Psychologist*, 28. 1: 43–50.

McCabe, Donald L., Linda Klebe Treviño, and Kenneth D. Butterfield. 2001. "Cheating in Academic Institutions: A Decade of Research." *Ethics and Behavior*, 11. 3: 219–232.

Teixeira, Aurora A.C. and Maria Fátima Rocha. 2010. "Cheating by Economics and Business Undergraduate Students: An Exploratory International Assessment." *Higher Education*, 59. 6: 663–701.

Treviño, Linda Klebe. 1986. "Ethical Decision Making in Organizations: A Person-Situation Interactionist Model." *Academy of Management Review*, 11. 3: 601–617.

13

PEER PRESSURE OR, I THOUGHT I WAS OUT OF HIGH SCHOOL

> **Key insight:** Our best intentions for student learning assignments may be undermined by what our colleagues do. Because students often compare workloads among professors and courses, especially among different sections of the same course, there may be subtle or overt pressure to match workloads and expectations with our colleagues. And, our student evaluations may suffer if students perceive our workloads or grading standards as more difficult than our peers'. This can become problematic if we experience those workloads as compromising our personal teaching paradigms for what students should be learning.

A colleague sent us a very interesting scenario he has faced multiple times that should resonate with many who both teach and follow trends in academia as a whole. We have experienced versions of it ourselves periodically. Consider this:

For the past ten years, you've taught a required course you like. You're effective at teaching this course, too: in the first several years, your course evaluations were very high and other student feedback indicated that they loved your course and valued its learning outcomes. However, although you manage the course in essentially the same way as you have since the beginning, and your teaching style has remained similar, your course evaluations have become not so great.

The reason behind this is that your students now evaluate your course's workload as much too heavy, especially in relation to others who teach the course. When you first were teaching the course and got great evaluations, over 90 percent of students evaluated your course's workload as "appropriate." Over time, now only 20 percent of students rate your workload in that way.

For students considering taking your course, the word on the street is that you are a very difficult instructor and your course carries an inappropriately rough workload. So, along with decreasing student evaluation numbers, you're also facing fewer students in your section and resentful colleagues, all in the context of a dramatically increased institutional focus on student retention and increasing class sizes. You consider your assignment load completely appropriate for the course material.

As you puzzled over your change in evaluation fortunes, you reviewed syllabi from colleagues who also teach this course and found out that, based on similar student feedback, they had been gradually decreasing the workload in their courses. It appears that other sections of this course now require only a group presentation (without a corresponding written assignment) and one multiple choice exam at the end of the course. Indeed, you do have the heaviest workload now out of anyone teaching that course, although there is nothing out of the ordinary in your assignment mix: multiple writing assignments, group written project, and two essay/short answer exams.

What do you do?

We would dare say we are all facing pressures to keep student numbers up, whether we're at tuition-dependent institutions or those with state-funded incentives for each student matriculated. At the same time, various stakeholders are demanding assurance of learning data and high-quality teaching environments. There may be some seriously competing goals working here and if you think you're hearing mixed messages, you are not alone. The conflicting values are an ethical dilemma that deserves our attention: should you lower standards but increase student satisfaction and your course evaluations? Should you maintain your own sense of rigor but risk continued poor course evaluations that may have seriously negative impacts on your overall performance appraisals? Should you give in to peer pressure and mirror their lower standards, but harbor your own gloom over what you believe is a personal values compromise over quality learning?

The choice our colleague faces above is more complex than whether he should simply lower course requirements to match others teaching the course. There are a bunch of things going on here, such as the empirical link between student grade expectations and our course evaluations (i.e., Clayson, Frost, and Sheffet, 2006) and an increasing emphasis on market-based "currency" exchanges like satisfaction and retention (Arum and Roksa, 2011). All seem to track back to watershed changes within higher education as a whole. Many have already written with alarm about the increasing corporatization of higher education; we experience the dilemma above as yet another manifestation of the "student as customer" metaphor used so frequently, and without irony. When learning becomes an exchange agreement, whether explicit or implicit, and administrative structures like reward systems change to accommodate it, we are in trouble. Marcis and Burney (2010), in their study of cognitive biases at play when students' expectations of grades do not match actual performance, describe the current academic environment as one "in which the potentially conflicting goals of maintaining academic rigor, maximizing student retention, and maintaining student satisfaction are advanced" (p. 32). And these conflicts are here to stay.

As we mentioned above, we have had a similar experience just this semester. Kathy administers an informal mid-term evaluation in her courses, and students in her capstone course section indicated that the workload was "crazy" and out of touch with their other responsibilities. Her initial reaction to this was, "This is your senior-level CAPSTONE course! Suck it up!" Later on, of course, she reacted more functionally, but certainly that feedback gave her pause about what they might say on end-of-term evaluations that matter, and caused her to think about possible options.

Similar to what we see when examining almost any ethical dilemma, the choices initially seem binary. Dilemmas seem to lend themselves to 'either-or' thinking: we either cave in and lower course requirements, OR, we will get poor evaluations. Although the choices seem binary, they are not. In Kathy's situation, she asked the three other instructors who teach the capstone course for their syllabi to see her course requirements in context, finding that she requires different assignments, but not more overall. Armed with this information, there was a very helpful mid-term evaluation debrief discussion that included students' anxiety over earning poorer grades as seniors than they had as first years or sophomores, and Kathy's concern about the grades – evaluation exchange. The worry, it turns out, was about their performance insecurities, not the workload.

For our colleague above, how about a meeting among all of the instructors of the course to hammer out some shared expectations and requirements? How about a frank conversation with students where these implicit exchanges become open for discussion? How about telling students the 'why' of rigor in college courses, and helping them see that holding them to tougher standards is not punishment, but a sign of truly caring about their learning? What about sharing a personal story of when we were held to what we thought was an 'impossible' standard, only to find enormous confidence in our abilities later on because of it?

There are forces at work that may unintentionally pit us against our students, to cause us to forget that our students are not our enemies. Students may be increasingly objectified as misaligned with the educational enterprise as a whole, when they are in fact simply unaware of why we hold them to the standards we do, and how they will benefit from them. Sir Ken Robinson, in his hugely popular TED Talk (Robinson, 2006), says that educational systems are designed by people who are most successful in them – those of us who stay in college a long time and earn PhDs! Getting out of our own framing and implicit biases may offer "better than binary" solutions to a common problem.

Discussion Questions

1. How are differences among course workloads, grading expectations, attendance, etc. resolved at your institution?

2.   Have such differences ever resulted in difficulties in student evaluations for you? If so, how did you handle it?

3.   If you were to receive poor student evaluations in which the main negative comment was workload related, would you receive support from your administrators, or would you expect to receive critique? Why do you believe so?

4.   How might students be engaged to understand the rationale among differences in workload, grading, course management policies, etc.? Is it even desirable to do so?

References and Additional Reading

Arum, Richard and Josipa Roksa. 2011. *Academically Adrift: Limited Learning on College Campuses.* Chicago: University of Chicago Press.

Clayson, Dennis E., Taggart F. Frost, and Mary J. Sheffet. 2006. "Grades and the Student Evaluation of Instruction: A Test of the Reciprocity Effect." *Academy of Management Learning and Education,* 5. 1: 52–65.

Marcis, John G. and Robert B. Burney. 2010. "Evidence of Cognitive Biases in Students' Academic Self-Assessment in the Introductory Finance Course." *Proceedings of the Academy of Accounting and Financial Studies,* 15. 2.

Robinson, K. 2006. "Do Schools Kill Creativity?" TED Talk. Accessed August 13, 2015. www.ted.com/talks/ken_robinson_says_schools_kill_creativity

14

TEACHING VERSUS PREACHING

Conversational Ethics in the Classroom

> **Key insight:** While we may be passionate about our disciplinary subjects and hold well-considered viewpoints on them, particularly when they are controversial, our passion and opinions are not always welcome by our students. This chapter discusses when "teaching" can move into "preaching" with attendant power issues at play.

The 2012 election season in the United States included many state-wide initiatives of great social importance, including marriage equality. Minnesota, where two of us work and live, was one of four states in 2012 where we had the opportunity to vote about a constitutional amendment banning marriage equality. Kathy's family woke up one Sunday morning, a couple of weeks before election day, to find that the "Vote No" yard signs had been stolen. Later that morning, her family heard a prescriptive message coming from a religious leader at their place of worship, a prescription they experienced very negatively. They felt trapped and forced to listen to views with which they strongly disagreed being put forth as the only truth. As we reflected on the day's events, it struck us that there are important parallels in the classroom. When might our students feel trapped, without voice, when we put forth information considered 'truth'? What kinds of classroom situations might make them feel like they need to believe what we believe to be successful in the course? As professors, our jobs are to engage students in the important issues germane to our courses – what we usually call 'teaching.' The 2012 election season – and certainly the subsequent 2016 season – gave us pause to consider the distinct ethical issue of when 'teaching' turns to 'preaching,' and when we confuse student learning with student proselytization or even indoctrination.

The great social issues we face are complex, and nuanced, and foster serious passion. The same is true of the significant issues facing managers and organizations today: how much regulation should we have in the markets? What is the most motivational and fairest way to compensate workers? How should we balance environmental realities with manufacturing needs in a global economy? We need to facilitate conversations with our students about topics that matter, but that is not easy when almost none of us is neutral about the best ways to respond to those issues.

Picture this scenario: you're having a rich and in-depth discussion with your students about a controversial ethical topic and it's going better than you had anticipated. Let's say it's about the social justice issues surrounding Arizona's immigration law, or the choices facing a local organization that wants to shift to renewable energy, when your state's economy is built on coal. Maybe it's about the politics of food subsidy programs that change dependent upon who occupies the White House. You've prepared deeply for this conversation, studying the facts. You're priding yourself on having finally gathered the courage and emotional stamina to take on this topic, and students will have varied and strong opinions about it.

The discussion is going along well, and a student asks you: "Professor Smith, what do you think about this issue?" Because you're so well versed in the subject now, you have a strong opinion on what should be done and you share this with the class. You believe you've presented your viewpoint clearly, backing it up with empirical evidence. As you finish sharing your opinion, you suddenly notice a change in the room's vibe, and as the silence lengthens, few students are making eye contact with you. You try to open the conversation again, but now, students are less willing to challenge each other, and the discussion that was so vibrant before now seems one-sided and forced. You answered that student's question honestly and fully, with a well-supported fact base.

What went wrong? And why is it an ethical issue?

Blurring the line between teaching and preaching can stifle discussion of differing opinions in the classroom, particularly about these difficult or controversial issues. In our courses, especially graduate seminars, we are both facilitators as well as participants in important learning conversations. As ethicists, we research salient ethics issues and usually formulate a pretty solid opinion about those issues. Critically considering topics in all our classes includes an ethical impact discussion. Students are normally quite interested in our view, but the trick seems to be deciding when our learning objectives include sharing our opinions. In other words, we have to decide if both the *process of sharing* and the *content of our opinion* are contributing to learning or, conversely, if either process or content could anchor the conversation in a certain way, or create an ideologically hostile space where some students feel trapped like rats listening to us.

Both anchoring and creating a hostile learning space are shades of preaching, and we need to be very careful about making that distinction.

For guidance on opinion-giving practices, we turned to the literature about "teaching versus preaching" in higher education. Sarah Pfatteicher (2001) notes that the roles of both preacher as well as professor are embedded in academic life but that instructors should be very careful about when each is appropriate. We can 'preach' on behalf of certain ideas with students, like global sustainability processes or better educational opportunities for low-wage workers, and we can 'profess' [teach] best practices for either idea based on empirical evidence, but we need to understand for ourselves the differences between those two roles and, we would add, signal as such to our students.

We also found that work about professor self-disclosure (PSD) was helpful. "Self-disclosure" itself is usually defined as any information a person divulges about him or herself to another person, usually to facilitate gaining trust or interpersonal liking. In the classroom, PSD is more often used to facilitate a learning outcome in lieu of fostering personal relationships with students. Wheeless and Grotz's work (1976) distinguished between *interpersonal* self-disclosure and *professor* self-disclosure because the goals are different – we are not sharing our opinion to foster an interpersonal relationship with students but rather to advance conversational learning about potentially difficult and/or affectively charged topics.

Cayanus and Martin (2008) indicated that PSD can help students learn complex concepts better, improve affective learning, and assist with student problems more effectively. Using computer-mediated disclosure tools like social media, Mazer, Murphy, and Simonds (2007) found that students appreciated knowing more about their instructor from the social media site profiles which contributed to a better classroom climate. From a communication perspective, PSD can contribute to greater intimacy in the classroom and make difficult conversations more accessible.

That's the good news.

Now, here's where things can go badly, and why PSD is indeed an ethical consideration for the classroom. Put yourself in students' shoes, or, maybe simply recall one of your own experiences where, stuck in a classroom setting, your professor regaled you with some wholly inappropriate personal opinion that not only didn't add to learning, it repelled learning. We remember several of those trapped-like-a-rat experiences from our student days like they were just last week, like when a professor in one of our undergraduate years regaled us with stories of his very difficult relationship with his mother. When our classrooms become ideological preaching sessions wherein students are forced to listen to our personal inclinations at the expense of being taught something germane to the course, we've crossed an ethical boundary. And, there's a second aspect of PSD that deserves attention – the power aspect. Ejsing's (2007) work shares the author's own illustrative story of what happened when she shared a personal experience designed to show empathy and connection to her students, but which spiraled into completely unanticipated student reactions.

Opinions can turn into sermons when we forget our authority role, which can be easy to do in this age of first-name bases and dialogical learning. In another way of thinking about opinion as power, think of this 'translation': *I can make you sit there and listen, and our hierarchical roles in the learning process could influence you to remain silent when in fact you have great objection to what I say. The undiscussed and implicit threat of course grades may delimit your response set, while I am free to say what I like.* Not good. Politics is especially enticing as opinion-imposing fodder for some folks, and there is no shortage of stories of questionable behavior.

Like most things, what's difficult about the teaching–preaching distinction and PSD is the operational stuff – how it's done, when it's done, and how much of it there is. Research by Cayanus and Martin (2008) indicates some conditions have to be met for PSD to be helpful and ethical. When it's *relevant* to the topic of conversation, PSD is helpful, but not when we are ranting about uninsured drivers. PSD fosters student learning when it's *appropriate in amount*, not when we come to class every time and talk about something going on in the community that we are interested in. Finally, PSD can be effective for student learning when we share mainly *positive* stories or examples, not when we share negative or derisive stories about a topic that make students squirm in their seats, unsure of even what expression to put on their faces.

Let's revisit the opening scenario – a composite of the few times this has happened to us. When we examine the PSD literature, one key thing leaps out: ultimately, what do we want students to learn? Does what we are saying contribute to students' learning, or to some other (unintended and unwanted) outcome? We don't think we can honestly now say that we advanced student learning by providing an illustrative opinion or a set of facts. We wanted to show students we had prepared for this topic, and that we could be relied on as a resource of "unbiased" evidence when we discuss complex issues. We should have said much less, and shared some of the evidence we used to come to our opinion, but not ALL of the evidence like we did. We should have been more alert to students' non-verbals, like when they sat back with their arms crossed, or when they stopped meeting our eyes. We should have invited their comments and challenges to what we were saying, rather than monologuing. Last, we should have been more alert to our power position in the class, and the delicate balance that conversational learning requires: providing an evidentiary discussion frame without quelling students' experiences. Although our PSD was certainly *relevant* to the conversation, we failed on the *appropriate amount* as well as using *positive* examples.

Understanding our own teaching versus preaching line demands self-awareness. There may be some topics that we just cannot seem to engage with objectively. How do you know when that happens? Student course evaluations (or some other systematic feedback mechanism) will usually coalesce around these topics, or maybe a colleague can come observe your classroom as you present certain topics for discussion and identify specific anchoring behaviors you exhibit. If you identify certain topics about which you have such strong beliefs that "teaching" them yourself seems risky, here are some terrific options.

- Invite guest speakers who hold differing viewpoints on that topic.
- Ask a trusted colleague to help facilitate the conversation with you, which would balance topical preaching toward teaching again.
- Borrow from law schools or political science departments by creating structured debates with defined roles to argue both sides of an issue. Pre-assigned teams of students explore defined sides or aspects of the topic, like the pros and cons of increasing the minimum wage, and present them in class. You advocate for both sides in turn, after students from each side speak. Because you speak on both sides, neither is privileged by your personal opinion signal.

As with most ethical issues, there are few hard and fast rules. While we think preaching is pretty much always suspect, it may be more so at an undergraduate level than at a graduate level. McElroy, a law professor, asks us to consider our teaching versus preaching stance: "we professors are still steering the ship, even if we do not endorse the 'sage on the stage' approach to teaching. Does that power dynamic dictate some sort of professional distance?" (2011).

Discussion Questions

1. When is it OK to share your own opinion about a controversial topic with students, in your disciplinary area? How might you manage the experience of 'preaching' that your students might have?
2. How do you allow for, or maybe even encourage, dissent in your classes?
3. When students passionately disagree among themselves, what is your role in 'refereeing' the conflict?
4. Are there any issues for which your opinion about them should never be brought up? Why?

References and Additional Reading

Cayanus, Jacob L. and Matthew M. Martin. 2008. "Teacher Self-Disclosure: Amount, Relevance, and Negativity." *Communication Quarterly*, 56. 3: 325–341.

Ejsing, Anette. 2007. "Power and Caution: The Ethics of Self-Disclosure." *Teaching Theology and Religion*, 10. 4: 235–243.

Mazer, Joseph P., Richard E. Murphy, and Cheri J. Simonds. 2007. "I'll See You on 'Facebook': The Effects of Computer-Mediated Teacher Self-Disclosure on Student Motivation, Affective Learning, and Classroom Climate." *Communication Education*, 56. 1: 1–17.

McElroy, Lisa. 2011. "What's Too Much Information for Students?" Guest post, Dorf on Law blog, www.dorfonlaw.org/2011/09/whats-too-much-information-for-students.html

Pfatteicher, S.K.A. 2001. "Teaching vs Preaching: EC2000 and the Engineering Ethics Dilemma." *Journal of Engineering Education*, 90. 1: 137–142.

Wheeless, Lawrence R. and Janis Grotz. 1976. "Conceptualization and Measurement of Reported Self-Disclosure." *Human Communication Research*, 2. 4: 338–346.

15

MY STUDENTS WANT TO FRIEND ME!

Boundaries and Relationships with Social Networks

> **Key insight:** In a digital world where social media are infused throughout almost every aspect of interactions, professors and students should examine boundaries and norms associated with "friending" each other. In this chapter, we explore what some of those boundaries might be, and discuss important considerations with this evolution of the teacher–student relationship.

Social Networking

The semester ended a week ago, with the usual flurry: exams, grading crunch, and anxious seniors making sure they passed our sections of their capstone courses. But this time, the end of the semester also brought something new: Facebook 'friend' requests from soon-to-be ex-students. They want to keep in touch, they say, and social networking sites (SNS) such as Twitter, Snapchat, Instagram, and Facebook have become important mechanisms to do so. For purposes of this chapter, we use Facebook (FB) as a 'generic' example of an SNS, largely since it is the most mentioned platform in the social networking and student relationships literature. An important distinction must be made here: career-related platforms such as LinkedIn do not carry the same potential issues as FB and other truly social networks, and it is appropriate to make connections with students on LinkedIn as ways to foster important prospective job and internship networking assistance.

We are still leery of FB and other SNS, being the "digital immigrants" (Prensky, 2001) that we are. We get easily shocked by what others post – what we consider to be deeply personal family issues are put out there for all to read and potentially react to – but it is not only the content about which we are apprehensive but the people FB finds for us to friend. The handy algorithm has already suggested we friend some of our students, even prior to the semester ending.

Would it ever be appropriate for us to send a friend request to a student? Under what circumstances? And conversely, what should faculty do when students, both prior and current, request to friend us? We have not ever friend requested a student, but we have responded both positively and negatively to friend requests from students. While plenty of colleagues and (real) friends offer advice, we checked into the literature to see what might be out there informing this newest of boundary-blurring activities. What are the new frontiers of ethical behavior here?

FB represents an interesting toggle between public and private – our professional and personal roles. Back at the end of 2007, Sara Lipka wrote "The old guy in the corner at a college party can come off as creepy. The same goes for a faculty member on FB, the online hangout first populated by students." Recent FB user information notes that college-age users (18–24) are now less than half of the membership, and the fastest growing demographic group is adults 30 and older, so its use has expanded well beyond its original identity as a site serving college students. Thus, the 2007 question of whether professors should join has been replaced by a new conversation: how to appropriately manage this new virtual relationship that we are able to craft with students.

While we might view our friending as a hip new entrée into the social networking world, our students might think we are crashing their party. Just as in the real world, even if students invite us to join their group, they may regret it once the party activities just this side of *verboten* start!

FB presents multiple ethical issues between faculty and students. Since we started our own FB accounts and experienced some of FB's unique student–instructor challenges, we have been periodically discussing these challenges with a variety of colleagues. Let's talk about a few of those issues.

Boundaries

Meyers (2009) rightly cautions about navigating the line between 'instructor' and 'buddy,' and helps us see that boundaries facilitate learning. Is it appropriate pedagogical caring when professors let students drive their cars, or routinely use their homes as study halls? We see FB as an extension of boundary setting in the real world. Boundary issues are by far the most prevalent in the few articles addressing instructor use of social networks with respect to students.

What seems clear among everything we have read is that students should be the ones making requests. Some researchers have surveyed students about appropriate and inappropriate instructor-to-student behaviors, and found that inappropriate behaviors included all the "comment" functions that FB provides: commenting on status, photos, links, etc. Students appear to want to keep those boundaries clear from instructor interaction. And, women were statistically significantly less likely to find professor–student interaction on FB as appropriate.

Thus, with respect to boundary crafting, we need to be cautious of intrusion into what Teclehaimanot and Hickman (2011) call "active" behaviors like commenting or messaging. There may be an implicit power-based threat for women, so navigating that line, particularly with male faculty and female students, will deserve extra attention and vetting, including backing off completely when requested.

Additional attention has been paid to the potential legal issues surrounding faculty–student SNS interactions from a boundary perspective. For example, potential problems such as defamation, harassment, administration surveillance, and privacy breaches are serious issues. A few states, such as Missouri, have tried to ban student–teacher friending, but those laws are coming under fire. Indeed, Missouri repealed its law only months after enacting it. School districts around the country are struggling with crafting policies that respect individual rights and the possible positive aspects of teacher–student SNS interactions while being cautious of blurring relational lines that make learning more difficult or impossible (Grisham, 2014).

SNS has lots of dimensions to consider: who 'owns' the social space in which interactions take place? When is it posting free speech, and when is it defamation? When does protecting students become an inappropriate invasion of privacy? Many cases seem to be occurring at an institutional, rather than individual level. However, when students 'evaluate' a professor negatively on FB, or conversely, when a faculty member gripes about some student's work on FB, the problems become very personal very quickly.

Roles and Expectations

A key consideration is from what vantage point students are experiencing us when using FB. Who is the "who" that is responding in FB? When we are using FB, we remain firmly in the real-world realm. Our FB friends are our real friends, many who hail from high school and undergraduate days thanks to the relentless connective algorithm. When we do FB activities, our vantage point is "non-work Paul" or "non-work Lorraine," not "Professor." Roles and expected correlative behaviors can become muddled on FB and it's smart to consider from what role we're responding. For example, Karl and Peluchette (2011) studied what happens when instructors want to friend students (but sort of curiously, not the other way around) and found that students reacted most negatively when professors of two certain types friend requested them: their worst professor and new professors. In their study, Karl and Peluchette found that friend requests from the worst and new professors engendered suspicion more than irritation… an interesting finding that would mirror the real world. Why would students continue a relationship with professors they suspect of having some kind of ulterior motive in doing so? Get through the semester, and make a break for it! Ethically, we should be honest with ourselves about our motives for friending.

We serve in different roles for different students, and social networks may assist in maintaining those. Some roles may be circumscribed by larger institutional or even national culture. A Chinese colleague who works in China noted that student–teacher friending crosses an accepted cultural boundary, and that such a relationship is viewed as inappropriate role spanning. In that case, we would probably do well to defer to such norms even if we personally thought friending students was OK.

If we have students with whom we have crafted relationships outside the classroom, such as with our research assistants, FB offers an avenue to continue some contact that would be mutually agreed upon. If we believe that faculty serve as resources for students in an ongoing way (letters of recommendation, networking points, etc.), a professionally oriented social network like LinkedIn could be appropriate. Some people maintain both professional and personal FB pages, which is also an option. The key seems to be to make sure students also view us in these mutually understood roles, and have these same expectations of an ongoing relationship.

Are We Caring, or Intruding, or...

Sometimes, FB may be the most effective and fastest way to get in touch with students who have otherwise disappeared. We may think we are caring about a student by tracking them down on FB and sending a note to see why they have not been in class. However, that kind of messaging was found to be a behavior students found pretty unwelcome coming from faculty, recalling the creepy partygoer.

FB may be the new communication and relationship frontier, but curious 'old school' paradigms seem to remain. While virtually messaging students to get in touch with us is seen is unacceptable, calling or texting their cell phones or tracking them down via institutional email are viable and expected options. In particular, some of the retention literature in higher education highlights the personal touch that using phone calls can signal. Additionally, while students may not want to interact with us and have us comment on their photo albums on FB, we know of many colleagues who have continued a tradition of inviting inter-national students over to their homes for American holidays, either because they would be alone and that's a drag, or, to offer international students culturally significant learning experiences like having Thanksgiving dinner or decorating a Christmas tree. Perhaps it's the longevity of this professor–student tradition that matters, or the transparency of the purpose for interacting? We don't know.

Increasingly, while institutions may have policies about participating in SNS activities, they also realize that SNS are where current and prospective students go to find information and connect. Thus, institutions are in a difficult space of needing to set behavioral parameters and risk-management policies on the one hand, and encouraging traffic to the social networking platforms that engage students on the other. A simple Google search for "university Facebook policy" yields a wide range of institutions that have formal, and sometimes extensive, policies regarding not only faculty–student SNS use but anyone connected with the institution's use of these sites.

Our former and current institutions are emblematic of the "one hand, other hand" situation above. Idaho State University (ISU; Kathy's former institution) has a confidentiality policy with respect to using social networks, blogs, or other internet sites with its overall Information Access policy statement. However, on ISU's home page, the entire bottom half of the site is devoted to feeds and posts on three SNS, including FB, Instagram, and Twitter. Gustavus Adolphus College does not have a formal policy governing faculty use of SNS, but, like ISU, has all the popular SNS icons embedded on the homepage, and features almost real-time feeds of anyone posting therein. The Mays School of Business, where Lorraine works, has an extensive social networking policy in place, indicating an essentially *caveat emptor* stance even while recognizing SNS ubiquity. Texas A&M's homepage also includes all those SNS icons at the bottom, and even includes Pinterest and YouTube as posting and following options. This type of ambivalence certainly sends mixed messages, leaving it up to individual faculty judgment or informal norms to navigate potentially difficult SNS relationships.

Which brings us to our closing thoughts…

Going back to the role distinctions, there are some really important implications when we lose sight of the blurring of roles that FB can engender. Perhaps we have all heard of instances over the last couple of years of colleagues posting examples of student work that is very poor, ostensibly as a "Can you believe what this student turned in to me?" commiserating moment. Once Kathy started her own page, she saw some of these posts first-hand. We have without exception found this to be rude and juvenile – and singularly unfunny. When a friend of ours (real and FB friend) engaged in this, and we pressed her for an explanation of how that could be considered at all appropriate, she replied, "My privacy settings would prevent my students from seeing it and besides, we don't run in the same circles." Clearly, we are not all interpreting the space represented by FB in the same way, despite well-meaning (and legalistic risk mitigation) policies. The above example seems like a no-brainer "never, ever do this" to us, but other faculty see FB space as their own, as a place in which to share exasperating examples of student experiences to get support or a laugh. They're professors, but also people who want to share what can be a common instructor experience. We say: When a post is at someone else's expense, don't post it. From an ethics perspective, we know we get into trouble with absolutes, but here, we can absolutely say posting this kind of information on FB is troublingly unethical.

Discussion Questions

1. Does your institution have a policy about social networking between students and professors? Do you think it helps with boundaries? Why or why not?

2. Is it OK, in your opinion, to friend current students? How about other connection forms such as cell phone texting or apps like GroupMe?
3. Federal Title IX reporting requirements make social media interactions more complex. How is your institution managing Title IX reporting with the realities of social networking? What are the policies, if any?
4. Has having a social network relationship with a student ever helped you be more successful with teaching and learning goals? Please share that experience and why you believe it was successful.
5. With your discussion group, share your responses to students who ask to friend you, on different social media platforms, and why you respond in those ways.

We recommend a faculty brownbag on this topic to help articulate and share what your college's norms about FB use are. Or, if you don't have FB norms with respect to students, it may be a good opportunity to craft some. These ethical issues are growing in number and complexity, and more faculty transparency here is better than less!

Resources

Here are a couple of FB resources about privacy settings that look promising and easy to understand:

- www.youtube.com/watch?v=_vqrXIsAPXk (YouTube video)
- http://michaelzimmer.org/2012/05/07/how-to-adjust-your-facebook-privacy-settings-2012/ (easy to follow document)

References and Additional Reading

Grisham, Laura. 2014. "Teachers, Students and Social Media: Where Is the Line?" *USA Today*, April 9. www.usatoday.com/story/news/nation-now/2014/04/09/facebook-tea chers-twitter-students-schools/7472051/

Karl, Katherine and Joy Peluchette. 2011. "'Friending' Professors, Parents and Bosses: A Facebook Connection Conundrum." *Journal of Education for Business*, 86: 214–222.

Lipka, Sara. 2007. "For Professors, 'Friending' Can Be Fraught." *Chronicle of Higher Education*, 54. 15: A1–A28.

Meyers, Steven A. 2009. "Do Your Students Care Whether You Care about Them?" *College Teaching*, 57. 4: 205–210.

Prensky, Marc. 2001. "Digital Natives, Digital Immigrants." *On the Horizon*, 9. 5.

Teclehaimanot, Berhane and Torey Hickman. 2011. "Student–Teacher Interaction on Facebook What Students Find Appropriate." *TechTrends*, 55. 3: 19–30.

16

WHAT DO WE DO WHEN STUDENTS DESPAIR?

Considering Pedagogical Caring

> **Key insight:** Pedagogical caring can take a variety of forms, and requires us to be alert to potential student struggles in unique ways. In this chapter, we share real incidents we encountered with students who needed more help than we were initially prepared to give, and frame our response around the Awareness-Motivation-Capability model. We discuss the pros and cons of reaching out to specific students who appear to be struggling with various aspects of the course beyond content itself. Pedagogical caring encourages reflection on the instructor–student relationship in a very different way than the social media relationships from Chapter 15.

Kathy graded her senior capstone students' first position/reaction papers late last week. As is usually the case on the first one, students do quite poorly, not making the conceptual leap from summarizing the contents of the article to making supported judgments about the article's assertions. It's a complex learning process, and as such she offers extensive handouts and scaffolding to lower their anxiety level. While the mean score is usually a low 'C' on the first paper, one student simply… how should we say it… bombed the assignment. "Bob" (not his real name, and he knows we are writing about this) did not follow any of the directions for either content or structure, and appeared to have no grasp of the assignment's intent.

What we have learned over the last five years is that our students would rather us contact them privately before they get their assignment back to let them know when they have done very badly, instead of being blindsided when getting the assignment back with their peers. This is true even when we contact them on a Friday, and they might stress about it all weekend before the assignment is returned in Monday's class. After emailing Bob with the unhappy news, he replied to Kathy with this message: "After hearing what everyone else did I actually came home ready to drop the class because I did not feel like I understood at all... When everyone else talks in class, I feel like I am not on that level."

So, they set up a meeting. Kathy also has a policy where students may redo the first assignment to make up half of the missed points, an opportunity Bob gratefully accepted. In his last email to her on Sunday, he wrote this: "I wrote my new reaction paper yesterday and would like to turn it in for half credit on Monday... Thank you for caring and not just giving up on me."

Now, at the risk of you thinking that Kathy is typing this while standing on a self-congratulatory soapbox, let us say she has come quite late to the student caring party. You'll note that it's been only in the last several years of a 20-year career that she alerts students to very poor performances beforehand. It's also only in the last several years that she has added other pedagogical caring behaviors to her student engagement repertoire, including contacting students who miss several classes to see what's going on, talking one on one with them about distracting classroom behaviors that are causing alarmingly fast drops in their professionalism scores, or sharing difficult feedback with them to which they are obviously blind in the Johari Window (Luft and Ingham, 1955) sense.

She is not proud that it took her that long to consider reaching out to students in trouble, and could offer you multiple explanations for it that served for years to support her non-engagement: as a strongly typed Myers Briggs Type Indicator "Thinking" type, she is reflexively not terrific at considering the possible negative impact of her classroom practices on students' psychosocial learning processes. In teaching adult students, she had never believed in following up with them about things that were, from her vantage point, firmly their responsibility, like contacting her if they had any sort of problem. And lastly, she just didn't want to spend precious time bringing up a topic with a student that could result in a long conversation – she had writing to do!

How far should we go to assist a student in distress? What is our ethical responsibility as educators to help a student connect to our classroom learning? During her subsequent conversation with Bob, she realized the problem went well beyond flunking one assignment. Sitting in a classroom and being paralyzed by an inability to either understand or contribute to the conversation is a daunting and terribly isolating experience. Bob is emblematic of other interactions we have had in recent years, in that, today's students are an odd mix of andragogic and pedagogical orientations: they have significant life experiences germane to course material they want to share, and yet, they still look to us for assurance that they can succeed, that they're not the only one who has struggled.

A dear friend and colleague co-wrote an article that has had immense influence on our student caring behaviors. Tom Hawk, with co-author Paul Lyons, gathered data over six semesters to ascertain how students experienced a lack of faculty caring behaviors. Their provocative article from 2008, "'Please Don't Give Up on

Me': When Faculty Fail to Care," is designed to help us be present to how we *don't* care for students when we recognize our own behaviors on their lists: we show a "complete disregard for whether or not I got the material," or, "ignored me for the remainder of the course even though it was clear that I didn't understand the material." Hmmm. Guilty. Hawk's 2017 update to that article, "Getting to Know Your Students and an Educational Ethic of Care," revisits the idea of engaging with students' often unique experiences of distress and offers new ways of considering how to positively engage with them.

How do we determine when to engage with student distress, and how do we do it most effectively? The robust and growing ethical decision-making and ethical behavior literatures indicate that all sorts of variables moderate our ethical intentions, reasoning, and ultimately, behaviors. What is clear, however, is that behaving well starts with *awareness* of an ethical situation. There are several classic frameworks (e.g., Chen, 1996; Miller, 1990) that are variations upon a process that could be very helpful here as we consider how to respond to student distress – *Awareness* of the problem (not always obvious!), *Motivation* to assist (it matters why we in fact engage), and *Capability* to help as the situation demands (we have to be able to reasonably assist with that student's particular needs).

In the above scenario, the student's dismal assignment performance was the first *Awareness* clue, and a relatively simple probe made it clear that Bob's issue was more holistic than just that one assignment. Student struggles may not be so clear, as is the case with the increasing numbers of Middle East war veterans returning home and finding repatriation a daunting, bewildering task. Domestic violence victims, too, tend to take pains to make their misery invisible to outsiders, as we have unfortunately seen with a handful of our female students. Awareness means we have to deliberately be alert to potential issues that plague certain groups of students, and not accept the *status quo* as OK. It also means we have to participate in sometimes emotionally difficult training, like being present to what post-traumatic stress syndrome might look like in practice.

Maybe the most unsettling part of the A-M-C framework in this context is the *Motivation* aspect. Why, ultimately, are we helping? Do we like this student a bit more than others? Would we help another student who we find kind of annoying who had the same problem? Are we hoping to deliberately manage our way to better teaching evaluations? Are we thinking that our intervention here will fundamentally boost this student's ability to learn in our class, and maybe even in his entire college suite of courses? Students pick up on our insincerity in a heartbeat, and their antennae ferret out our instrumentality when we help for the wrong reasons.

Finally, we need to assess the extent to which we can reasonably assist with a student problem – our *Capability*. Returning again to the scenario with Bob, Kathy was clearly able to help, and it was her role to be proactive in doing so. Years ago, she had a student whose sibling died, sending her entire family into a paralyzing spiral of denial and pain. When she came to Kathy to discuss her options for passing the course, it became a counseling session she was not qualified to conduct. We need to know when we are out of our league of expertise, and so in that case, continuing to 'assist' would have been unethical for Kathy. Thankfully, our student counseling center was available, and she remains grateful to this day that they took over for her.

Our *Capability* to assist is also impacted by the sheer number of students we may have in any given semester. Some courses are small enough where managing individual student needs is workable; what about the huge 300 student lecture courses, where we don't interact with students personally? While perhaps we could monitor individual student grade patterns, it would be pretty much impossible to engage in caring in the same ways as with a 25 student seminar. What might caring look like in these mega-courses? Ultimately, what's in your assistance toolkit, and what's not? Honestly assessing our own skills is critical.

We have experimented with caring behaviors after we understood that some of Hawk and Lyons' (2008) students could have been talking about us. The results of our little experiments leave no doubt at all as to our power to fundamentally change a student's experience from negative to positive, from disengagement to immersion. Consider this comment from a student who joined Kathy's course late, into the second week, and was obviously struggling with course norms and expectations.

> At first I didn't like her teaching style but she took interest in me and drew the best out of me which in turn created interest from me in the class and has resulted in a great experience. I will choose her as a professor in any classes she offers that I need in the future.

The "before" Kathy would have seen that he was struggling, but not spoken to him, since that was HIS responsibility to come see her. The "after" Kathy spoke to him after class in week 3, alerting him to several course policies he was violating to the detriment of his entire course grade, and encouraging him to modify how he participated in the class.

This is still a process – we don't have this all figured out. And it is still a very conscious, cost–benefit calculus for us to decide to have these conversations. There have been, however, zero instances where our caring behavior toward a student was for naught, where we did not notice a dramatic change in performance, attitude, or both. What's clear to us, for better or worse, is that we can no longer blissfully deflect obvious student distress under the guise of students' owning their own learning experiences.

Discussion Questions

1. Share instances in your own teaching experiences of student despair, how you handled it, and whether you would do things differently.
2. What are the costs to caring? What are the benefits?

References and Additional Reading

Chen, Ming-Jer. 1996. "Competitor Analysis and Inter Firm Rivalry: Toward a Theoretical Integration." *Academy of Management Review*, 21. 1: 100–134.

Hawk, Thomas. 2017. "Getting to Know Your Students and an Educational Ethic of Care." *Journal of Management Education*, 41. 5: 669–686.

Hawk, Thomas and Paul Lyons. 2008. "'Please Don't Give Up on Me': When Faculty Fail to Care." *Journal of Management Education*, 32. 3: 316–338.

Luft, J. and H. Ingham. 1955. *The Johari Window: A Graphic Model of Interpersonal Awareness*. Proceedings of the Western Training Laboratory in Group Development. Los Angeles: University of California Press.

Miller, George E. 1990. "The Assessment of Clinical Skills/Competence/Performance." *Academic Medicine*, 65. 9: 63–67.

Noddings, Nel. 2005. "Caring in Education." *Encyclopedia of Informal Education*, www.infed.org/biblio/noddings_caring_in_education.htm

17

FROM CONTENT TO RELATIONSHIP

Key insight: With a host of significant external forces pushing for change in academic institutions, the entire enterprise of teaching and learning has come under the microscope. Long-established and widespread teaching practices are increasingly considered obsolete in terms of adding clear value to students' collegiate learning experience. In this chapter we explore some of those key forces, and the ethical ramifications of compelling changes we must make in teaching and learning. Specifically, we want to talk about what those changes mean for adding value to students' college experience, and the way we must help our colleagues reimagine and retool their teaching practice. In rethinking what "college" means, professors can remain compellingly relevant to students' learning and college experience.

As a business school professor, beginning with the new millennium, the 2000s have not been the kindest years. From stunning corporate ethical breaches (for which business schools were blamed in creating amoral executives), murky finance field dealings, and a global recession that changed the fabric of millions of people's lives, forces for change have accelerated their impact on us. A Carnegie report (Colby et al., 2011) continues to impact how we consider the value of higher education *per se*, and we want to talk about that in this chapter. The report, "Rethinking Undergraduate Business Education: Liberal Learning for the Profession," brought significant challenges facing business educators into sharp relief. Anne Colby and colleagues began their research around the working assumption that something had gone seriously awry in business education over the last couple of decades – and they are correct. They argue that business education has privileged only one type of thinking – practical reasoning – at the expense of encouraging more holistic types of thinking, including reflection and acceptance of multiple frames, or 'truths.' In divorcing practical reasoning from traditional liberal arts-based thinking, we have graduated business students who lack holistic thinking skills and empathic understanding of the impact of business practice. Given the last 15 or so years, we see no viable way of arguing with those conclusions.

In other "Wow, we're not in Kansas anymore, professor!" news, we were struck by the attention that Moody's (yes, the credit rating agency) is giving higher education as a whole. A January 16, 2013 Moody's report downgraded higher education's outlook as an entire industry, an evaluation the agency reiterated in a December 5, 2017 report. The agency continues to be concerned with business models and revenue outlooks. The firm noted that higher education as an industry has been too slow to adapt to changing income availability (we can't just keep pricing tuition higher and higher) and reduced student demand (they will not continue to take on gothic debt levels). The challenges we face seem unarguable.

These significant and persistent external forces, changing almost every important and hallowed aspect of higher education, have been planted firmly on our radar. So, what does this mean for ethics in teaching?

The Ethics of Value

Higher education has been disrupted with innovations that challenge our entire teaching and learning enterprise. We clearly need to rethink the value proposition of what we are providing, or risk being lumped with another industry that persistently and arrogantly ignored key external innovations that disrupted its status quo – the US auto industry. That's the first key ethical issue for this chapter.

The teaching model we have used for so very long has been all about sharing *content* – deliver a lecture about some relevant topics, assign homework about those topics, and test students' "knowledge" of those topics. Even "transformational teaching" advocates still anchor the college learning experience on content mastery (see, for example, Slavich and Zimbardo, 2012). A college degree represents a composite credential testifying to the fact that students have taken certain courses and have theoretically mastered certain course content, and right now, employers still look for the college degree credential.

But massive open online courses (MOOCs) have disrupted the game. College course content is now commoditized and is increasingly cheaply available. While critics have pointed to the low completion rates of MOOCs as evidence of their overhype and failure, dismissing MOOCs as the "disruption that wasn't" is a grave error. Although many MOOCs now charge a fee, the standard is $49 USD for courses available from the most prestigious institutions in the world (Cook, 2016). MOOC course offerings from educational institutions and corporate 'universities' are growing exponentially. In an example of this growth rate, it's like moving from "160,000 learners at one university in 2011 to 35,000,000 learners at 570 universities and twelve providers in 2015" (Cook, 2016). The perceived gap between an online experience and an in-class experience is also shrinking. Thomas Friedman (2013) envisions the day when students will "create [their] own college degree by taking the best online courses from the best professors from around the world... paying only the nominal fee for the certificates of completion. It will change teaching, learning, and the pathway to employment." Friedman's futuristic path to employment means the credential for employment may no longer be a program-focused college degree, but rather a series of inexpensive exams that students take to certify their knowledge, which are accepted by employers in lieu of 'whole' college degrees.

If content delivery can be so easily replaced by an online course or a MOOC course, and employers would someday be willing to accept a test as 'learning' verification, how can we justify spiraling tuition costs? CNN reports that 151 colleges and universities charged more than $50,000 in annual tuition, fees, room, and board for the 2012–13 academic year. That's an increase from 123 schools in 2011–12, and 100 schools in 2010–11. And in 2015, 50 colleges and universities charged more than $60,000 per year for those same services. Moody's seems to think we're not providing $200,000 worth of teaching and learning value for students in a four-year undergraduate program. So if our old model is out... what's the new model?

Learning through Relationship, Gen Ys and Beyond

The answer has to be in reimagining what "college" means for student learning. It means engaging with the idea that we are in it to develop students as holistic persons, as participants engaged with communities we help them enter, and as lifelong learners. It goes even beyond the classic liberal arts model – we have to be much more high-touch with students, meaning, building mentoring relationships with them that persist well beyond their graduation. In short: we actually have to care about them as they develop!

In one example, Bill Ferris reimagined the professor–student relationship as one of a senior partner guiding a novice junior partner, a form of apprenticeship (Ferris, 2002). Ferris' metaphor strikes us as more hopeful and more responsible than the "student as customer" comparison, but it comes at a cost: mentoring junior partners is a long-term relationship, where our graduate remains linked with our institution as part of an active community, where support and help are readily available at any life stage. It's already happening at some institutions; Kathy's undergraduate alma mater, Notre Dame, has systematically nurtured its alumni and mentoring community for decades. We are all part of our institutions' alumni community charged with helping other graduates succeed. Now the value of that institutional support network must become part of the relationship package we provide students.

Pedagogically, we need to provide much more compelling learning environments where experiential and active learning experiences are the norm. The 'sage on the stage' monologuer must give way to the 'guide on the side' facilitator. This shift is chronicled in the 'flipped classroom' concept, wherein content is delivered outside of the classroom via some technological platform, leaving class time for hands-on, personalized engagement with students. It's a relational model that underscores how content is only a piece of what we offer in learning – an entree, if you will, to the real value of one-on-one engagement.

That means sharing power, control, and authority with students to create a co-learning community. It means a fundamental shift from "college" being synonymous with content, to "college" being the holistic, relational process of student development. Yikes!

Helping Each Other

And that brings us to our second ethical issue of the chapter: how do we help each other reconfigure what we do every day? For most faculty, moving to high-touch, long-term relational teaching goes against everything they have been trained to do, against the very model of being a content area expert acquired through doctoral programs and research streams. We cannot just flip a switch where faculty suddenly know the new rules for experiential teaching methods, mentoring students, and fostering alumni relationships. We owe our colleagues mentoring and foundational help in making such a dramatic switch in how their jobs are to be done. We owe our students professionally refreshed faculty who understand that the *process* of learning has trumped the content of course delivery.

To move to the practices associated with learning in relationship, colleges must commit resources for faculty development. We have long held the philosophical orientation toward the workplace that no one wants to be obsolete. No one wants to experience the message that everything they know how to do, and everything they have been trained to do, no longer works. Teaching in engaged and relational ways is not obvious, and if faculty decide to 'wing it' in the classroom, bad things can happen (Keith-Spiegel et al., 2002; Lund Dean and Jolly, 2012).

Many teaching and learning societies and communities exist where our colleagues can become part of the answer to higher education's challenges: the Management and Organizational Behavior Teaching Society (www.mobts.org) has shared relational and experiential learning techniques for decades. Most professional associations now provide a set of teaching workshops devoted to innovation as part of their annual meetings. The National Society for Experiential Education (www.nsee.org) supports a community of teaching and learning professionals devoted to learning through experience. The Teaching Professor annual conference (www.magnapubs.com/2017-teaching-professor-conference/) provides a multidisciplinary space for active and engaged learning, sharing nuts-and-bolts tips and techniques with hundreds of conference participants.

There are many others, but a key ethical idea is to resist the temptation to be impatient with colleagues who appear to resist new teaching methods – they may understand their pedagogy has to change but may not know with what to replace it. And that's where our own senior–junior partner mentoring must come in. In the same way we should not ignore our own development and learning about teaching, so, too, do we have a responsibility to our students as part of a community of teachers to help keep all professors up to date. Our industry's survival may depend on it!

Discussion Questions

1. What are the key external forces shaping teaching and learning as we look ahead to the next ten years, from your perspective?
2. Have you and your colleagues held any structured, dedicated conversations about what these changes mean for the future of teaching and learning at your institution?
3. What ideas might you have about helping our 'sage on a stage' colleagues retool their relational teaching practice?
4. What conferences or other developmental opportunities have you attended that might be good for others in your institution? Please share your experience with them.
5. Although supporting students and relationships appears like a no-brainer good thing, what are some of the potential costs and downsides? What are the ethical issues of relational teaching from your vantage point?

References and Additional Reading

Berrett, Dan. 2012. "How 'Flipping' the Classroom Can Improve the Traditional Lecture." *Chronicle of Higher Education*, February 19. http://chronicle.com/article/How-Flipping-the-Classroom/130857/

Colby, Anne, Thomas Ehrlich, William M. Sullivan, and Jonathan R. Dolle. 2011. *Rethinking Undergraduate Business Education: Liberal Learning for the Profession*. Stanford, CA: Carnegie Foundation for the Advancement of Teaching.

Cook, Merrill. 2016. "State of the MOOC 2016." *Online Course Report*, www.onlinecoursereport.com/state-of-the-mooc-2016-a-year-of-massive-landscape-change-for-massive-open-online-courses/

Ferris, William P. 2002. "Students are Junior Partners, Professors as Senior Partners, the B-School as the Firm: A New Model for Collegiate Business Education." *Academy of Management Learning and Education*, 1. 2: 185–193.

Friedman, Thomas. 2013. "Revolution Hits the Universities." *New York Times*. January 26. www.nytimes.com/2013/01/27/opinion/sunday/friedman-revolution-hits-the-universities.html

Flipped classroom description: http://learning.blogs.nytimes.com/2011/12/08/five-ways-to-flip-your-classroom-with-the-new-york-times/

Keith-Spiegel, P., Whitley, Jr., B.E., Ware Balogh, D., Perkins, D.V., and Wittig, A.F. 2002. *The Ethics of Teaching: A Casebook*. Mahwah, NJ: Lawrence Erlbaum Associates.

Lewin, Tamar. 2013. "Students Rush to Web Classes, but Profits May Be Much Later." *New York Times*, January 6, www.nytimes.com/2013/01/07/education/massive-open-on line-courses-prove-popular-if-not-lucrative-yet.html?pagewanted=all&_r=0

Lewin, Tamar. 2013. "Universities Abroad Join Partnerships on the Web." *New York Times*, February 20. www.nytimes.com/2013/02/21/education/universities-abroad-join-mooc-course-projects.html

Lund Dean, K. and Jolly, J.P. 2012. "Student Identity, Disengagement, and Learning." *Academy of Management Learning and Education*, 11. 2: 228–243.

Moody's Investor Services. 2013. "Moody's: 2013 Outlook for Entire US Higher Education Sector Changed to Negative." January 16. ww.moodys.com/research/Moodys-2013-outlook-for-entire-US-Higher-Education-sector-changed–PR_263866

Moody's Investor Services. 2017. "Moody's: US Higher Education Sector Outlook Revised to Negative as Revenue Growth Prospects Soften." December 5. www.moodys.com/research/Moodys-US-higher-education-sector-outlook-revised-to-negative-as–PR_376587

Rae, Tushar. 2011. May 12. "Postdocs Can Be Trained to Be More Effective than Senior Instructors, Study Finds." *Chronicle of Higher Education*, http://chronicle.com/article/Postdocs-Can-Be-Trained-to-Be/127525/

Slavich, George M. and Phil G. Zimbardo. 2012. "Transformational Teaching: Theoretical Underpinnings, Basic Principles, and Core Methods." *Educational Psychology Review*, 24. 4: 569–608.

Solomon, Ethan A. 2013. February 8. "MOOCs: A Review." *Tech*, MIT, http://tech.mit.edu/V133/N2/mooc.html

Thrift, Nigel. 2013. February 13. "To MOOC or Not to MOOC." *Chronicle of Higher Education*, http://chronicle.com/blogs/worldwise/to-mooc-or-not-to-mooc/31721

18

IT'S NOT JUST RATE MY PROFESSOR ANYMORE!

Ethics and Student Evaluations

Key insight: In this chapter, we want to examine the thorny and multi-dimensional ethical issues around student evaluations of teaching (SET). Using Quinn's Competing Values framework to guide the conversation, we look at who uses SET, who wants to use them, and ethical issues of context, competing concerns, and most saliently, validity problems. We also consider how we use SET data – whether formatively or summatively – and what process assurances we may owe our colleagues to improve their teaching practice. We finish with a brief conversation with an administrator, Associate Provost and Dean Darrin Good, who headed up one institution's SET modification effort.

With every end of semester comes a variety of closure experiences, and among those hallowed rituals is the administration of student evaluations of teaching (SET). In doing some research, it has become clear to us that very few aspects of academic life inspire the kind of emotion that SET do. We lost an entire half day just reading a couple of blogs about SET and those blogs' comments. Opinions run high and diametrical: Schuman (2014) thinks they are biased and worthless, while Burt (2015) thinks that even with embedded bias, they are useful to consider how power works in teaching and learning. Others, like Patton (2015), say that using SET data for faculty evaluation, pay decisions, and as a retention criterion is fraught with problems, leading professors to obsess about hitting a particular evaluation rating number. There's a lot of hostility out there.

Our institutions have undertaken, in fits and starts, revisions to a SET instrument, a thankless task akin to running into a stiff headwind. So the timing seemed right to take a look at SET from an ethical perspective. Revising SET is a tricky undertaking, because there's more at stake now than there was when SET were initially created. Using Quinn's Competing Values framework helped us think about the original and now changing roles and uses for SET. Briefly, the Competing Values model says that the evaluative work associated with administrators toggles among roles in a 2x2 matrix, with structure considerations on the vertical axis and focus considerations on the horizontal. The structural continuum ranges from flexibility to control, while the focus continuum ranges from internal to external. It's on those continua that we want to base the conversation here to highlight how SET construction and data usage are subject to strongly competing claims among different stakeholders.

Focus Considerations: Internal versus External

The creation of SET can be traced back to the 1920s, and is generally attributed to Herman Remmers' work at Purdue University. Only a handful of universities collected SET data through the 1940s and 1950s, but student demands for more instructor information pushed SET usage into many institutions in the 1960s.

The original intent behind SET was to help faculty develop their teaching practice, and to offer a feedback loop among those closest to the teaching and learning craft – students, instructors, and perhaps departmental chairs or an academic dean. It was a way to offer a window into an often opaque process between instructor and student, ideally as a continuous improvement tool (Galbraith, Merrill, and Kline, 2012). Consistent with Quinn's "internal process model" roles, SET have also been integral parts of a professor's performance evaluation, such as with promotion and tenure packets, or when being considered for instructional awards.

These internal roles have persisted, but SET have taken on added weight in ways that we doubt were anticipated by their creators. The data that had cozily resided among a select few has now been pushed outside academic systems and sometimes outside academic control. Now, many people are interested in SET data, and recent evidence shows the migration of SET data from internal stakeholders to those outside the institution. The goal of this migration has been to "prove" that there is some consistent mechanism by which those outside academic walls may be assured that faculty are providing quality instruction and overall value (see Spooren, Brockx, and Mortelmans, 2013). The push for evaluation information has led to new types of SET housed outside of university walls, such as Rate My Professors (RMP) and community impact evaluations adopted by some Campus Compact branches. It's a brave new world of transparency, where anyone with a computer can offer comments on a professor's performance. Administrators and faculty have little or no control over these sites, which presents inherently ethical problems.

Externally, SET information has become one of a laundry list of statistics that some would use to cull poorly performing professors, cut funding, or conversely to market specific professor skills. And it's these added "functions" of SET that have my colleagues around the country very cautious about what to change, and how to change it. The ethics of SET has become complex and murky. We think the biggest three issues include lack of context, competing concerns, and probably most importantly, validity issues.

Lack of Context

Some of the people who would like access to SET information lack the context by which to interpret the data with integrity. A parent, for example, might see low SET ratings for a particular professor and conclude poor instruction, not realizing that the course may be a rigorous Gen Ed pre-requisite with traditionally low grades, a relationship that has been shown to exist in a variety of disciplines (see Clayson, Frost, and Sheffet, 2006 for a particularly clever experimental design). Or, a student may rate an instructor poorly because he/she has little interest in the subject matter, or because the instructor has a teaching style the student doesn't like. A state board of education member seeing those ratings may not take student characteristics into account. Interpretive context matters.

Competing Concerns

There are sometimes competing concerns among stakeholders. For example, SET ratings are not generally released to students in the same way that performance ratings are usually kept between employee and manager. Professors have a right to performance information being kept close at hand, for sure. However, students, fed up with the lack of information by which to choose effective in lieu of ineffective teachers and having to rely on sometimes sketchy word of mouth to avoid awful professors, have moved SET outside academic walls to sites like RMP. Students tell us, too, that they post on RMP when it appears over time that nothing has changed with a professor's teaching despite repeated SET input about what could be improved. Some of their word-of-mouth information about instructors is surely inaccurate. However, conversations we hear each semester among students remind us of two lessons: first, that such informally shared information can indeed be spot-on, and second, how much people in any organization dislike what we call "the illusion of participation," or, being asked for their considered opinion when that resulting opinion has no impact whatsoever. So while confidentiality of SET ratings is appropriate for some reasons, their release could also be seen as the right thing to do for students.

Consider this analogy, posted by "Bill" in response to a blog post about releasing SET data publicly (Khan, 2012):

> I honestly fail to see why profs should be allowed some sacred space in which to be arbitrary, unfair, illogical or irrelevant with both the impunity

which they ALREADY LARGELY HAVE in most institutions and also ANONYMITY to their patrons, that is, the people who will pay $5000 + for their classes. This is no different from saying that Consumer Reports shouldn't be able to run customer satisfaction surveys.

Clearly, Bill has had a negative past with his professors in which he experienced their performance as unethical. And it annoys us that someone thinks our performance evaluation information is no different than the information we get when we research computer tablets on Consumer Reports. But, although we've rejected the "paying customer" metaphor in academe, does Bill have a point about wanting information about an experience for which he will be paying a significant amount of money? We think he does. One of the compelling issues for professor evaluation information is balancing our right to privacy with others' (including Bill's) right to know.

Validity Concerns

This is, in our view, the Big One. The increasingly broad usage of SET information has placed a spotlight on validity concerns. While SET are generally reliable, here's the empirical bottom line about validity: All of the literature we examined as well as web-based writings and recent research (Flaherty, 2016) tell the tale of an instrument that is widely used yet maddeningly resists efforts at validation. Gender discrimination with SET outcomes is also being carefully documented throughout many disciplines (Boring 2017) – there is evidence of systematic lower ratings for women, and such evidence should be front and center when SET data are used for any kind of performance decisions.

Measuring "teaching effectiveness" is conflated with "student learning" (Stehle, Spinath, and Kadmon, 2012), a messy, convoluted, and possible non-relationship (Uttl, White, and Gonzalez, 2017). Anyone can post on RMP, whether they actually had a course with an instructor or not. Even though there is research indicating that RMP "can" be valid for a couple of important evaluation constructs, RMP's "hotness" chili pepper rating detracts from taking it seriously.

More broadly, the advent of assurance of learning mandates, particularly by accrediting bodies, manifests external stakeholder frustration with a roundly perceived lack of institutional and professorial accountability and responsiveness. We understand that, and are in many ways sympathetic to their gripes. State governments, communities, and parents are among those who have successfully pushed for more transparency, more action, and more tools with which to get institutions to pay attention to teaching quality. But, and this is a big but, using SET in punitive and holistic ways, and as the only data points, by which to assess professors' classroom performance, is quite simply wrong.

A Special Case

The Board of Regents at the University of Kansas voted in December 2013 to restrict professors' right to express views via social media, saying they want to protect the institution (Summers 2014). In an age where institutions are beholden to donors and the fear of controversy looms large, we get it. What they are really worried about are the responses from, well, anyone who doesn't like a professor's pedagogical methods or course goals and raises a public stink. We see this as a special form of an über-invalid SET from people without context, and with agendas that compete with our role as encouraging difficult, unpopular, or power-contesting viewpoints. As Schuman (2014) asserts, "A bunch of know-nothing randos on the internet should not be able to get professors fired." This is a patently unethical new horizon, since we are against "know-nothings" having so much potential say in our performance evaluation as a whole.

Evaluation and Support Focus: Flexibility versus Control

The other axis in Quinn's model, for our purposes here, is how we want to use this information. We are fans of developmental performance appraisals rather than simply evaluative ones (student evaluation gurus use the terms "formative" and "summative" in lieu of developmental and evaluative). When we managed others in industry and were doing a performance appraisal, our focus was always about laying out expectations and supporting the employee in achieving them. The appraisal *process* was more important, to us as managers, than the *content* of the appraisal itself because we knew we did not have complete insight into any employee's performance. We think the same should ideally be true of SET and how we use those data. Because there are such well-documented validity issues with SET, and because there are so many nuances in a professor's 'effectiveness,' the idea that they should inflexibly be considered as-is, and as THE evaluation data of an instructor's classroom effectiveness is unethical. Seeking more quality control over academic instruction is a good thing, for everyone, but it's that process of inclusion and ownership that must be integrated, and an ethical HR process is more flexible than controlling, in our experience.

The idea of 'control' in academe deserves attention. We have never seen anyone linearly, directly, and measurably make a student learn something. Our control over what students learn is minimal – if in fact what we really want to effect by "teaching effectiveness" is student learning. Thus, those who view SET data as a control systems tool overestimate the teaching–learning relationship. Part of the wonder of our jobs is watching that "a-ha!" moment that differs for each learner. We wish we could say we had more design over when that happens, and for what students, but alas, in our combined 87 years we have not found that formula. Being evaluated as "effective" is irreducible to a single instrument at one point in time.

Staying at the Table

It's not a newsflash to recognize that student evaluations in some form are here to stay. Despite validity issues, despite being used acontextually, and despite being used summatively instead of developmentally, efforts are underway to expand SET usage, not rein them in as a sort of failed experiment. And the sooner we engage with this inevitability, the more voice we will have in how SET will come to look, and how they will be used.

When we argue for more engagement with student evaluation development, not less, it's because we think there are lots of analogies between resisting SET and resisting other serious external forays into our academic enterprise. The most analogous example for us is how we handled assurance of learning documentation efforts. All higher educational accrediting bodies include some form of assurance of learning, which came about in the early 2000s and requires documented connections between learning objectives and student learning outcomes. While Kathy has written about philosophical concerns with such a documentational approach to learning, we vividly remember some of our colleagues' outright dismissal of assurance of learning. We heard, for example, at one of our prominent conference venues: "Assurance of learning? They can't make us do anything we don't want to do!" Uh, well, yes they did. And we see a very similar trajectory with resistance to expanding student evaluation administration and data usage. We can't give up our seats at this table. We can't put our heads in the sand that "they" can't make SET usage more integral to our teaching practice, and that "they" cannot find ways of using those data that run counter to our best interests as professional educators. Stakeholders both inside and outside of our institutions deserve to know how we're doing as instructors, and we *must be there* to shape how that evaluation process will go.

We think we are in a liminal space with respect to SET administration. There's a lot of attention being given to a normative recommendation for how SET should go. The Gates Foundation, for example, is funding research into creating valid, credible, and useful SET on a post-secondary level, modeled after their sweeping K-12 evaluation research projects. Those projects recommend a multi-pronged evaluation approach including classroom observation, student achievement scores, and yes, some kind of SET instrument. As with most evaluations, triangulation is a good thing, and faculty need to advocate for expanding evaluation data points in institutions for which only SET reign supreme.

The Ethics of the "Now What?"

The ethics of SET include responsibilities on multiple 'sides' of the instruments. The almost wholesale resistance to sharing what happens in a classroom, citing academic freedom, has resulted in a pendulum swing over which we have less control than before. *Professors* have a responsibility to take student input seriously, even as we understand the sometimes significant limitations of student-derived comments and suggestions. Students may, for example, evaluate a professor's teaching harshly and negatively, only to find later in life that the lessons imparted are life changing and valuable. This is the nature of our work, but not every student comment is borne of this kind of experience. Some of their feedback is true, and we need to engage with it. We administer both a mid-term and end-of-term evaluation instrument, and we find student suggestions and comments invaluable. What helps a lot is priming students for them, and coaching them as to what kinds of comments and suggestions are helpful. Over every semester there have been creative nuggets for improvement that we never would have thought of ourselves. It has been our experience that when we signal and model how their input matters, we get suggestions that energize our teaching practice.

Students have a responsibility to offer comments and suggestions in the spirit of fairness and goodwill. Student evaluations have a bad name in part because of the sometimes breathtakingly painful and personal criticisms that students write. We need to coach them on how to give developmental feedback in ways with which professors can engage and from which professors can learn, including a focus on course issues rather than on personal instructor issues. Similar to our manuscript peer-review process, where some of our reviewer colleagues need to learn how to offer feedback in responsible and developmental ways, we should not assume students know how to offer candid SET data without veering into unhelpful personal critiques.

Administrators have a responsibility to offer instructors a mechanism by which to reflect on SET information, such as an annual evaluation process, an annually renewed statement of teaching philosophy, or a peer-coaching group. They should resist the urge to use such data punitively without also offering improvement coaching and support. They have a responsibility to disseminate the data about potential bias in SET, and contextualize their use in any form of faculty evaluation. Even in the last ten years, we have observed massive changes in teaching practice, from the lecture-based 'sage on the stage' to the 'guide on the side,' complete with learning management systems, flipped classrooms, and increasingly daring experiential learning opportunities such as community-engaged partnerships. Faculty can't just pick these new practices up, be confident in crafting learning outcomes, and carry out affectively charged learning experiences as if we're changing classrooms. We need protected professional development funding and support to actualize the possible in new teaching frontiers. And when we try something and it falls flat, resulting in gothic SET that semester, we need help picking through the pieces of that experience and learning what we could do differently.

External stakeholders hold responsibility, too. It is true that academe has resisted calls for reform, for transparency, and for some kind of accountability for the quality of academic instruction. But revolution does not happen overnight, and it should not happen top-down, in ways that inspire fear and risk aversion.

MOOCs, for example, brim with the promise of unprecedented learning access, but in domestic bailiwicks the conversation centers more around the fear that MOOCs will be used as a cost-saving lancet, reducing academic positions. While SET can capture some interesting data, they do a poor job capturing how professors help students become their best selves with learning that resists spreadsheets and test scores. Perhaps you've helped Sherry overcome her crippling fear of speaking in front of a group, or helped Sid gain the confidence he needs to apply for law school years after he graduates with his baccalaureate degree. Life changing, yet probably not on your SET, and external folks must honor the complex and longer-term character of learning outcomes.

Moving Ahead

OK – now, having said all that, we will also say we are in favor of using student evaluation data, however flawed, to help us get better at our craft. We only say that if SET are used in the developmental or formative way discussed above. The key seems to be, as they say in recovery groups, taking what we need and leaving the rest behind, and using that information in ways that help us learn how to be better teachers.

To get an idea of what that might look like, Kathy talked with Darrin Good, who served as Associate Provost and Dean of Sciences and Education at Gustavus from 2012 to 2015, and who now serves as Vice President of Academic Affairs and Dean of Faculty at Whittier College. While at Gustavus, Darrin led the effort to revise the SET.

The holistic conversation about SET is not only about what questions should go on the SET – what we want to validly measure – but how that information will be used. Although Darrin told Kathy first things first – we need to work on getting a better instrument that faculty trust – we're asking interesting questions: Should SET data be used in ongoing performance evaluations, even post-tenure? Who should have access to SET data in addition to the professors themselves? What kind of support will be available for those instructors with negative and "needs improvement" ratings?

Given the far-reaching impacts of the answers, it is no wonder that, while the committee (and all Kathy's colleagues that she spoke with about the SET) agrees that the current instrument needs revision, committee members are having a hard time converging on something different.

When Kathy asked Darrin how to respond to SET validity issues, he said, "A SET can hold up a red flag, not necessarily exactly the right thing to pick out that needs attention, but a good committee can see a data point and spend time on it if needed with the faculty member." (By "committee" he is talking about an informal coaching circle or triad of colleagues who are devoted to helping each other distill SET comments and classroom observations into helpful practical teaching improvement.) He added,

It's important that we understand where we can and can't get good information from students, and that leads to those red flags. There are instances
where students may not be able to define or articulate what's wrong with a
professor's teaching, but they know there's something not working in a
professor's course, and that's where a committee can see the need to dig
deeper and work with the faculty member to see what's going on.

We really liked his description of this supportive process, and it links back with
respecting process over content for performance evaluation as a whole.

We also believe he's right when he says,

There is only a small percentage of faculty that do not want to improve, and
get better at their teaching. If there is an instrument people trust, with valid
feedback, and a committee truly helping the faculty member improve in a
non-threatening and informal community-based way, teaching will improve.

Thus, here's the last thing we will say for this chapter – which seems to sum up
the gist of the thing nicely, also from Darrin.

We know a lot about good pedagogy. What we want to see is if that
instructor is doing things that generally lead to good learning outcomes. Are
there pedagogically sound behaviors and assignments? There are many ways
to be successful in the classroom, just like there are many different leadership
styles. We want to focus right now on the instrument itself and increasing
validity and meaningfulness.

Discussion Questions

1. What would it mean for your institution to have SET "done right"?
2. What would the content look like, and what about the process of using
   them?
3. Should SET be voluntary or mandatory? Why do you think so?
4. If you could choose the questions for your SET, what would they be, and why?
5. What could we do in terms of administering SET that would increase their
   usefulness for professors? What should we be asking students to do to
   increase their helpfulness?
6. In what ways have you seen faculty manipulate SET ratings? Given that
   SET generally serve as the major or only data source for teaching evaluation,
   could it be considered simply smart practice to "teach to the evaluation"
   criteria similar to the way we may encourage students to complete assignments
   with the grading rubric in mind?
7. Do we owe special consideration or protections for PhD students and their
   (usually) poor ratings as they learn the craft of teaching? As job candidates,

they will probably be asked to share SET data, which will probably be at their lowest point in their professional career. Is there anything we ethically owe students in this respect?

8.   Does your institution use a different instrument for pre-tenured, post-tenured, and senior faculty? Why or why not? Is it fair, in your opinion?

References and Additional Reading

Boring, Anne. 2017. "Gender Biases in Student Evaluations of Teaching." *Journal of Public Economics*, 145: 27–41.

Burt, Stephen. 2015. "Why Not Get Rid of Student Evaluations?" *Slate Magazine*. www.slate.com/articles/life/education/2015/05/a_defense_of_student_evaluations_they_re_biased_misleading_and_extremely.html

Clayson, Dennis E., Taggart F. Frost, and Mary Jane Sheffet. 2006. "Grades and the Student Evaluation of Instruction: A Test of the Reciprocity Effect." *Academy of Management Learning and Education*, 5. 1: 52–65.

Flaherty, Colleen. 2016. "Zero Correlations between Evaluations and Learning." September 21. Accessed October 16, 2016. www.insidehighered.com/news/2016/09/21/new-study-could-be-another-nail-coffin-validity-student-evaluations-teaching#.V-LSMoCLo_g.mailto

Galbraith, Craig S., Gregory B. Merrill, and Doug M. Kline. 2012. "Are Student Evaluations of Teaching Effectiveness Valid for Measuring Student Learning Outcomes in Business Related Classes? A Neural Network and Bayesian Analyses." *Research in Higher Education*, 53. 3: 353–374.

Khan, Matthew E. 2012. "Should a Professor's Teaching Evaluations Be in the Public Domain?" www.samefacts.com/2012/04/everything-else/should-a-professors-teaching-evaluations-be-in-the-public-domain/

Patton, Stacey. 2015. "Student Evaluations: Feared, Loathed, and Not Going Anywhere." https://chroniclevitae.com/news/1011-student-evaluations-feared-loathed-and-not-going-anywhere

Schuman, Rebecca. 2014. "Student Evaluations of Professors Aren't Just Biased and Absurd, They Don't Even Work." *Slate Magazine*. www.slate.com/articles/life/education/2014/04/student_evaluations_of_college_professors_are_biased_and_worthless.html

Spooren, Pieter, Bert Brockx, and Dimitri Mortelmans. 2013. "On the Validity of Student Evaluation of Teaching: The State of the Art." *Review of Educational Research*, 83. 4: 598–642).

Stehle, Sebastian, Birgit Spinath, and Martina Kadmon. 2012. "Measuring Teaching Effectiveness: Correspondence between Students' Evaluations of Teaching and Different Measures of Student Learning." *Research in Higher Education*, 53. 5: 888–904.

Summers, J. 2014. "Educators Not Satisfied with Revised Kansas Social Media Policy." *National Public Radio*. Accessed February 18, 2017. www.npr.org/sections/ed/2014/05/25/315837245/educators-not-satisfied-with-revised-kansas-social-media-policy

Uttl, Bob, Carmela A. White, and Daniela Wong Gonzalez.2017. "Meta-Analysis of Faculty's Teaching Effectiveness: Student Evaluation of Teaching Ratings and Student Learning Are Not Related."*Studies in Educational Evaluation*, 54 (September): 22–42.

19

STUDENT RECOMMENDATIONS

To Give, or Not to Give, That Is the Question

Key insight: Although writing letters of recommendation may be a common task, there is much more to these letters than meets the eye! In this chapter, we discuss a variety of ethical angles to student recommendations based on who the requesting student is. We consider recommendation requests from long-graduated students who contact us (sometimes out of the blue); the online recommendation phenomenon, such as with LinkedIn, that utilizes 'blanket' or generalized recommendations; potential legal issues about what we say in recommendations with respect to privacy laws, including what might change for us writers when students can examine our letters before we send them; and finally, an ethical issue raised by different cultural interpretations of what's OK.

In Chapter 15, we focused on the ethics of student–instructor social networking, and when it might be appropriate to friend students in that very gray area of relationships that social network sites provide. That subject was prompted in part by the end of the semester coming, and our receiving a spate of "friend" requests from students. Another touchstone experience at the end of any semester is the rush of requests for recommendation letters. Like many of you, we get lots of requests each term to craft letters of recommendation for students moving on in any variety of ways, particularly when we teach seniors or graduate students. Some are easy – a student "Shawn" who earned a high score in a very competitive graduate course and was one of those students who, when he spoke in class, earned his peers' clear admiration. Some are... not so much. "George" was a better-than-average performer, but was so unpleasant and arrogant that his request for a recommendation seemed more like a demand. Or, consider "Tina," whose performance was wholly unremarkable – not terrific, but not terrible either. Does she get a letter, or, do we reserve those for the Shawns of the world?

Writing recommendations has a significant ethical angle in our increasingly competitive world that students enter. A solidly crafted recommendation can be the deciding factor for a student gaining an opportunity s/he would otherwise not have had and we must consider our gatekeeper role. Whenever we get a request for a recommendation, they tend to fall in a few categories. Let's go through those and tease out the ethical issues.

The Student Requesting the Recommendation was a Poor Classroom Performer

We don't want to talk about the no-brainer, high-performer "Shawn" cases here. When the requesting student simply did not have the level of performance we would agree merits our recommendation, we have to stop and consider what to do. We could agree, fudge a letter for him or her, and avoid the potential conflict – *caveat emptor*, right? Although it may be tempting, particularly for a persistent student and for expedience, passing along inaccurate or incomplete information about a student's performance is simply the wrong thing to do. And we owe students an honest conversation about why we cannot write a positive letter for them. In requesting a recommendation, they are in effect indicating they think they can do the work required of a new and more rigorous role. We agree with Verba (n.d.) that when we have any reservation about a recommen-dation, we have a sometimes difficult conversation with the student, offering him or her evidence-based feedback that may conflict with their very idea of who they are.

It's not easy, and we wish sometimes such discussions were formulaic in what to say. We have had a couple of different reactions from students. Most know their own performance issues and can sheepishly admit they are not academic rock stars. Others, though, seem to not have an accurate under-standing of their performance and exhibit occasionally bullet-proof blind spots about it. All we can do is be frank without being nasty, and offer evidence as to why we are saying no. We have never had a student who, after this con-versation, suggested that we write the recommendation anyway – a patently unethical suggestion.

Schall (2006) said,

> Sometimes, the kindest, most responsible thing we can do for a student is to refuse to write a letter of reference… The pushiest students might insist that you really are the best recommender they've got, and that your letter is critical to their very existence.

When we have had these instances, we are alert to something else going on, and our conversation with that student is even more straightforward. We experience pushiness as confirmatory data that we are making the right decision to decline writing that letter.

We Don't Know the Student Well Enough to Make a Candid Recommendation

Occasionally we get requests to comment on more holistic aspects of a student's performance, such as personal integrity or patriotism. Students going to work for the federal government with security clearances, or in certain financial fields, need questions like this answered. We have found this issue not as difficult to handle. If a student asks for a letter, and we can't make a judgment, we have some options. We can decline, correctly citing a lack of knowledge. We can decline that section of an evaluation, citing a lack of direct experience. We can try to find out by talking with the student and filling in the gaps. Or, we can ask others for their experiences with and recommendations about that student, as long as we say in the letter where we got the information.

Scholars agree that the unethical thing to do is guess, or affirm simply because we have not seen or heard information that would contradict those criteria. Declining to answer does not doom the student's chances, in our experience, but makes the other aspects of the recommendation more credible.

The Student Is Annoying and We Really Dislike Her/Him

It's sure hard to write glowing things about personality-challenged students. From an ethics perspective, though, it has to come back to performance. Unless whatever is annoying you will have a demonstrable negative effect on the student's future prospects, the recommendation should proceed with the usual inclusions and evidence. Recalling "George" from the opening of this chapter – what happened? Because the program to which he was applying was clearly in his skill set, we did the letter. Maybe it was also part of our ultimate decision to do it when we realized George's field (and that particular employer) was full of people just like him! We wrote the letter, carefully documenting how his skills matched the program's needs, and decided to let his ubiquitous "Hey dude!" greetings speak their own volumes.

The Student Had Average, or Unremarkable Performance

These seem to be increasing in frequency due to the persistently challenging economy and students' need for any competitive advantage or differentiating factor. When we get a request from a "non-Shawn" or, a student whose performance does not make writing a recommendation obvious for us, we consider our gatekeeper role. An especially helpful process we use comes from Hosmer's *The Ethics of Management* (2010) and other work of his, in the form of The Four Questions. If we do the recommendation,

- Who gains, and how much?
- Who gets harmed, and how much?
- What do I owe others (i.e., the people involved), if anything?
- What do others owe me, if anything?

The first two questions are outcomes-based, while the last two are duty-based, so it's a terrific structured evaluation process that helps us think about important aspects of a decision. Although it's too long a calculus to wholly record here, let's briefly consider each aspect.

If we write the recommendation, the average performer "Tina" may get a position that taps into her passions, and her performance may be rejuvenated. It could be, literally, a life-altering opportunity, such as the internship experience one of our Tinas got that turned into a professional position in lieu of the secretarial one she otherwise would have had to take. With respect to the harms question, we have often considered the performance appraisal process to be our ally. If we write Tina a letter and her moderate performance follows her into the workplace, she will most likely be culled out on her own (lack of) merits. If we don't write the recommendation, the harms may be more widespread and longer term in her not getting her foot in the door.

The duties questions seem more interesting to us here. We absolutely think we owe the recommendation reader an honest evaluation of a student's performance, so we are careful to not embellish or use broadly based language. A "Shawn"-like comment might be, "Shawn's group process skills are well-developed and he has earned the respect of his peers" while a "Tina"-like comment might be, "Tina's peers appreciated her promptness to group meetings," when we have peer-evaluation evidence that this particular aspect of her performance was solid. So, our evaluations are more narrow and focused. We think we owe Tina our effort to craft a letter that takes into account some skills, because we have come to realize that for under-the-radar performers, it may be one of the few times a professor has ever said anything affirming about them. What do others owe Tina, or us? Perhaps an honest shot at the job for Tina, but that is true for many job candidates. And, we think the job market over the last ten years has been very short on duty fulfillment, so we are more concerned about how our interaction with Tina affects her prospects as well as our own sense of honest evaluation.

The internet and social media sites have made it not only possible, but probable, that students we had years ago can find us, even at different institutions. And, changes in the law can also affect our recommendation-writing behaviors. Here are a few more possible scenarios for consideration.

The Long-Ago Graduated Student Finds You Again, Requesting a Recommendation

As social networks make it possible to find people long gone in the 'real world,' a former student "Sydney" contacted us for a recommendation even though she had graduated 13 years prior and we had not kept in touch with her. Although we remembered her, we did not remember at all any of her performance in our classes. Should we write a letter for her? If we cannot speak to particular performance criteria and talents the student has now, it becomes our responsibility to decline writing the letter. Although we might be pushing some employment opportunity out of reach for our Sydneys of the world, these former students should have been cultivating more current relationships with those who could speak to their abilities credibly and completely. This student did not seem surprised when we declined; on our more suspicious days we wonder if her performance since graduation had simply been so weak that she was reaching for any available voice to assist her.

A Student Wants an Electronic "Blanket" or Generalized Recommendation, Such as Those Found on LinkedIn

"Blake" asked for an electronically housed recommendation on LinkedIn. While he was a very strong performer, his request was for a general or blanket recommendation highlighting more global skills such as ability to work in a group and writing skills, rather than for a particular job position. How useful are these types of recommendation? As we trolled for information, we hit upon what seemed to be a particularly helpful evaluation from Susan Adams at Forbes (2012).

Similar to old-school recommendations, the more specific, realistic, and skills-based the recommendation the better. Adams talks about too flowery language (not good), overkill at 50 recommendations (did your mother ask all her friends to write one?) and vague or indifferent language (also not good). She also indicates that such recommendations can indeed be helpful, but employers are not at the point of candidates having an e-recommendation or losing out completely. So, the ethical frame remains ultimately the same: if you can fairly, accurately, and specifically point to skills that many employers might like, such as time management or conflict resolution, then e-recommendations appear to be at least neutral. On the other hand, if you cannot positively assess such transferable kinds of skills, it is probably best to decline. Although LinkedIn is subscriber-based, as an internet option it is out there, with the potential for many, many people to see the letter you write. We did write a LinkedIn recommendation for Blake, and made very specific references to his work skills. It was easy, because he was terrific as a student and we had just finished the semester with him so it was fresh. But we did make clear that we were willing to write the recommendation specifically about those skills and he was appreciative of that.

The end of the story is that he did get the job he wanted, and the LinkedIn recommendation played a positive role.

Dicey Legal Issues with Recommendations, Particularly FERPA

The Family Educational Rights and Privacy Act, or FERPA, was designed to protect student educational performance information and allow students themselves to decide who gets that information. FERPA has been interpreted differently around the country, but with respect to recommendations, the legal implications are clear. Students have a right to see what you write in your letter unless they explicitly waive that right, something most graduate and professional school admissions offices require. Requiring students to waive their FERPA rights ostensibly allows us as recommenders to be more frank with admissions folks about the student's abilities. As importantly, keeping our letter content confidential does not allow the student to hunt down letter writers, looking for the people who "kept me out" of the desired program. Being blamed for the lack of invitation to join a program does happen, so many professors themselves require the FERPA waiver. Investigating this informally, we have learned of colleagues who will only write a recommendation, for any program or job, if students agree to waive their FERPA rights to examine it.

While we have only done a few recommendations for a non-business graduate or law school in the last ten years, we have done a million of them for MBA programs. What has worked for us is having very straightforward conversations with students about their abilities and potential success in the graduate programs they are considering. By doing so, the results have seemed binary to us: either the student is very qualified and we write a recommendation that we have no problem with them seeing, or, the student's performance does not merit our recommendation and we decline it altogether. Now, a key factor may be that we seem to get requests from students with whom we have crafted a solid relationship, while those with whom we have not do not ask us. While we still think our process could work, we have not been exposed to the retributive and blaming students our colleagues have. Ethically, all resources we have tapped appear to be consistent on the requirement of evidence-based commentary, meaning, discuss only those performance aspects for which you have direct experience and evidence.

While it seems kind of sad to us that the recommendation process has become such a potential gatekeeper that real contention and legal trouble have arisen, we understand that pressures to succeed and get the next credential can override seemingly sane people sometimes. We have to protect ourselves while serving students with this important source of information, and the line is not black and white.

How About a Cultural Interpretive Difference?

A colleague who was raised and still resides outside North America sent this scenario, which we will paraphrase and disguise a bit:

"John" teaches quite large class sections of over 100 students each, so he does not really get to know his students all that closely and thus receives few recommendation requests. One student asked for a recommendation, a request John declined because he could not reasonably speak to the student's performance in the criteria the organization requested. Indeed, the student's request was the first time John had actually met this student and based on the few assignments the student had turned in, she was a below-average performer. The student, when John indicated he could not do the recommendation with any integrity, indicated that her father would pay John for the recommendation, and seemed confused when John refused yet again.

Perhaps to a North American worldview, this is a clear "Sorry, can't help you" situation. But John reported this student seemed genuinely confused by his refusal to help. Culturally, this could be partially explained by a brief article from 2012 in the *Harvard Business Review* (Currell and Bradley, 2012) that detailed compelling factors leading to bribery in emerging markets, including stifling bureaucracies and multinational corporations' own time pressures for market penetration. Students raised in environments where 'grease money' does not carry the same negative weight as it does in Western countries have a right to know why we won't help them, in clear but not denigrating discussions. John was not at all equivocal, but increasing global reach and diverse classrooms will guarantee we will see more of these kinds of requests, and concurrent reactions.

For students you agree to recommend, there are a variety of forms for recommendations but they should include

1 *An honest vetting of the student's abilities, past performance, and projected capabilities within expected new roles.*

Verba (n.d.) notes that, "If, after doing a careful review of a candidate's strengths and weaknesses, you cannot write a supportive letter, it is important to have a candid discussion with the student." Evidence used in the evaluation should be clear to the reader, and when projecting new responsibilities, tapping colleagues in those fields is most welcome. For example, a law school recommendation should include why that student might be successful in a J.D. program, and consulting with law school colleagues can add valuable weight to a candidate's evaluation. If you've considered the student's abilities and you don't believe you can write a positively supportive recommendation, it is time to talk to the student.

2 *Explanations of any perceived weaknesses in the student's record.*

Evaluators will want to know why, for example, an otherwise outstanding academic record included very poor grades for a particular time period. With the student's permission, it is OK to disclose family illnesses, or other conditions that resulted in red-flag performance issues. We had a student who was a domestic violence victim whose performance, quite understandably, tanked for an entire spring semester. We got her assistance through a local agency, she repeated most of the courses after getting out of that situation, and she asked us to help her get into a non-local graduate program. It was an easy letter to write based on her holistic performance, and we collaborated on language explaining her prior household situation. Even if a performance issue is not glaring, it is important to offer critique of any possible holes in the student's record and how the student will overcome them. For example, a student's problems with sentence structure and mechanics will be ameliorated by her use of a professional copy editor at her own expense.

3 *Explanation of your relationship with the student – how do you know what you know?*

Student contact can come through myriad forms and the reader should understand how you've been able to evaluate the student's performance. Were you the instructor, or the faculty advisor? Mentor for a client consulting project? Offering context helps the reader understand your role and adds credibility to the student's overall evaluation.

Why Risk It?

Letters of recommendation are a big deal – they can be a make-or-break factor for students gaining access to a prestigious graduate program, or a coveted promotion, or funding for a grant proposal. They can also serve as the spark to ideological battlegrounds over who gets to evaluate whom. We cannot help but think about that high-profile dispute from 2003 where a Texas Tech student sued his biology teacher, Professor Michael Dini, for refusing to write a letter on the student's behalf. The professor had, on his website, a set of guidelines under which he would write such letters; one included an acceptance of evolution as a basic biological underpinning. The student refused to affirm evolution on religious grounds, dropped out of Tech, and sued the instructor.

The Texas Tech case was complicated, and fortunately, most recommendation situations do not invite litigation. In the majority of cases, these letters are a delight to write: affirming the student's hard work and providing a connection within that important developmental space between undergraduate to graduate, or mid-level manager to executive ranks. But they are important enough to warrant our attention about who deserves one, and who does not. Joe Schall (2006) wrote about the reciprocal nature of letters of recommendation: "None of us got where we are professionally without the help of recommendation letters written on our behalf. Most of us therefore feel obliged to write letters for students whenever they ask." While we agree with his first assertion, it's the "whenever they ask" part that deserves our ethical consideration, as Schall well notes later on in his essay.

Discussion Questions

1.   Tell of a time when a student asked you for a recommendation and you hesitated. Why were you hesitant? What was going on? What ultimately did you do, and why?

2. When would it be OK to refuse to write a recommendation even if the student is a strong performer?
3. Share effective verbiage from your own letters you've written, or effective phrasing of student performance aspects you've evaluated.
4. What happened when a student asked you to include information about him or her that was simply not true, but would have really helped their chances?
5. Does anything change about your letters when students have a chance to see it before you send it?

References and Additional Reading

Adams, Susan. 2012. "Everything You Need to Know about LinkedIn Recommendations." www.forbes.com/sites/susanadams/2012/02/08/everything-you-need-to-know-about-linkedin-recommendations/#55d12a3562d3

Currell, Dan and Tracy Davis Bradley. 2012. "Greased Palms, Big Headaches." *Harvard Business Review*, 90. 9: 21–27.

Hosmer, LaRue Tone. 2010. *The Ethics of Management*. New York: McGraw-Hill.

Schall, Joe. 2006. "The Ethics of Writing Recommendation Letters." *Academe*, 92. 3: 41–44.

Verba, Cynthia. n.d. "GSAS Guide for Teaching Fellows on Writing Letters of Recommendation." Derek Bok Center for Teaching and Learning, Harvard. http://isites.harvard.edu/fs/html/icb.topic58474/Verba-recs.html

20

THOUGHT LEADER

Robert A. Giacalone on "Broken When Entering"

Key insight: Bob Giacalone and Mark Promislo co-authored a 2013 article in the Academy of Management Learning and Education entitled "Broken When Entering: The Stigmatization of Goodness and Business Ethics Education." In this chapter, we first react to their work, and then share some of our conversation with Bob Giacalone about the article. We have also fielded and included in this chapter some reactions from Kabrina Krebel Chang of Boston University, who serves as Executive Director of Boston University's Susilo Institute for Ethics in the Global Economy and who is directing the School of Management's comprehensive ethics education effort.

Robert A. Giacalone: A Brief Introduction

In a departure for this book's section, we are writing about teaching ethics itself as a content area, rather than ethical issues in teaching. After reading Bob Giacalone and Mark Promislo's (2013) article about students being ethically broken when they come to us, we wanted to write about two particular challenges we face when teaching ethics, and particularly business ethics: coming clean about the organizational costs to behaving ethically, and what we can do in the classroom to acknowledge these costs and move forward. Bob and Mark argue that through the use of 'normal' business school language, modeling, and metrics, we perpetuate 'broken' student perspectives and behaviors with respect to ethics. They say that ethics education is tougher than we already knew it was, because students aren't even coming in at the ground floor – they are coming into our classrooms with persistent and troubling assumptions about what 'business' is about and what their leadership responsibilities are. We wanted to talk with Bob about some of their suggested 'fixes' to this problem that they articulate at the end of the article, and we also wanted to know his continuing thoughts on this topic.

Bob is one of the most well-published and thoughtful scholarly leaders in ethics education as well as in the management, spirituality, and religion domain. He serves as the Raymond and Eleanor Smiley Chair in Business Ethics at John Carroll University and previously held the Daniel's Chair in Business Ethics at the University of Denver. Prior to holding the Daniel's Chair, Bob was part of the Temple University faculty for nine years. Kathy enjoyed working with Bob for many years in the Academy of Management's Management, Spirituality, and Religion group, and she was the invited papers editor for the *Journal of Management, Spirituality, and Religion* when Bob was Editor-in-Chief, roles that ended in 2012. Bob is no stranger to provocative articles in *Academy of Management Learning and Education*. His 2004 article, "A Transcendent Business Education for the 21st Century" is a staple in calls for transforming business education by challenging *status quo* metrics of success. The *Handbook of Workplace Spirituality and Organizational Performance*, now in its second edition (2010), was co-edited with Carole Jurkiewicz and is among the most-cited scholarly sources in the entire management, spirituality, and religion domain. And in his spare time, Bob co-edited with Mark Promislo the *Handbook of Unethical Work Behavior: Implications for Individual Well-Being*, out in 2014. He has been teaching business ethics for 30 years.

Kabrina Krebel Chang and her holistic reframing of how Boston University's School of Management is approaching organizational ethics were featured in a 2013 *Wall Street Journal* article. She is co-author of *Cyberlaw: Management and Entrepreneurship* (2015) and her work explores the intersection of online applications and ethics. She is a lawyer who teaches business law and ethics at Boston University, and her research includes how social media is fundamentally influencing employment decisions. She has been teaching ethics for 12 years.

Broken When Entering

The essential thesis from Broken When Entering (BWE) is that not only are students entering b-schools soundly unequipped for ethical reasoning and moral decision making, we faculty can make it much worse by the language we use and the norms we perpetuate. The materialism that underlies our entire cultural values set and subsequent vocabulary pervades our students' holistic sense of what business is and does, and skews their expectations about their role in the business world. Giacalone and Promislo describe the language b-school professors use that supports that skewed sense and in fact degrades it further, and then describe the "baggage" students carry as they enter our classrooms. Such ideological burdens include "a mindset that disparages virtue," "demonizing those needing help," and "the stigmatization of goodness," all of which serve to undermine our efforts to develop students' moral selves. Indeed, Christian Smith and his sociology colleagues offered "depressing" evidence that students lack the ability to understand situations as requiring ethical reasoning and the language with which to describe them (2011). BWE ends with some suggested techniques to counteract both language and baggage, and it's there where we think some conversation should continue.

In reading BWE, we were struck by the starkness of the language they use in describing our broken culture – how plainly they called it out. We use this language to embed certain norms in business schools – norms the authors say are at the root of b-school professors' pernicious complicity in furthering bad behavior in organizations. "Econophonics" is a "powerful, dominating language in which money is used to dictate and justify all actions" while "potensiphonics" is also a dominant language "but its emphasis is on power and supremacy" (Giacalone and Promislo, 2013, 88). Potensiphonics is Bob's creation from the Latin root for power, "potentia." And while we understand the materialism focus as mainly operational in for-profit organizations, both econophonics and potensiphonics have made their way into almost every organizational space. Witness, for example, the over-the-top show of power and authority on the University of California Davis campus with the now infamous pepper spray incident (2011; see the Wikipedia entry), or the sad, sad abuses with Jerry Sandusky at Penn State.

In every organizational role we have had, whether as a corporate manager or business owner, as a researcher or as a consultant, as a teacher or community organization board member, the scene tends to be the same. Nothing will fundamentally change with respect to ethical behavior in organizations until we engage with the compelling incentives that reward bad behavior and the shockingly short-term time horizon that now rules American organizational practices. So, cultural norms and short-termism are key aspects of our ethics courses with respect to the 'why' of unethical behavior. But BWE goes further – the language we use in business schools encompasses our students like the Seahaven dome under which Truman Burbank was raised in *The Truman Show*. Like Truman, students accept what is around them as 'truth' and when we seamlessly integrate both types of language as normal, how can students ever get a plausibly different view of the range of business activities and behaviors available to them? They can't. And that is one of the reasons why we ethics instructors may be seen as hopelessly out of touch, or experienced as idealists with little relevant knowledge to impart.

The "baggage" the authors characterize seems to come at our students in both directions: not only is real need vilified as a state of being deserving of our attention, but neediness' positive sister, goodness, is also rejected as being built on a moral principle threatening individualized actions that can lead to wealth and power and status (Giacalone and Promislo, 2013, 92). Our society's culture gets students, if you will, coming and going. Having a lasting effect on how our students view their business roles and responsibilities is an exercise in futility if we don't help students drop those bags.

Giacalone and Promislo also make an argument about the sinister nature of being oriented toward values-based behavior: "[others'] commitment to virtues over purely economic concerns creates the impression of a personal agenda that makes them unpredictable" (Giacalone and Promislo, 2013, 93). So it's not just that some people act in virtuous ways that others may think are ridiculous as they pursue their own agendas toward wealth and power, but that the virtuous themselves represent a disruption to carefully cultivated bottom-line norms that may be emotionally disconfirming to the extent that virtuous employees must be stopped.

The Costs of Ethical Behavior

The authors talk about being transparent with our students about the costs associated with morally grounded behavior, just as we might warn students about belonging to a counterculture during the organizational behavior course discussion of organizational culture's social control mechanism. Ethical and principled behavior is destabilizing to important, instrumental relationships in business, and there are costs to that.

Bob's and Kabrina's examples of how costs are 'paid' and how people make those personal calculations can be powerful. Their examples can offer students a kind of inoculation approach to ethics decisions: If they can think about certain types of situations beforehand and test out possible avenues of action, they may be more ready to do the right thing when an actual 'test' comes along.

BWE discussed those costs overtly, recommending we talk with students about them, too. Here is where we wanted Bob and Kabrina to weigh in. Kathy asked both of them questions related to BWE, in the interest of extending what BWE has to offer us.

Question: The article touches on the personal nature of and potential costs associated with ethical decisions we make in any organizational setting. Can you add to that discussion?

Bob: I would say that virtuous people in organizations represent as much of a threat to the status quo as incompetent people, probably more. The reason is that, while incompetence threatens the overall functioning of the organization, virtuous people may screw me directly, so self-interest is also built in. If you do something that is virtuous that causes me to lose a bonus or miss my numbers, then you have done harm to me personally, just because you had the audacity to do the right thing. So you must be stopped. If you're not stopped, you're a clear and present danger to my welfare.

Ethics isn't free. There is a cost to it. You make a choice every day as to whether you're going to pay. For me, it's a matter of every day choosing to define yourself in a way that says "This is what I stand for, and this is what I am willing to pay for standing for that." I'm not judgmental about it. While I may not like what he does, I can respect any thief who can admit he's a thief; I can respect the fact that he knows who he is, is upfront about it, and owns up to it.

What I cannot respect are those who say they are virtuous but then turn around and do things against what they say they are. That, I can't live with. So when we talk, I tell my students that and get them to respond.

Kabrina: I am at a b-school in the northeast and students are uber-motivated. Being in a business school, sadly I take it as a given that we will need to break much of the money=happiness equation. Breaking the equation has to happen in more than one class, and they have to see real examples. I use a bunch of different examples that have been effective in getting students talking.

A long time ago there was an article in the *New York Times* about the unemployability of whistleblowers so they read that. When we talk about virtue in my ethics class I use other examples. One is Barry Schwartz's TED Talk on the "Loss of Wisdom" where he talks about the job description of hospital janitors and how willing we are to look past people like that. Another is a video of a guy in Cincinnati getting beaten up in a parking lot robbery and two guys come to help him. It turns out the two heroes are homeless men and in interviews with them they start talking about the stigma of being homeless. One last example is hearing the 911 [telephone] operator pleading with staff at a retirement community after an elderly woman goes into cardiac arrest and no one will perform CPR. Not even the nurses! The 911 operator is baffled as to why no one will help her.

Question: The article offers some potential solutions and action items in the concluding remarks. They include increasing critical thinking skills, leveraging the student voices who do speak up against dominant language, and modeling what we want to see from our students. Of those, I found the leveraging student voice suggestion most potentially difficult in practice. As you reflect on that article since it was published, how might you give specific guidance to students about voice? Do you have any other recommendations about taking action when students see or experience unethical behaviors in their workplace?

Bob: Behaving ethically is complex. What we're claiming we want people to do is not clearly understood. There are both direct and indirect effects of choosing any behavioral path X. You can't say easily that doing X or Y is the right thing because you may not know! I see only direct impact – I can't see indirect impacts like, I don't see what happens to you in the community, or when you go back to your family. Mark and I have collected information about the impacts of serious stress on not only the people themselves under stress, but on the people around them. There is a systems aspect to ethical decisions we haven't thought that much about. And we need to.

While we tend to look at ethics as something different, it's simply another aspect of life. It's a decision making aspect. People do it all the time. Yet we believe in it as a one-off experience, like if we make a bad decision it will stick with us forever. And that's just not the case. We don't do a good enough job telling students that they will make mistakes but that they can learn from them, that it's expected, and that's critical thinking and taking the risk to speak up in class.

With respect to the second recommendation [leveraging student voices], you could get stories from students in advance about the ethical dilemmas they have faced, and how they have had to confront ethical issues. Have them write them down ahead of time, talk about them in class, anonymously, about what they did. Talk about the amount of courage it took. Talk about the amount of altruism it took to do that. Then look at the impact – what would have happened if they had not done that? We can talk about what the good students have done in glowing terms, even anonymously, as a message against dominant language they encounter.

Kabrina: My focus is on the critical thinking skills – getting them to broaden their horizons when it comes to decision making will have a real impact on their ability to make decisions that will take into account the betterment of people and not just the betterment of their business. [BWE] mentions that in a few paragraphs at the end. I am reluctant to leverage those few students who do focus on the human side of decisions; I wouldn't want to embarrass them or pit the class against them. I welcome that voice in class, but I don't think I could use them to counter the other arguments all of the time. That could be a lot of pressure for them and they may be embarrassed.

For example, two women who were really standouts in my freshmen class seemed not so burdened by the 'baggage' Bob and Mark talked about. I incorporated their views by getting on their side; they were not embarrassed if I said the things they wanted to say. I sided with them whether I agreed with them or not. So there were three of us rather than one challenging these prevailing views. I advocated for the alternative view by adopting that view, sort of playing a role on purpose so they were not the lone wolves. I bet many of us already do this and I almost never simply say "You're wrong," but start from what they are saying that's right and we work on it together. But even the ones who are burdened should not be shut down, because then they react defensively. My take on ethics and the take I employ now and will certainly take with the freshman class is not to teach them right and wrong but to teach them that there's more to think about with a decision. I expect them to be burdened coming in, but I cannot ostracize them when they are 18. My job is to help them broaden their perspective by teaching them analytic tools.

Afterthoughts: Here's Why We Are Hopeful

Where is the hope? Why, if BWE is right, do we persist in "ethics education?"

While we cannot control students' baggage and we have little control over the monolith of our society's culture, we still can take action. We have to be the ones who tell students about these costs, and help them think through who they want to be, and what lines in the sand they will draw for themselves and their own self-respect. We need to be the ones who demonstrate the process of making good decisions, and we have to model it. Programmatic immersion like the Boston University School of Management effort, the Susilo Institute, or stand-alone ethics centers, starting with freshmen, offers great hope in iteratively exposing students to different language, different business models, and different goals.

And, similar to the one-off oddities that Truman experiences in his otherwise perfectly seamless life/show, we can hope that if they happen often enough, and such alternatives are offered by people students know and trust, then like Truman, students will eventually realize that there are alternatives to the dominating cultural 'rules' that prevail and start to question, start to think for themselves.

Discussion Questions

1.   What examples of econophonics and potensiphonics do you hear in your own college of business?
2.   What would alternative language and business paradigms look like for you? How would you talk about them outside of the "burdened" language presented in BWE?
3.   What has happened in your classrooms when students have challenged the status quo of business norms? How did you manage that, and what might you do differently now?
4.   How can you support ethical critical thinking skills for your students, in ways that make sense to them? What examples might you use?

References and Additional Reading

Giacalone, Bob. 2004. "A Transcendent Business Education for the 21st Century." *Academy of Management Learning and Education*, 34: 415–420.

Giacalone, Bob and Mark Promislo. 2013. "Broken When Entering: The Stigmatization of Goodness and Business Ethics Education." *Academy of Management Learning and Education*, 12. 1: 86–101.

Korn, Melissa. 2013. "Does an 'A' in Ethics Have Any Value? B-Schools Step Up Efforts to Tie Moral Principles to Their Business Programs, but Quantifying Those Virtues Is Tough." *Wall Street Journal* (Eastern Edition). February 6. www.wsj.com/articles/SB10001424127887324761004578286102004694378

Smith, Christian, Kari Christoffersen, Hilary Davidson, and Patricia Snell Herzog. 2011. *Lost in Transition: The Dark Side of Emerging Adulthood*. Oxford: Oxford University Press.

UC Davis Pepper Spray Incident. 2011, November 18. Many news descriptions are available, the Wikipedia entry is especially helpful: https://en.wikipedia.org/wiki/UC_Davis_pepper_spray_incident

PART III
Ethics in Professional Life

21

CODES AND CONFLICTS OF INTEREST

> **Key insight:** Most faculty members at various points in their careers will take on leadership roles in one or more professional organizations. Conflicts of interest are likely to be one of the main ethical dilemmas that face faculty who are in these leadership roles. Codes of ethics exist in many professional organizations, but are aimed at the general membership rather than the leadership.

Introduction

Part III of our book on ethics in the Academy examines ethical dilemmas that face us in our "service" or "professional" roles in the Academy. In effect, we view our role here as journalists on professional life issues. Compared to research or teaching, it may be more difficult to define this sphere of ethical issues. Research means reading, analyses, writing, presenting, submitting to editors (and in our case, often resubmitting after editorial rejection), and publishing pieces for a variety of outlets: journals, books, book chapters, working papers, policy reports, case studies, and other scholarly purposes. The ethical issues this process raises are myriad, but the process has an intuition that most can grasp pretty easily, and many of these issues are covered in Part II of this book.

Likewise with teaching. Even before we became academics, we "knew" what teaching entailed. We saw it played out over years of primary and secondary education followed by years of university undergraduate and graduate school training. Again, ethical issues related to teaching are wide ranging, but teaching activities themselves seem, at least at first glance, to be relatively easy to get our arms around. They are what we do to help students learn in the classroom, during office hours, and elsewhere on campus. Many of these specific issues are covered in Part II.

That leaves professional life, which we might describe as the sphere of "everything else." We divide it into two hemispheres: academic institution life issues, and professional organization life issues. Activities giving rise to ethical issues in our respective departments, colleges, and universities include activities such as: committee work, recruiting, running departments and institutes, meeting and voting on curriculum and promotion issues, and speaking to members of the broader university and surrounding communities. Then there are ethical issues linked to activities in various professional organizations like the International Social Science Council, American Sociological Association, the Academy of Management (AOM), or the American Economic Association:; committee work (again); attending/organizing/participating in conferences and meetings where members present papers, debate, and recruit; and – when in leadership roles – making decisions crucial to the maintenance and growth of these organizations and the profession more generally. These are big – really big – hemispheres. So with little fear of running out of ethical issues in either hemisphere, let's start with a big one: conflicts of interest.

Conflicts of Interest: So What?

Here we are rummaging about primarily in the professional organization hemisphere. An important and sometimes understudied ethical issue relates to how we deal with actual and apparent, potential conflicts of interest that professional organization leaders occasionally face. Leadership of a professional organization entails responsibility for deciding how money gets spent, how people contribute and get recognized, and how important events unfold.

Here is an example from our own experience as business academics. Our largest professional organization, the AOM, has a multi-million dollar budget, lists nearly 20,000 members from 105 countries, gives out 60 annual awards to members for various achievements, and runs each August the single biggest annual meeting somewhere in North America – and perhaps one year soon outside of North America. There are more than 700 AOM members listed in the "Leadership Directory," with a 14-person Board of Governors at the top (AOM, 2017). AOM may be the biggest organization in our field, but many other professional organizations in social science disciplines have similarly distributed organizational structures and leadership.

Which is where conflicts of interest can arise. Leaders make decisions in the best interests of the organization. They are fiduciaries holding a position of trust. A conflict of interest (COI) occurs when that trust might conflict with the leader's personal interest. A leader responsible for allocating funds between two members for two organizational projects might allocate more money to a member based on a personal relationship rather than based on criteria set down in organizational by-laws. That is an actual COI. The same leader may allocate more to the same member based on criteria in the organizational by-laws, but others know that the leader also has a personal relationship. That is an apparent, potential COI.

Both matter. An actual COI disserves the best interests of the organization and undermines the legitimacy of other leaders in the organization trying to do the "right thing" for members. An apparent potential COI can still end up with the leader serving the organization's best interests, yet still undermine the legitimacy of other leaders. Without action by the leader in question and his or her colleagues to deal with the apparent COI, members might very well view the decision selectively and cynically.

What Can We Do? Disclosure +

What is a leader of a professional organization to do? One common response from academics working in these organizations (e.g., Moore et al., 2005) is simply to disclose prior to making a decision. Tell fellow leaders and members what the COI is. But perhaps, too, we need to do more than merely disclose. A "disclosure +" response may be as simple as adding an assurance that the decision is still based on criteria set down by the organization. Disclosure + could also entail disclosure and then delegation of the problematic decision to another authorized leader without a real or apparent COI. Or the response could be disclosure followed by giving others at the decision-making table the opportunity to exclude you from the decision-making process altogether. There are many responses that meet a disclosure + standard, all with the aim of showing that leaders have a fiduciary commitment to the organization. As the amount of money, the number of people, and the scale of events increase, so too does the importance of some "disclosure +" response when COIs arise.

What Can Our Organizations Do?

What can our organizations do to help leaders deal with conflicts of interest? One organizational approach might be this one: Do nothing and rely on the professionalism of the leadership. Though smaller than the AOM, the Society for the Advancement of Socio-Economics (SASE) boasts a broad range of academic members drawn from different fields including business, economics, political science, sociology, and law (SASE, 2017). SASE members come from more than 50 countries and meet annually around the world to promote many of the same academic research presentations, discussions, debates, recruiting, and networking aims that the annual AOM meeting promotes. Like AOM, SASE has a distributed leadership with a president and board largely drawn from academic ranks. The money, people, and events are there, so one would guess that COIs occasionally arise, too.

Yet, there is no written guideline for dealing with COIs at SASE. To be sure, there are SASE by-laws (SASE, 2017) that include, for example, processes to remove SASE officers for "inability or failure to carry out the duties of office in a reasonable and prudent manner and/or a serious violation of the rules or norms set forth within these by-laws" (Article VII, Number 1 of SASE By-Laws). But there are no explicit guides for, say, disclosing and remedying COIs. Presumably, the obligation to deal with COIs is implied as a matter of any SASE leader's professionalism and fiduciary commitment to the organization.

The AOM does have a written code of ethics for members and the code does address COIs (AOM, 2017). Members are urged to avoid taking on roles within the AOM where their "interests or relationships could reasonably be expected to: (1) impair their objectivity, competence, or effectiveness; or (2) expose the persons or organizations with whom the relationships exist to harm or exploitation." Members need to disclose information that would otherwise give rise to the appearance of a COI. They also need to reflect on the potential for bias when decisions might affect others with whom the decision maker has "strong conflicts or disagreements" (AOM Code of Ethics, Section 1.5). This sort of language is not unique to the AOM. Such codes are standard for larger professional organizations across higher education (see, e.g., Gallant, 2011)

Yet another professional organization in the business Academy, the Academy of International Business (AIB), sits somewhere between SASE and AOM in number of members, countries represented, initiatives supported, annual events run, and distributed governance practices (AIB, 2017). And again, there are leadership decisions involving money, people, and events that can give rise to COIs. The AIB has recently developed a new code of ethics with quite detailed guidance for leaders dealing with COIs. It provides a detailed definition of COIs with examples related to personal, research, and other professional ties that could give rise to COIs for AIB officers. There are different gradations of COIs based on whether the COI is "visible" or "invisible" to others, as well as its "minor" or "major" scale. At the "bottom" of the COI scale, a minor and invisible COI might arise when an AIB officer shares research interest with someone who is up for a vote to be appointed to some committee. At the "top" of the COI scale, a major and visible COI arises when that same AIB officer is married to the possible appointee. The AIB code lays out various responses involving disclosure and remedies ranging from recording the disclosure to disqualification of the officer from further involvement in a problematic decision (AIB Code of Ethics, Section III).

What's Right for You and Your Organization?

We are reluctant to endorse any one individual or organizational approach to deal with COIs. On the other hand, we will disclose that we helped write the detailed AIB code for dealing with COIs. Perhaps that puts us in the "more is better" camp on this issue: disclose + and + and maybe more +; provide more written guidance on dealing with COIs under different circumstances. Such guidance is probably more important as the organization gets bigger, more diverse, and the leadership more distributed.

We tell our business school undergraduate students that they are going to be in leadership positions within a firm sooner than they think. So it is with business academics who join professional organizations very early in their careers – often as graduate students – and find their way into leadership positions sooner than most thought when they first joined. The good news is that we almost all bring to our work energy, good will, and good sense that the organization's interests matter first and last. The bad news is that many of us bring little previous experience in dealing with COIs. Professionalism as well as professional codes can help bridge the experience gap and help us do our work for professional organizations more effectively and enjoyably.

Discussion Questions

1. Explore your main professional association's website for ethics codes or specific guidelines to handle COIs. What does it say and do you agree with these guidelines?
2. What about your home institution? What ethics guidelines exist for both broader ethics issues as well as specific to COIs? How might you interpret those for your daily work and responsibilities?
3. Why might a perceived COI be as damaging as a real one? Do you agree that they can be equally damaging or not?
4. Consider sharing an experience you've had where a COI situation has arisen and needed to be resolved. What happened, and how was it resolved?

References and Additional Reading

AIB. 2017. Academy of International Business. Information on the professional organization, applicable codes of conduct, and guides for managing conflicts of interest is available electronically at: https://aib.msu.edu/

AOM. 2017. Academy of Management. Information on the professional organization, applicable codes of conduct, and guides for managing conflicts of interest is available electronically at: http://aom.org/

Gallant, T. 2011. *Creating the Ethical Academy: A Systems Approach to Understanding Misconduct and Empowering Change in Higher Education.* New York: Routledge.

Moore, D., D. Cain, G. Lowenstein, and M. Bazerman. 2005. *Conflicts of Interest: Challenges and Solutions in Business, Law, Medicine, and Public Policy.* New York: Cambridge University Press.

SASE. 2017. Society for the Advancement of Socio-Economics. Information on the professional organization, applicable codes of conduct, and guides for managing conflicts of interest is available electronically at: https://sase.org/

22

WHEN IS A JOB OFFER REALLY A JOB OFFER IN THE ACADEMY?

> **Key insight:** Job offers and acceptances are part of what we do as academics. We extend them. We accept or reject them. But job offers can be fraught with complications, which provide lots of fodder for ethical dilemmas. In this chapter, we discuss some ethical issues associated with job offers in academia and how to handle them appropriately.

When is a job offer really a job offer? It may sound like a silly question, the beginning of a joke, or a question on the final exam of a first-year law student's Contracts course – yet another forum for silliness. But it's not so silly when you receive a phone call, email, or letter from some departmental, college, or university official asking you to move across the country or across the world to take a new job. And it's not so silly when you are on the other end of that transaction doing the asking – some might say wooing – to get a would-be colleague to move across the country or world.

Offers and acceptances are part of everyday life, and getting an offer of paid work in our field after a long doctoral program can seem like finally getting to the end of the tunnel. We tend to think that we know them when we hear, read, or write them – they're pretty standard, right? But it might be a little more complicated when it comes to a job offer, especially when the job is for a senior faculty position with tenure. And some of the complications have, we think, substantial ethical dimensions. Even if the job offer doesn't include tenure, there are some less-than-obvious process issues worth thinking about so that academics on both sides of the prospective transaction do the right thing. In this chapter, we provide our own take on ethical issues associated with job offers in the Academy. what they should include; how they should be conveyed; what contingencies might render a "job offer" moot; and how to respond to contingent and non-contingent offers so that you are fair to both your current and prospective future institutions.

'Tis the (Challenging) Season of Offering

In many parts of the world, December marks the season of giving, but in the academic world, January–April is the season of offering. When a department is hiring, candidate visits often start at the end of January and will run into February with the hope that an offer can be made and accepted by sometime at the end of February, but more realistically by sometime in March with delays letting negotiations bleed into early April.

At least two trends have made the art of wooing newly-minted PhDs, junior faculty, and senior faculty more challenging of late. Here is one trend. The supply of new PhDs, which was never that large to begin with, has recently shrunk. According to the National Center for Education Statistics, there were 3,116 business PhDs produced in 2015 (2015). That's 10–20 percent down from a decade earlier. The proportion of business PhDs produced among all doctoral degrees has declined from about 2.7 percent in the early 2000s to an estimated 1.7 percent in 2015 (Association for the Advancement of Collegiate Schools of Business International (AACSB), 2013). PhD programs are apparently not so easy to maintain, let alone expand, particularly when local economies go into recession and universities start cutting in response. When one of us started a PhD program at the University of Minnesota in the early 1990s, there were six other students also starting in the same department. Now, that same department takes in only two to three students each year.

So supply is down, but demand for PhDs is up. That's the other trend. Again, the AACSB estimates that there are about 14,000 business schools around the world. Though most are still found in North America and Western Europe, growth in new institutions is in the developing world, where they are scrambling to find business PhDs with the promise, if not proven track records, of publishing research in respected peer-reviewed academic journals. There's also something of a scramble – well, maybe an amble– in North American and Western Europe. If a 2011 *Wall Street Journal* article has it right, then the driving force here is demographic (Gardiner, 2011). Waves of faculty hiring in the 1970s and 1980s are giving way to waves of faculty retirements in the 2000s and 2010s. Even with a rise in part-time faculty, the AACSB tells us that the typical business school is still 60–70 percent composed of full-time tenured and tenure-track professors. Some move on each year to other institutions or careers. Increasingly, though, they simply "move" from active to emeritus status. In either case, there are pressures to search out, interview, and offer faculty positions to new PhDs, as well as junior and senior faculty at other institutions to fill ranks and expand into new areas of teaching and research.

The Offer: What, Which, and How?

So the search committee has done its work, and a candidate has come and wowed the faculty with cutting-edge research, teaching evaluations, and engaging banter in office visits. The department wants to make her an offer. Let's keep it simple and limit this to either an offer with tenure to a senior faculty member at another institution or a tenure-track term offer to a newly-minted PhD or junior faculty member at another institution. At least three questions then come to mind: What kind of offer to make; which terms to include in that offer; and how to convey that offer. By "what" question, we mean whether to make an offer with or without tenure. This distinction is important, vitally important for what the offer really is. If the decision is to make an offer without tenure – a tenure-track offer – then the process is straightforward for the department and/or college to complete with the university playing little or no role in the whole process.

But if the offer is made with tenure, then it gets complicated. The complication is that the offer is typically then only a contingent offer that does not lose its contingent status until all of the departmental, college-, and university-level reviews and votes are completed. That process can take weeks or months to complete. Until then, the candidate probably does not have a real offer to respond to, just an intent to make an offer given favorable assessments after those different reviews and votes. We say "probably" because some offers do include the alternative of a non-tenure appointment if the tenure review process stalls or results in tenure denial. But let's get back to that situation in a moment.

And the "which" and "how" questions. By "which" terms we mean articulating offer terms such as the candidate's salary and related benefits, teaching loads, and some articulation of research and service expectations. *All* of the terms of the candidate's offer don't need to be spelled out (though some candidates will press for more detail), just the "material" terms. The material terms are the ones that, if changed, could also change the candidate's mind from accept to decline, from yes to no. Such terms include: title, appointment date and length (with or without tenure), base salary, departmental assignment and teaching load, recurring and non-recurring expense reimbursement terms related to moving, and the like. Other terms could also be included, like spousal job accommodations or hardware/software purchases.[1] We don't mean for my list of material terms to be the final word, but in our experience, the list is representative of current practice and expectation.

Then there is the "how" question. We find it remarkable when we hear that an offer was made over the phone or face to face with some expectation of immediate response from the candidate. The movie producer, Samuel Goldwyn, once remarked that "[a]n oral contract is as good as the paper it's written on." We think it nearly as remarkable and suspect when an offer is made through a series of messages sent via email rather than in a single letter. The candidate is being asked to pull up stakes and move herself and perhaps her family across miles, countries, maybe even continents. In this context, there has got to be a way to handle the what, which, and how questions that is fair to her and to others involved in this wooing process.

Some Ethics of Offer Fairness

Back to that contingent offer issue for tenured offers. Let us do that now by repeating an earlier point. Until the tenure review process is completed successfully, there is no tenured offer on the table for the candidate to consider. Nothing. The tenured faculty offer is contingent, an intent awaiting decisions out of the control of either the offeror or offeree. And those decisions will not be resolved for weeks or months. In this context, we think it unfair to ask the candidate to "accept" a non-offer. Yet, letters from the department or college or university often include such requests. Most institutions do this.

Needless to say, we think it unwise for any candidate to sign and return such an acceptance request. Doing so is tantamount to accepting an offer to buy the Brooklyn Bridge. Business schools intending (but not yet in a position) to make a tenured offer to a candidate should not ask the candidate to commit to accepting an offer before the offer is really there. It is wrong. It should stop. We're less incensed when the letter includes an alternative non-tenured offer that can be accepted while the tenure case is being processed. At least there is now some actual offer to consider. But candidates looking for a tenured offer are unlikely to accept this alternative, even as a short-term back up. If the application for tenure stalls, then the candidate is much more likely to stay put at their current institution. Much better to leave out requests to accept the intended offer before its contingencies are resolved. Much better to call the letter what it is, a *contingent* offer letter.

Once contingencies like tenure review and approval are resolved and there is a real offer on the table, then the candidate has an obligation to respond in a timely manner: accept, accept with the following changes in terms, or decline (gracefully). As with non-tenured offers, the wooing institution may have an offer expiration date, an "exploding" offer. We have no problem with exploding offers as long as they give the candidate a reasonable time period to consider and respond before the fuse runs out.

While we are on the subject of letters, let us suggest to universities and candidates that the *only* way to convey an offer or contingent offer is in a letter. We have no problem telling a candidate face to face, over the phone, or in an email that an offer (or contingent offer) is *likely* to be made. But it is better to have it all written out in a letter on departmental, college, and university letterhead from an authorized representative like the department head or academic dean. Taking the time to do this gives the wooing institution and the candidate an easily identifiable, common document to use in discussing and negotiating material terms.

An offer letter also makes things easier for the candidate's current institution. Many candidates will prefer confidentiality until they have a letter in hand. Once an offer (or contingent offer) letter is generated, the candidate can share it with her current institution, typically by giving a copy to her current department head. We don't think she has an obligation to share this letter, but it's wise to do so. Most importantly, sharing that letter gives the department head an opportunity to respond, perhaps with a counter-offer. Also importantly, sharing that letter lets the department head plan the next semester's teaching and service schedule with some notice of the candidate's possible departure. Sharing the letter does not mean that the candidate is leaving. It certainly does not amount to the candidate's letter of resignation. It is a matter of courtesy. It is also a matter of credibility because the letter spells out in writing what the prospective institution is offering (with or without contingencies) to the candidate. This sort of clarity helps all parties reach the right decision in the end.

So When Is a Job Offer Really a Job Offer in Academia?

We said it wasn't so simple to identify and act on a job offer. Here are seven take-aways we think will make the process a bit less complicated and maybe less silly: 1) be aware that many offers simply aren't – they are contingent offers with some-times substantial contingencies like tenure review and approval; 2) such contingent job offers should be stated up front to the candidate, preferably in a letter; 3) such contingent job offers should *not* include language seeking the immediate acceptance of terms from the candidate – generally, there is nothing yet to accept; 4) offer or contingent offers should be made through letters on institutional letterhead from authorized representatives; 5) those letters should summarize all of the material terms; 6) once received, candidates can and probably should share such letters with the department head of their current institution; and 7) once contingencies are dealt with, candidates have an obligation to respond to an offer in a timely manner.

Good luck to all candidates looking for a job and to all institutions looking for a candidate. Let the wooing begin.

Discussion Questions

1. If your institution hasn't incorporated the seven "take-aways" above for ethically offering a job to a candidate, how do you raise awareness about them with your colleagues?
2. What are the options for a job offer when making a tenured position offer must in fact go through a lengthy acceptance process at your institution but you really want the candidate to take your position?
3. What about the reverse – what are the best ways to respond when you've made a job offer in good faith, with all the "right" information, and your candidate drags her or his feet in giving you a response?

Note

1 See   www.vpul.upenn.edu/careerservices/files/Academic_Job_offer_letter_checklist_
negotiating.pdf for a representative checklist of job issues related to academic jobs. More
generally, we also recommend Malhotra's suggestions for substantive job terms to
negotiate (Malhotra, 2014).

References and Additional Reading

Association for the Advancement of Collegiate Schools of Business International. 2013.
"Sustaining Scholarship in Business Schools." Available at: www.aacsb.edu/~/media/
AACSB/Publications/research-reports/sustaining-scholarship-in-business-schools.ashx .
Gardiner, Beth. 2011. "We're Hiring: Many Business Schools Have Trouble Filling
Faculty Positions." *Wall Street Journal*, November 11. Available at: www.wsj.com/arti
cles/SB10001424052970204224604577032232809553166
Malhotra, D. 2014. "15 Rules for Negotiating a Job Offer." *Harvard Business Review*, April.
Available at: https://hbr.org/2014/04/15-rules-for-negotiating-a-job-offer
National Center for Education Statistics. 2015. "Doctor's Degrees Conferred by Post-
secondary Institutions, by Field of Study: Selected Years, 1970–1971 through 2014–
2015." Available at https://nces.ed.gov/programs/digest/d16/tables/dt16_324.10.asp?
current=yes

23

ATTENDING PROFESSIONAL MEETINGS

Key insight: Are there ethical dilemmas involved in attending and participating in annual meetings and conferences of our professional associations? Here we look at the etiquette and obligations involved in getting together with one's peers at professional meetings. There's more involved than just showing up.

Showing Up

The US comedian and movie director, Woody Allen, once said that 80 percent of success is showing up. When it comes to professional meetings, there's more than a little truth in his claim. Think about an American Psychological Association annual convention, a Modern Language Association annual conference, or an Academy of Management (AOM) annual meeting. They would be rather short and uninteresting events if only a few showed up. Each if those organizations host annual conferences for which thousands of members submit their work to be reviewed. At each, there are several opportunities to hear paper presentations at competitively selected panel sessions, symposia, caucus meetings, keynote addresses, receptions, and informal gatherings. Not every paper or presentation is ready for *verbatim* publication in one of the discipline's top journals. But over the years at each meeting there are great opportunities to see, hear, and learn from a diverse group of scholars and scholarship. And it happens in one place over a few days. Quantity has a quality all of its own. And when you show up, you promote both.

In this chapter, we think about some of the ethical issues raised in showing up to professional meetings and doing your part for your own professional development as well as that of your colleagues.

What's Right (and Wrong) for You (and Us) in a Professional Meeting?

In 2017, there is no shortage of professional societies to join, meetings to attend, and related service to promote the maintenance and growth of both societies and meetings. In our disciplines of law and business, it's an alphabet soup running from AAoM to AEA, AIB, AOM, EURAM, EGOS, IABS, IEEE, ORSA-TIMS, SASE, SBE, SMS, and beyond. Indeed, the National Academy of Sciences tells us that professional academic societies have exploded in the 2000s with more than 600 representing sciences, social sciences, and humanities (2005). Many of us have limited budgets and time to submit papers, proposals, and/or attend them on an annual basis. Here is a very rough rule on annual meeting numbers. Try and submit papers to and attend two or three professional meetings annually. For example, we three are business academics, so we regularly attend the AOM meeting in August. Then, we might also attend the Academy of International Business (AIB) meeting in June–July, and/or the Strategic Management Society (SMS) meeting in late October–November.

What's right for you depends. Our own view is that a meeting should provide at least three learning opportunities: 1) to learn about your field – through presentation of your own research to others or from listening to and discussing the research of others; 2) to learn about your profession – through presentation by the association leadership and journal editors, interviews with prospective job candidates (including, perhaps, you as the candidate), and discussion with vendors such as publishers; and 3) to learn about your colleagues – see familiar faces and reconnect to find out what is happening in their professional and personal lives, and to make new contacts and friends. These factors make it difficult to miss the biggest professional organization meeting each year, the AOM, but a bit easier to let an AIB, SMS, or other annual meeting slip by in the same year. The same is probably true for those in other social science fields. Our language colleagues never miss a Modern Languages Association conference and our psychological sciences colleagues would not dream of missing an American Psychological Association meeting, even if it meant missing smaller or regional meetings.

Of course, there are other factors in play. There is registration expense, travel, and accommodation expense, the opportunity cost of time away from home and work. And there's the work of preparing an original submission six to nine months earlier than the date of the meeting. We often justify those submission deadlines as prompts to help us finish writing a paper that was only an idea and a few data correlations. The December–January winter vacation window for submission to AOM, AIB, and SMS fit work habits in Northern Hemispheric locations. We then attend the meetings in the following summer and fall months.

Learning, time, and expense factors are part of the calculus leading to decisions about which meetings to attend. Here are a few other factors that probably shouldn't be part of that calculus. Maybe location matters – Atlanta in August may not appeal to everyone. On the other hand, humidity is not and probably should not be the reason to attend or avoid a professional meeting (in an air-conditioned hotel or conference center). Then there are other factors that simply shouldn't be part of the calculus: the number of receptions with an open bar (and top-shelf liquor); and the likelihood that some faculty colleague will make a spectacle of himself or herself (at one of those receptions). Call us judgmental but these and many other "cosmetic" factors strike us as irrelevant. We're there to learn and help others learn. It's the quantity of such learning-motivated attendees that gives a meeting its quality.

The No-Show Problem

Over the years, we have occasionally strayed into professional meetings in other academic fields. If we are interested in studying the role of electoral politics in prompting more or less foreign investment in developing countries, then a great place to learn more about electoral politics of foreign investment may be at a professional meeting of political science scholars. The American Political Science Association (APSA) meets annually in late August or early September while the Midwest Political Science Association (MPSA) meets annually in late March or early April. Both meet in North America.

Competitive paper sessions at APSA and MPSA have an additional element we've never found at meetings in our own field. At specific sessions, the presenters, chairs, and discussants fill out forms to verify their attendance. Apparently, there's a no-show problem. Scholars submit papers and get them accepted for presentation. Others sign up to serve as chairs or discussants. And then they either don't go to the professional meeting or go but don't attend their scheduled session. We confess to substantial ignorance regarding the extent of this problem in political science, in management, or in other fields. We can imagine the potential for abuse. Maybe the faculty member signs up to chair a session and then uses such scheduled participation in the program to get his/her trip paid for by the department or college. It's an interesting way to ask for, say $1,000–$1,500. Maybe it's a little risky, too. If the meeting organizers learn that you ducked out of your session as chair, discussant, or presenter, then, supposedly, your participation in subsequent years could be put in jeopardy. In any case, the no-show problem is an issue and rightfully so. Failure to show and participate as scheduled detracts from the learning experience of others in the same session, and indeed, in the meeting more broadly. Your missed session is also a failed opportunity for another scholar to participate, making it perhaps more of an ethical issue because your behavior directly and negatively influenced someone else's chances for learning, exposure, or engaging with other scholars.

Setting Examples: In Person and Electronically, from the Top Down and the Bottom Up

The no-show problem is not unique to political science. It happens at many professional meetings, including business meetings. One recent instance was at the

AOM meeting when a doctoral student was presenting a paper in a competitive session. The scheduled discussant was a chaired professor at a major research university in the US. Not only did s/he *not* attend the session as discussant, but s/he was found across the hall sitting quietly at another session where his/her doctoral student was presenting. When confronted afterwards by another participant in the doctoral student's session s/he hardly feigned regret at the failure to show up. Being present for his/her doctoral student apparently trumped other obligations to the meeting organizers.

In a digital world with instant and also asynchronous communication it has probably become easier to be a no-show at meetings. It's late July and a track chair gets a brief email late at night from a faculty member in the state or the country of Georgia saying that she won't be able to attend the AOM session and present the paper they were invited to present after submission the previous January, review in February, and scheduling into the program in April. Sometimes, there is good reason for the email: health or family emergencies; for foreign faculty coming to the US, visa issues. Stuff happens. But sometimes the late-night email just says "Can't come." No explanation. Those are the emails that vex track chairs who put in hours trying to allocate scarce paper presentation slots. Those are the emails that vex session chairs and discussants who put in hours reviewing and preparing comments on papers. Those are the emails that prompt us to think about ways to identify and sanction habitual no-shows.

We think such vignettes represent exceptions to a well-accepted duty to attend and actively participate in professional meetings. But no matter how exceptional, each incident sets a bad example for others to follow. After observing a chaired professor blow off a session across the hall with no apology, a doe-eyed doctoral student thinks about when seniority and self-importance will let him/her blow off scheduled meeting obligations. The umpteenth email from Georgia – state, country, and/or person – begging off at the last moment leaves the track chair weary of ever volunteering for such service again. The umpteenth no-show at a paper session leaves the session discussant wondering how s/he got conned into reading a paper and preparing a constructive review for someone s/he doesn't know and is now probably less interested in knowing. There is much to lose for the no-show and for others at the meeting and in the profession.

These examples seem pretty "top down" in nature. Faculty scheduled to attend a meeting don't, and other peers or more junior colleagues learn the wrong lesson. Here's a "bottom-up" example. It's a cliché to say that doctoral students represent the future of our field. It's a bit less cliché-ish to hold that those same students are the biggest potential beneficiaries of *and* biggest contributors to professional meetings. They get all of the learning opportunities we outlined above. And it is all new to them: the people, the papers, the various networking opportunities. There's a naïve excitement often palpable and energizing in the questions and comments we get from doctoral students who attend a symposia, paper session, or other session we attend and contribute to. They remind us of our own past, and help rekindle some of the excitement that got us into this business in the first place. Our own view is that we should be encouraging and financially supporting doctoral students to attend professional meetings as soon as possible and as often as possible. When they show up, they tend to do so with more gusto as consumers and catalysts of learning.

Intellectual *Ginbura*

A few years ago, one of us was a track chair for the AIB annual meeting in Washington, DC. There was an opportunity to identify papers for presentation in competitive sessions and papers for less formal "interactive" sessions. Interactive sessions include six to eight paper presenters sitting around a table, taking five minutes each to summarize key points and implications for the session theme. The session chairs double as discussants, often commenting on individual papers immediately after their presentation and then summing up commonalities across papers. And there are comments and questions from other session presenters and attendees. It's a busy affair.

One idea was to visit some of the interactive sessions in the meeting track. It would set a good example to have the track chair show up to sessions that might otherwise attract less attention and attendance than, say, some symposium composed of senior scholars. Maybe wander in after an interactive session started, and then stay for 30 minutes before wandering on to another session. It would be like the Tokyo shopper who wanders the streets of the Ginza with no specific purchase in mind. But reasons for such an intellectual *ginbura* changed after the first two interactive sessions attended. They were both so interesting. Asking presenters to be brief and to highlight connections to previous presentations encouraged real dialogue on common themes around the table. The session chairs were fantastic at drawing out implications from a single presentation or from a few presentations addressing common themes. It was just the kind of learning experience conference organizers hoped to prompt at the AIB meeting, but not where those same organizers expected that learning experience to happen. Sure, no-shows are a problem for those of us who attend expecting to learn from them. But maybe we have an obligation to think more broadly about who else made it there and how they may surprise us with something unexpected and exciting.

Professional Obligations, Not Merely Etiquette

Maybe that's a great place to conclude. Woody Allen is probably right that 80 percent of success is simply in showing up. For professional meetings, showing up is a big part of overall success in learning and developing professionally. We have an obligation to show up when we submit a paper or proposal and have it accepted for presentation. We have an obligation to show up when we agree to serve as a chair, discussant, facilitator, consortium faculty member, judge. We have an obligation to play our role in professional meetings with diligence and care. It's not just a matter of etiquette – observing some niceties in person or electronically when pulling out of a specific session's duty or from the meeting generally. Others are depending on your presence and active participation. Others are observing and learning from your behavior. You matter. You should be there. And if some emergency keeps you from attending, then you should try to mitigate the loss by reaching out to co-authors and colleagues who might fill in with diligence and care.

And for those who do show, well you're 80 percent of the way to success. To increase that percentage, reflect in advance on how this professional meeting will enrich your learning. Maybe you could also reflect on how some surprise learning might happen. As the *ginbura* story illustrates, it makes sense to do a little exploration for learning opportunities in less familiar venues of a professional meeting.

Discussion Questions

1. Do you agree that no-shows represent an ethical problem, or is it more of just an annoyance? Why or why not?
2. What should happen to those who are no-shows? If you think some type of sanctioning should occur, at what level (peer, institution, conference/professional society, etc.) and who should be in charge of doing so?
3. Should professional associations have sign-in sheets like they do at political science meetings? What are the pros and cons of having session participants sign in?
4. Is there an alternative process for filling session slots that would not rely on firm attendance that you can imagine? Would it be desirable to make such a change?

References and Additional Reading

National Academy of Sciences. 2005. *Facilitating Interdisciplinary Research*. Washington, DC: National Academies Press.

24

PEER REVIEWING

Key insight: One of the most frequent – and most underappreciated – tasks we do as university professors is writing peer reviews. We review each other's papers. We write letters of recommendations for students and other faculty, reviewing each other's work. We are constantly evaluating and being evaluated. Peer reviewing is part of what we do. However, some of us do a lot more peer reviewing than others. Is there an ethical issue here?

Incredible Generosity

For many, December is a holiday month of gift giving, but the experience of one of us as a track chair for the Academy of International Business (AIB) annual meeting persuaded him that the real gift-giving time, at least professionally, is from mid-January to mid-February. It was during those weeks that so many AIB peers gave their time and attention to read and review the hundreds of papers submitted to the track for competitive or interactive presentation at the upcoming AIB annual meetings. The goal was to get multiple reviews for every submission and get them in less than four weeks. Virtually every AIB member submitting a paper to the track also got a paper to review. Several got more than one paper to review. More than a few got several papers for the track as well as papers from other AIB track chairs, and from counterparts over at the Academy of Management (AOM). Four weeks later, practically everyone had submitted their reviews, whether it was just one or several from those "overfished" reviewers. It was amazing to observe. And it's critically important to preserve and nurture. So that's our topic for the chapter: peer review and its importance in our professional lives; peer review and the motivations of peer reviewers; and how we might do a little less overfishing of some especially good and generous peer reviewers.

Peer Review in Publication and Professional Life

Our profession is shot through with peer review. Think about the publication process. There is friendly developmental peer review – the comments on a first-draft paper you solicit from departmental colleagues down the hall or from former grad school classmates across the globe. There is pre-submission peer review – papers given at departmental seminars, invited talks at other institutions, symposia, or conferences like the AIB annual meeting. Then there is post-submission peer review – the multiple rounds of single- or double-blinded review that more often (in our cases) lead to editorial rejection but occasionally lead to publication in journals, conference proceedings, authored books, and edited volumes.

But wait, there's more. Post-submission peer review means that the book quarried from your dissertation may get another round of review and write-up in an applied professional journal like the *Economist* or a newspaper like the *New York Times*. The book or journal may be judged for purposes of awarding various prizes: best of the conference, the year, the decade. There will be total citation counts as well as citation counts in this, that and yet another citation count database that we've never heard of but apparently should have (because our citation counts there are considered a little low). In other fields, this sort of post-submission peer review applies to databases, films, websites, and software.

And then there's, perhaps, the most important peer review. It is the institutional peer review in tenure and promotion cases. Department, college, and university committees are formed. Letters are solicited from outside academics. Stacks of papers, working papers, books, book manuscripts, reviews of the same, works in progress, and candidate statements get submitted. That stack gets read, reread, counted, and weighed (metaphorically and maybe literally). This peer-review process usually takes months and multiple meetings. By and large, our peers do their best to read it all and read between the lines to figure out what the quality of the candidate's overall contributions to the profession and institution really are, and whether they merit the recommendation of appointment "without time limit" (tenure) or promotion to "full" professor or "distinguished" professor or "chaired" professor or some other position of distinction in the field. The candidate's job in all of this is to not let the peer-review process consume him or her. Relax. Just let it happen. In the end, reviewers usually do the right thing… usually.

Peer Reviewers: Democratic, Representative, and Motivated by...

We're neither attacking nor defending the system of peer review. (If we were, we might defend the system like Churchill defended democracy, as the "worst form of government except all the others that have been tried.") Instead, let us talk about people behind the peer-review system: the reviewers. Without them, the whole system of scholarly publication and career development would quickly grind to a halt. So who are these people? Why do they do it? And why do a few of them do so much of it? The quick answer to the first question is nearly *everyone*. To get track papers reviewed for the AIB annual meeting, it was necessary to tap a mix of old and new AIB members, located in the US and overseas, from large research universities, small colleges, government-funded research institutes, and even a few businesses – yes, businesses. It's a similar story over at the AOM. The rank and file play an important role in figuring out what is presented in what forum at annual meetings.

Other smaller professional meetings may rely less on the *vox populi* and more on review committees drawn from the broader membership. It's similar with many scholarly journals where experienced and well-published representatives of the profession are invited to join editorial review boards. The boards are smaller if editors prefer to stay up all night reviewing manuscripts themselves. The boards are larger if editors prefer to stay up all night keeping track of the reviews board members agreed to complete but haven't yet. These journal boards are not democracies – reviewers and their reviews are merely advisory to an editor's decision – but they are nonetheless representative. Journal boards are comprised of members from across our global profession.

It's similar with the choice of outside reviewers in tenure and promotion pro-cesses. The process is far from democratic – committees don't solicit outside let-ters from anyone in the profession. Those tenure and promotion reviewers are leaders in their respective fields, an elite. There might have been a time when that elite resided at just a few research universities in North America and Western Europe. Increasingly, that elite is dispersed across many institutions and regions of the world. So even the pool of tenure and promotion reviewers is becoming more representative.

It may be a weekend spent reviewing a candidate package and writing a tenure letter. It may be a day spent reading and writing a review for a journal. Maybe it's 30 minutes on the phone with a grad student talking about the first draft of a paper for conference presentation. In these and other contexts, it's useful to ask what motivates these peer reviewers.

Think about those AIB annual meeting track reviewers. They did reviews so quickly and helpfully, and not merely because they were asked to by a peer. It's pretty sure that they saw it as part of their job, as a chance to learn, as their opportunity to matter in the process of scholarly discovery. Maybe they also saw it as a shot at harpooning some big cigar under the cover of double-blind review. It certainly wasn't about money. We think there is little, if any, *homo economicus*, that is, narrow self-interest, motivating most peer-review work. We think there's much more *homo sociologicus* at work here. It's part of how we define our career, our sense of a professional community. We're lucky.

Peer Reviewer Overfishing

There are a few peer reviewers who do an awful lot of work for the rest of us. We sit on an editorial review board for a top-tier management journal like the *Academy of Management Journal* and get a new or revised manuscript to read and assess about once every six weeks. Other members do it more frequently, much more frequently. Almost every summer or early fall, a few of those elite professors get multiple requests to write outside letters for tenure review and promotion cases. And then there's the AIB annual meeting anecdote. A few members got a disproportionate share of reviews from the track chair. It isn't random. It's over-fishing. And we're guilty anglers.

As our careers develop and we interact with colleagues at different institutions, often through peer-review processes, we gain insight on who can and will do the reviewing, do it carefully, do it constructively and candidly, and do it on (or about on) time. What's their reward? They get more of it, a lot more of it when annual meetings are looming, when journal editors seek their reviews for journal submissions. Boards seek their reviews on grant requests. And then there are the tenure and promotion letters. A few really great peer reviewers get requests from too many of us. We're overfishing. And the danger is similar to what we get when we overfish any pool. The "stock" collapses. Overfished reviewers drop out from the process, in part to protect their time for research, maybe also in part because it's just taxing to judge and judge and judge again. There's a burn-out factor that matters over the time and intensity of review work.

Nobody wants that to happen. It slows down the whole journal review process for our papers (Ellison, 2002). Some have suggested that payment to reviewers might help (Mason, Steagall, and Fabritius, 1992). In a recent study, Raj Chetty, editor of the *Journal of Public Economics*, tested whether shortened deadlines and cash incentives increased the speed and quality of peer reviews (Chetty, Saez, and Sandor, 2014). During a period of 20 months, 1,500 referees of his journal were randomly assigned to different groups: 1) A control group with a six-week (45-day) deadline to submit a referee report; 2) a group with a shortened four--week (28-day) deadline; 3) a group rewarded with $100 for meeting the four-week deadline; 4) and a social incentive group where referees were told that their reviewing times would be posted publicly.

Chetty and colleagues reported that shortening the reviewer deadline from six to four weeks reduced the median review times by 12 days – they sped up their work under a shorter deadline. Receiving cash incentives for submitting a timely report reduced review times, but when the cash incentive stopped, reviewers in this group reverted back to slower reviewing practices – money mattered. The social incentive treatment reduced median review times, especially with tenured faculty – peer pressure mattered, too.

Putting these results together suggests that reviewers care about different factors including financial ones. Social factors related to peer standards and pressures seem especially important. As we figure out how to deal with overfishing in the review process, those social (and financial) incentives might provide answers.

Two Ideas: Less Rains, More Recognition

But maybe we should first try to do a little less of that overfishing. Here are two ideas for that. One idea is to be a little bit less like Claude Rains, that is, Claude Rains playing the corrupt but still loveable Vichy Captain Louis Renault in the 1942 classic movie, *Casablanca*. More than once in the movie, Rains' character responds to news of a crime with the cynical command: "Round up the usual suspects." Those of us with a tendency to overfish might do well to think about his words. We go back to the same generous, reliable peer reviewers perhaps too reflexively. We're rounding up the usual suspects. Don't, or at least don't so much. The AIB review process uncovered a dozen new scholars providing great reviews. They're now on an expanded list of reviewers for future work, in part so that we can move a few of the usual suspects down the list. Maybe we could all benefit from checking our written or mental list of "go-to" reviewers. Try adding a few more names so that the "go-to" reviewers you've relied on in the past don't become the "go-to-too-much" reviewers of the future.

Here is another idea that comes out of the study by Chetty and colleagues. Try to give more recognition for this important work. We said earlier that self-interest probably explains little, if any, motivation for so much of the peer-review work we do. Even so, we like to know that it's appreciated. Reviewers enjoy getting a note from an associate editor after submitting a review, or getting a letter from the editor-in-chief at the end of the year. It seems so little but it means so much. The plaque for best conference reviewer is just a plaque, but it means a lot to new and not-so-new members of an association or institution. These tokens remind us of what we do to build a profession bigger than any one career within it. You can't send too many notes. You can't hand out too many plaques. They are social incentives like the publication and time-framing incentives in the study by Chetty and colleagues.

An AIB track chair gets to nominate a few papers for awards. That is often tough to do. There are so many interesting and worthy papers. There are other nominations for a track chair to make, including those for best paper reviewers. Again, it can be difficult as there are so many worthy candidates, and they come from institutions around the world. You do your best to make a thoughtful judgment regarding nominations for best reviewers. Those judgments send a signal of appreciation for all that reviewers do to help the work go forward and help the profession grow and thrive. Reviewers really are some of the most generous people you'll meet in the profession. Every day's a holiday when they do their important work for us.

Discussion Questions

1. Across every academic discipline a disproportionately low number of colleagues do the bulk of reviewing work (see Bergeron et al., 2014, for a discussion), often at costs to their own scholarly output. Do you think peer review should be managed more intentionally to spread the work? Why or why not?

2. Scholarship can't happen without peer review. How might institutions tackle this issue and engage more people in performing peer review?

3. What types of recognition or rewards should excellent peer reviewers get?

4. Should someone be able to make a promotion and tenure case using excellent peer reviews as scholarly work? Why or why not?

References and Additional Reading

Bergeron, D., C. Ostroff, T. Schroeder, and C. Block. 2014. "The Dual Effects of Organizational Citizenship Behavior: Relationships to Research Productivity and Career Outcomes in Academe." *Human Performance*, 27: 99–128.

Chetty, R., E. Saez, and L. Sandor. 2014. "What Policies Increase Prosocial Behavior? An Experiment with Referees at the Journal of Public Economics." *Journal of Economic Perspectives*, 28. 3: 169–188.

Ellison, G. 2002. "The Slowdown of the Economics Publishing Process." *Journal of Political Economy*, 110. 5: 947–993.

Mason, P., J. Steagall, and M. Fabritius. 1992. "Publication Delays in Articles in Economics: What to Do about Them." *Applied Economics*, 24. 8: 859–874.

25

MANAGING UNIVERSITY
SERVICE WORK

Key insight: University faculty are evaluated on three key dimensions of performance: research, teaching, and service. One might think that doing more service is a good thing, leading to higher performance and greater rewards. However, we think there are ethical dangers attached to doing too much service, which we explore.

Why We Don't Say "No" More Often

This chapter discusses issues related to service, that is, the part of your job that is not about research publication or teaching. It is important for the life of your university and profession, but it can become all-consuming without guides for when to decline it.

So let's start this discussion with a familiar situation. It's mid-afternoon, mid-semester. You are in your office reading an article, writing a paper, or putting down the phone after a chat with an academic colleague. There's a quick double knock on your nearly closed door followed up by its swift swing open to reveal the department head. S/he's smiling slightly, holding a sheaf of papers rolled up tightly in the left hand, casually waving you into the department office with the right hand, and mumbling three words that should turn on any faculty member's time-management radar: "Got a minute?" Twenty minutes later, you've somehow consented to joining a departmental committee to overhaul the undergraduate curriculum, on a college committee tasked to identify and recruit a new director of college alumni affairs, or maybe on a university task force investigating the causes and consequences of teaching assistant unionization.

What Were You Thinking?

It's a question we've asked ourselves many times. We're the ones who have trouble saying no to service, whether it be for professional or university communities. And we're not alone. Service goes with our job. It always has. Ancient universities of Western Europe saw (and still see) college fellows debating Plutarch in the morning, and then debating alternative investment strategies for the college endowment in the afternoon. Historically, they did administrative jobs as members holding equity rights in the college akin to property. Today, they do so as faculty members holding (or hoping one day soon to hold) property-like tenure in a department, college, or university. With rights also come obligations. Larger and wealthier academic institutions may have resources to contract out many administrative obligations to non-faculty employees. But whether contracted out or retained within the faculty, the jobs need doing. And faculty, starting (but not ending) with the dean, are responsible for seeing that the jobs get done and that the college moves ahead with its academic mission. Such assumptions are central to maintaining faculty governance over any academic institution. They're our jobs. It's one important reason we might find it difficult to say no to our department head, dean, provost, chancellor, or president.

There are other reasons aside from the weight of history and/or the dearth of non-faculty employees. Maybe it's also a matter of personality. Let's be stereotypical for a moment and think of two extreme responses to a service request. At one extreme, think of a brash in-your-face confrontational colleague who not only declines the current invitation to serve on a committee, but also tells the department head exactly where the next such invitation can go in advance of any knock on the office door. At the other extreme, think of a reticent go-along-by-getting-along colleague, who accommodates this and almost any other service request. Neither extreme is appealing. If the more realistic colleague is a mix of each, then perhaps a dash more reticence and getting along is a better long-term strategy. On the other hand, there's a good chance that brash, in-your-face confrontation will get you more time to finish reading the article or writing the paper in the short to medium term.

Maybe it's also a matter of gender. We claim no expertise on the topic, but there's a substantial research tradition in psychology and related fields theorizing about apparent differences in the moral decision-making processes of men and women. Decades after its initial publication, Carol Gilligan's book, *In a Different Voice* (1982), can still start a lively debate over the proposition that men base their moral judgments on individual rights and abstract principles of right and wrong, while the moral understanding of women is contextual and emphasizes human needs, empathy, and interdependence.[1] For proponents of this view, it's easy to see how female faculty members might find it more difficult to decline service requests. Add to this requirements at many universities to include female faculty on committees dealing with hiring and diversity. It sums up to more service requests aimed at faculty who may be less pre-disposed to declining them.

Maybe it's also a matter of taste. To choose an academic career is, to some substantial extent, to choose a life devoted to the generation, presentation, and publication of new knowledge. Many academics are good *only* at that. But some can also create the context for knowledge generation, presentation, and publication by others. Such doubly-gifted academics know how to motivate their colleagues with the right kind of faculty seminar theme, teaching schedule, or research grant program. They may even occasionally enjoy saying yes to such service. Developing that taste can be dangerous for junior (untenured) faculty where the focus begins and ends with scholarly research publication. For other established senior scholars, the taste for service can co-exist, even complement and enhance research agendas. For a few, service acumen can lead to the dean's suite.

How FAR to Go with University Service

So there are many reasons service calls and we answer. How often should we answer in the affirmative? How much of our job is to be devoted to service, particularly university (not professional) community service? One way we answer the question is by looking at annual "faculty activity reports," or FARs. It's the form many of us fill out annually to tell our colleagues what we've been doing (and gotten done) in terms of research, teaching, *and service*. Our colleagues, including our deans, then get to tell us how well we've performed and what kind of (relatively small) adjustment in remuneration last year's performance merits in the coming academic year. FARs differ across institutions but you might think these weights are reasonable: approximately 40 percent of the performance assessment is based on research; 40 percent is based on teaching; and 20 percent for service. FARs for untenured assistant professors are weighted more on research (60 percent) with less on teaching (30 percent) and service (10 percent).

So in terms of proportion of time devoted to service, a simple answer is 20 percent of time on the job. It might be difficult to stick by this guide on a given day or week, but over the month or semester we can reasonably rely on certain guides – hours preparing for and attending committee meetings – to tell us whether we're on or off track time-wise. Of course, effective service is not merely a matter of time input, but also results output. Did the faculty search committee we chaired come up with a pool of viable candidates leading to multiple campus visits, an offer of employment, a successful tenure-review process, and then an acceptance? In answering these questions, we also need to account for results that we can control more or less.

Let's complicate things just a bit more. A 20 percent service goal includes service to the university and the profession, which often means professional academic organizations such as the ones discussed in earlier chapters. In prioritizing between these two, the university often loses out. Service to a professional organization may be recognized and rewarded by your university colleagues *and* by your professional colleagues located throughout the world. Not so with university service. Recognition and reward follows from colleagues who could be with you for an entire career or for a single quarter. For this reason alone, university service is often last hired and first fired for academics thinking strategically.

We're not so strategic when it comes to the choice between professional and university service. Departments and colleges (not professional organizations) are where key career decisions are made regarding tenure and promotion, curriculum, and expenditures. For senior (tenured) faculty, there can be some immediate and substantial rewards from service to those ends. More self-interestedly, committee service means being able to set in place preferred standards and processes for allocating scarce university resources. More altruistically, committee service means (re)shaping a department, college, or university for years to come. It means leaving a legacy that redounds to the benefit of others in the future.

Many might disagree, but I believe that some of these critical committees are precisely where junior faculty should serve at least briefly. A newly-minted assistant professor should, for example, serve on a department- or college-level committee charged with making recommendations about the granting of tenure. It strikes us as an unconventional but quite effective way to acquaint junior faculty with research, teaching, and service norms of the institution. Either as a voting or nonvoting member, this sort of committee work will also give new faculty rich insight on the sort of frank discussion and sometimes tough decision-making that their more senior colleagues are called on to make for the good of the institution.

Two Ideas for Managing Service Work: A Handy List and a Yes-if Policy

Recall the scenario we described at the beginning of this chapter. A faculty member meets the department head and comes away with some additional service work. Should the faculty member have said "no" to the request? Like many ethical questions, the answer is often "it depends." For us, it would depend most importantly on how much else was on our professional and university plate. If we're well over that 20 percent threshold, then we're likely to decline the department head's request and get back to work. If we're well under that 20 percent threshold, then we're more likely to accept, especially if it fits our own service interests. In making that decision, it helps to keep handy a one-page list of current (semester or academic year) service appointments and estimated time each month devoted to such appointments. Keep the list right next to the office phone just in case the department head calls rather than stops by in person.

Our junior faculty colleagues might also have the same sort of handy list, and use it when mulling over the occasional service request from a department head or college administrator. Even so, s/he may find it more difficult to decline a request. No matter how congenial and collegial the work environment might be, there's always some power distance between senior and junior faculty members. And that may make it harder for the junior colleague to decline a request. So here's a suggestion for the junior colleague. Don't say "no." Say instead "yes if." If the department head wants you to serve on a new department- or college-wide committee and if such service seems difficult to shoulder at the moment, then try a response that begins: "Yes if you can also help me get these other current service obligations met as well as this current teaching and research work you want me to prioritize." Many times, the department head isn't fully aware of all service appointments that the junior faculty member is currently filling. Alternatively, the department head just needs a little update on current teaching and research efforts as a reminder about near-term priorities. In either case, the handy list and the yes-if policy can help junior faculty members respond to service requests. They can also help senior faculty better manage service obligations and improve their academic institutions for future generations.

Discussion Questions

1. What might be ethical issues with the power differential between senior and junior faculty noted above?
2. How might senior faculty raise their awareness of when junior faculty are being asked to carry too heavy a service load? What might they do to protect junior faculty's time while getting required work done?
3. Would the "yes-if" response work for you in your institution? Why or why not?
4. Do you see or have evidence that female faculty take on a larger service burden than men? Describe what you know and how you might rebalance that load.
5. As service loads increase across higher education, how do you think faculty should respond? What might "yes-if" responses do to committee and university work as a whole?

Note

1 A similar analysis about differences in workplace negotiation based on gender comes more recently from Katty Kay and Claire Shipman in their 2014 book, the *Confidence Code* (Kay and Shipman, 2014).

References and Additional Reading

Gilligan, C. 1982. *In a Different Voice: Psychological Theory and Women's Development.* Cambridge, MA: Harvard University Press.
Kay, K. and C. Shipman. 2014. *The Confidence Code: The Science and Art of Self-Assurance – What Women Should Know.* New York: HarperCollins.

26

TRIBALISM

> **Key insight:** Regardless of your discipline or your professional "home" (department, school), tribalism is a constant problem in academia. By tribalism, we mean that researchers in one discipline tend to ignore work on a common topic of interest when that work is being done by scholars in another discipline. We are silos in a common university home. This chapter investigates the challenges associated with discipline-based tribalism, how to confront it in professional life, and perhaps how to exploit it for beneficial career development.

A Great Paper from "Outsiders"

We'll get to the topic momentarily, but first a vignette about an article. Research interests for some in business schools relate to international business (IB), that is, issues about multinational firms and cross-border transactions. Those faculty are usually readers and occasional contributors to the *Journal of International Business Studies* (JIBS), the leading IB field journal. Here is a JIBS article some IB scholars might find particularly interesting. It's a 2010 article by Nathan Jensen, Quan Li, and Aminur Rahman about apparently unaddressed challenges associated with using data from certain cross-national firm-level surveys popular with IB and related management scholars (Jensen, Li, and Rahman, 2010). They develop and test a theory of under response and false response biasing measures derived from those cross-national surveys, which ask questions about bribery and corruption faced by local businesses.

Here's their theory in brief. Individuals from firms in politically-repressive countries are less likely to respond at all or respond truthfully to questions about bribery and corruption. Respondents in those countries fear that their response will get back to the local mayor, chief of police, or party official shaking them down for a "contribution" important to continued business survival and success. Better either to not respond or respond that there's little or no bribery or corruption. Here's their evidence in brief. Non-response rates in a prominent cross-country survey by the World Bank increase with lower levels of press freedom in a given country. False report rates also increase with less press freedom. Respondents tell the World Bank surveyor that corruption isn't as severe as alternative non-survey measures indicate. The end result is that some of the most frequently used survey data on bribery, corruption, and related cross-country business issues (e.g., quality of the business environment) are biased. At a minimum, there are important adjustments for researchers to make if using these survey data. Most haven't, so publications based on such "evidence" merit renewed scrutiny and revision.

Jensen, Li, and Rahman might not be familiar names outside their disciplines of political science and economics: Jensen and Li are political scientists, and quite productive researchers in journals within the political science field. Rahman is an economist at the World Bank. They're "outsiders" to my discipline who crossed disciplinary and professional boundaries to submit, revise, and publish provocative research with a stinging critique of an empirical research stream in our field. Way to go.

Why doesn't this happen more often? The answer is tribalism. Finally, our topic!

Disciplinary Tribalism

There is more than a little tribalism in the Academy. By tribalism, we mean that researchers in one discipline have a tendency to ignore much of the work on a common topic of interest another group of scholars are addressing in another discipline. Maybe it's research and researchers in psychology and management asking common questions about why individuals and firms escalate commitments in an apparently irrational way. Maybe it's research and researchers in law and political science asking common questions about constitutions and the quality of government. Maybe it's research in religion and environmental studies exploring common questions about why some religious groups tend to resist policies reversing environmental damage from climate change. In any case, we tend to look inward at our disciplinary "tribe" for reference regarding which scholars, ideas, and publications are relevant for a given topic of discussion and debate. We look less often, if at all, outside our field for insight on the same topic. Discipline-based professional associations, conferences, and journals reinforce this inward-looking tendency. As Golde and Hanna (1999) note, tribalism is cultivated in us from the start of our doctoral education, then continues throughout our academic careers.

We'll admit that we need some tribal lines in order to define intellectually distinct fields, set professional standards and qualifications, and more generally bring order to what is and isn't immediately relevant to our work. That aside, though, the inward-looking trope is probably not a good thing. Tribalism raises barriers. It limits outside voices in discussion and debate. It leads to intradisciplinary navel gazing.

Crossing Tribal Lines: Individually and Collectively

There are things we can do as individuals and as groups to deal with some of tribalism's negatives. Individually, it's possible to look outside in many ways. Offer a class with a cross-listing in another department (good) or in another college (even better). Serve on a masters or doctoral thesis committee in another field dealing with a research topic that overlaps with your own interests. Attend, serve on a panel, submit, and present research in progress at a professional meeting in another disciplinary field – economics, political science, engineering, sociology, law.

Of course, published scholarly research is foundational to career development in research universities. So submitting to, revising, and ultimately publishing in high-quality journals outside your primary field constitutes a strong blow against tribalism. But it's difficult. Tribalism has some strong defenders, and as we noted earlier, their defense is sometimes justified, and often well meaning. For researchers looking to cross lines, the barriers put up by their own tribe can be substantial. The range of acceptably "high-quality" journals is almost always longer within your disciplinary field (tribe) than it is in almost any other field. That's usually because we know less than we think about those other fields. In the Department of Strategic Management and Entrepreneurship (SME) at the Carlson School of Management, there is no list of high-quality journals in management – we're supposed to just know what they are. That may be relatively easy to figure out for journals in the disciplines of strategy or entrepreneurship.

But what about journals in other disciplines? What are the top journals in SME related to, say, political science? That might be much more difficult for faculty members to identify. And tribal defenders in the SME department may have a very short written or mental list of outside journals that "count" for tenure and promotion purposes. That can be a pretty strong deterrent to crossing lines for research and journal publication outside your primary field. That helps us understand why articles by the Jensen, Li, and Rahmans of this world are infrequent.

Collectively, there are other initiatives worth thinking about to combat tribalism. We've mentioned some teaching and service initiatives for individuals to consider. Commendation of (or at least indifference to) such efforts from departmental faculty colleagues, departmental chairs, and college deans would be helpful. Research-wise, we can think of few more important individuals to fight tribalism for the rest of us than journal editors. It was not an accident that Jensen, Li, and Rahman submitted their manuscript to JIBS. Their submission followed presentation of the paper at an interdisciplinary conference with editorial team members from JIBS in attendance. No doubt, they received encouragement to go further and submit the paper to the journal for review.

The JIBS editor-in-chief at the time – also one of the authors of this book – made it part of her mission to attend and speak at conferences outside IB and management. She emphasized the interdisciplinary nature of the journal and its openness to research submissions from other disciplines. Such efforts to fight tribalism paid off with more submissions from scholars outside the IB and management rank and file, and more notice of (and citation to) JIBS articles. We are pretty sure the outside submissions got just as tough a review as rank-and-file IB submissions. We noted three revisions over more than a year for the Jensen, Li, and Rahman article. It was no quick hit. Tough, constructive reviews from JIBS editorial board members likely made the article better for an intended audience that begins with IB and management scholars but goes beyond that to others outside our tribe.

How often does that happen at other journals?

Your Tribe, but Also Your Career

As we said earlier, some tribalism is inevitable and not unwelcome. For doctoral students and junior faculty striving to develop a research agenda and reputation, tribal lines help. Early in a career, the lines help us understand which people, institutions, conferences, and publication outlets will support that agenda and recognize that growing reputation sooner. But an academic career isn't always so instrumentally driven. We are lucky. We get paid to find interesting intellectual debates, learn the issues guiding them, and then weigh in with sound thinking grounded in rigorous theory and broad-based evidence. As careers develop, maybe the location of those debates should matter a little less. If they are outside your department or college, go forth and weigh in. Push that further. Find those outside debates, weigh in, and then translate their implications for others in our home department and college – our tribe. Prompt colleagues down the hall to look outward rather than inward.

Discussion Questions

1. Have you ever published or presented work outside your immediate disciplinary area? Talk about that experience. What worked well and what might you do differently?
2. How should we resolve the tension between keeping scholarly disciplines distinct for research purposes and engaging other disciplines for research richness?
3. What might you write in your cover letter to an editor when submitting to a journal outside of your own discipline? How could you make the case that your manuscript should go under review at that journal?

4.   Identify some cross-disciplinary teaching or service opportunities at your institution, and commit to following up on at least one of them.

References and Additional Reading

Golde, C. and Hanna, A. 1999. "The Challenges of Conducting Interdisciplinary Research in Traditional Doctoral Programs." *Ecosystems*, 2: 281–285.

Jensen, N., Li, Q., and Rahman, A. 2010. "Understanding Corruption and Firm Responses in Cross-National Firm-Level Surveys." *Journal of International Business Studies*, 41: 1481–1504.

27

OUTSIDE APPOINTMENTS

Key insight: Outside appointments are enjoyable, educational, and mutually beneficial to home and outside institutions. What's the problem? Where are the ethical dilemmas in outside appointments? We argue there can be several and survey some in this chapter along with simple guides for minimizing the problems those dilemmas can prompt.

The Producers' Problem

Some of us love movies. Among the co-authors of this book, a favorite movie is *The Producers*, and here we mean the original version directed by Mel Brooks and starring Zero Mostel and Gene Wilder (IMDb, 1968) (not the 2005 remake starring Nathan Lane and Matthew Broderick). For those of you unfamiliar with this comedy, here is the basic plot. A ne'er-do-well Broadway director (Mostel) and his accountant (Wilder) hatch a scheme to make money by producing a play that flops. The duo will go to backers and raise thousands more than is needed to produce a play. Of course, they'll have to sell more than 100 percent of the profits to raise all of that money, but as long as the show flops – preferably closes on opening night – the backers will expect neither the return of their invested principal nor any profits. The duo can take the remaining money and head to Rio de Janeiro. Ah, but if the play is a hit then they're in big trouble, because they've promised much more than 100 percent of the profits to the backers. Of course, they end up inadvertently producing a hit musical comedy (improbably titled "Springtime for Hitler"), which lands them in jail for fraud, where they start producing and overselling yet another musical (more appropriately titled "Prisoners of Love"). That's Mel Brooks.

So what does *The Producers* have to do with ethics (other than accounting ethics)? Well, there are times when we might be offering more than 100 percent of our time and attention professionally. It's rarely if ever done illegally, but ethical lines can get crossed and faculty can get into all sorts of hot water. One way this can happen is with outside appointments, that is, appointments faculty may take up outside of the home institution appointment. That includes everything from a visiting professorship at a foreign university to a research affiliation across the street with a "sister college" in the home university. If there's an appointment outside your home institution, there's almost certainly someone back at your home institution asking whether (and, perhaps, assuming that) your outside appointment is taking you away from research, teaching, and service you owe the home institution. In this chapter, we discuss this problem – *The Producers* problem – and think of ways to keep from crossing lines, keep from getting into hot water with colleagues, and keep from promising (or appearing to promise) more than 100 percent of your time and attention to research, teaching, and service.

It's Nice Outside

Aside from the Church, the Academy is probably the closest thing to a global community. You can go almost anywhere in the world, find a university, and draw an invitation to live, learn, teach, and write temporarily. Indeed, one of the perquisites of an academic life is the occasional opportunity to step away from the home institution and visit another near or far. Visits during sabbatical leave are typical. After six years of service, a professor applies for and receives permission from her home institution to take a year's leave. The professor also applies for and is given a visiting faculty position at another university, often in another country. The professor rents her home, packs up spouse and kids, goes abroad, sets up a home overseas, enrolls the kids in local schools, comes to an understanding about what the trailing spouse will do, and then goes to work in a new place for a year.

Outside appointments come up in other ways. An organizational theorist sits in a business school but takes a courtesy appointment in the sociology department located in another college. An international business professor sits in a US business school but takes a research affiliate position in a European business school as a condition of receiving a European Union research grant. A political science professor takes a senior fellow position at a public policy think tank in Washington, London, or Tokyo. The difference with the sabbatical leave scenario is that these alternatives do not involve the faculty member also taking leave from the home institution. She's still on the home institution rolls with all of the pay and benefits and all of the research, teaching, and service obligations.

At most home institutions, there are policies to guide such non-leave outside appointments at foreign universities. Take the University of Minnesota's Carlson

School of Management. There, it is assumed that faculty with a "particularly strong international reputation" will visit another institution at the full professor level. Other lower-grade outside appointments may be as visiting lecturers. Again, they are great opportunities for travel, to live in, contribute to, and learn from a different research community. And that seems to be the overall aim of non-leave outside appointments. Home and outside institutions benefit from faculty exchange and collaboration on research, teaching, and service initiatives.

But Will You Miss Library Committee Meetings?

So outside appointments are enjoyable, educational, and mutually beneficial to home and outside institutions. What's the problem? There can be several, as Donna Euben points out in her article for the American Association of University Professors (2004) and as the University of Minnesota's Carlson School handbook guidelines point out (2017). Carlson School guidelines on outside appointments explicitly state limitations on non-leave outside appointments. The guidelines also refer to limiting terms lurking in different offices and on different websites of the University of Minnesota. For example, references to outside appointments in the Carlson guidelines are paired with references to "tenured" faculty – perhaps assistant professors need not apply. There are also references to the maximum number of days that faculty may "consult" for other organizations. There is even a conflict-of-interest bar on taking outside appointments involving teaching that might contribute to a program that "competes" with the Carlson School for students. Then there's reference to other University of Minnesota policies limiting outside appointments. It gets complicated pretty quickly, but the overriding principle in working through these guidelines seems to be this: You can take an outside appointment when not on leave if it is good for your professional career, if it is good for the reputation of your home institution, and if it doesn't leave you short in terms of fulfilling your home institution duties (Carlson, 2017). Euben echoes those points, suggesting that the Carlson School guidelines are not outliers. They track standard guides for many universities.

That last "and" in those guidelines can be problematic. Permission to take a non-leave outside appointment usually starts with a conversation with your department chair, then with your academic dean, then perhaps with your dean. Then there's a written proposal for permission to take an outside appointment, then completion of various forms, then review by that same chair, academic dean, and dean, and perhaps a provost or two to see that university guidelines have been observed. It's a people process like so many others in a university community.

And different people bring different perspectives to the process. A department chair responsible for covering courses with instructors may ask whether this outside appointment will lead to class cancellations because a visit to the outside institution during term was extended due to an unforeseen complication, like an airline pilot strike. A dean may ask whether the outside appointment will lead to absences from critical committee meetings because they conflict with periodic briefing sessions you have with a state governor dependent on policy recommendations from your think tank. If your departmental faculty colleagues know about your outside appointment request, they might wonder – and wander into the department chair's office to wonder – if you'll still be available to do the "drudge work" of service on, say, the library committee, the curriculum committee, the you-name-it-but-what-does-it-really-do committee. It's a people process and those people have an interest, a self-interest that might lead them to conclude that your outside appointment will overload you – be more than 100 percent of your time and attention – and force them to shoulder some of that overload. It's one version of *The Producers* problem.

It's a Hit! And It's Mine (Not Yours)

It's also a problem even if nothing comes from the outside appointment, that is, if it's a "flop" in terms of research, teaching, and service outputs. Still, the outside appointment could be a "hit" producing new journal articles and other outputs valuable to institutions seeking recognition, enhanced reputation, and the financial support following both. Fantastic, but now your "backers" want what they think is theirs. The home and outside institutions both want to count your publications as their own for purposes of measuring historical faculty research productivity and asking for future government-funded research grants. Both want to claim intellectual property rights to the software algorithm you developed, copyrighted, and patented in connection with the new research and journal articles. Chances are both want 100 percent, but you may not have 100 percent to hand out to both – another version of *The Producers* problem.

As in the movie, you might choose to keep one institution or the other (or both) in the dark. Keeping information from your home institution regarding outputs from outside appointments – including how much you were paid under that appointment – is likely to get you into a lot of hot water, perhaps even to the point of legal action leading to discipline and/or termination. Better to let home and outside institution know everything, then let them sort it out, dean to dean, provost to provost.

Two Guides: Make Forward and Be Forward

Here are two other guides worth considering as you disclose to home and outside institutions. One suggestion is to "make forward" teaching and service work in advance of seeking an outside appointment. It's an easier conversation with a department chair when you can point to a surplus of teaching credits and/or committee work. "Making forward" means you are less likely to fall behind and have to "make up" teaching and service obligations during the term of the outside appointment.

Here's another suggestion. "Be forward" with that same department chair (and associate dean, dean, provost, etc.) about everything you can regarding the proposed outside appointment. If there's a letter or memorandum detailing the terms of the outside appointment, including terms related to expected work, compensation, and the treatment of any output, just give it to those home institution decision makers. Let them contact the author. Let them draw their own conclusions about what the outside appointment will do for you, for the home institution, and for your ability to discharge other home institution obligations. If, in the end, they think the outside appointment will push you past 100 percent, then maybe it isn't worth taking. Being forward will help everyone make an informed decision, which is then more likely to be in the affirmative.

It's a privilege to work in an institution dedicated to creating and disseminating knowledge. It's a gold-plated privilege to have occasional opportunities to change institutional venue, be part of a different learning community, and bring new insights back home. Make and be forward as you take advantage of that gold-plated privilege, and as you give it all 100 percent (and no more) of your time and attention.

And leave the comedy to Mel Brooks.

Discussion Questions

1. Does your institution have outside appointment or non-leave policies in place? Investigate and see what you find, and discuss them with colleagues. What do they say?
2. "Being forward" is a transparency norm that can help make sure everyone in both institutions is on the same page. Discuss how that would work in your institution, i.e., who should be involved? What is the timing for having conversations? What barriers or politics do you anticipate needing to overcome?
3. What conditions would make an outside appointment untenable for you and/or your institution? What would make you decline such an invitation?
4. Conversely, what conditions or benefits would make an outside appointment irresistible for you? If such a leave were unavailable to you for some reason, how could you go about getting those benefits without the leave?

References and Additional Reading

Carlson School of Management. 2017. "University of Minnesota Carlson School of Management Employee Handbook." Available at: http://assets.csom.umn.edu/assets/137700.pdf

Euben, D. 2004. "Faculty Employment Outside of the University: Conflicts of Commitment." Washington, DC: American Association of University Professors. Available at: www.aaup.org/issues/resources-conflicts-interest/outside-university-conflicts

IMDb. 1968. *The Producers*. IMDb summary information on the movie available at: www.imdb.com/title/tt0063462/

28

CONSULTING

Key insight: Individuals, firms, government agencies, and non-profit organizations often seek out academics for advice and analysis related to their areas of research and teaching expertise. Outside consulting by academics can be rewarding financially and otherwise, but consulting also raises important ethical issues related to conflicts of interest and prior duties to provide diligent research, teaching, and service to the institution and profession they represent. In this chapter, we survey those issues and offer practical advice on when academic consulting is less likely to raise conflicts, how some conflicts can be managed, and what role consulting should play at different stages in an academic career.

Purists, Industrialists, and Opportunists: All Potential Consultants

Career advancement in the Academy depends substantially on the ability to publish high-quality basic research and attract high-value grants from conventional sources such as government agencies and foundations. Excelling at those two pursuits lets colleges, universities, and other research institutions bathe in the reflected glory of faculty publications as well as advance the institutional mission financially with overhead income that might top more than half the dollar value of the grant. Institutions love this "purist" faculty profile and reward it with faster advancement in professorial rank, larger compensation packages, and other benefits.

But there are at least two alternative career profiles that also attract faculty interest, particularly in professional colleges such as law or business schools. One alternative has faculty pursuing applied research publications in practitioner-oriented journals and industry collaborations with working professionals who can often wrangle high-value grants to support those collaborations. Institutions may bathe in less reflected glory from these publications, but overhead income from industry grants to faculty can still be substantial, thus making an "industrialist" faculty profile still attractive and worthy of some recognition and reward.

Another alternative faculty profile prompts indifference or even suspicion among institutions. Faculty pursue neither basic research with general application nor applied research in a specific industry. Instead, they research, write, and present analyses valuable to specific individuals, firms, and organizations. Results from past engagements may find their way into "how-to" books found in airport stores or advice columns found in newspapers and trade magazines. But they are just the icing on a financial cake baked with lucrative consulting contracts that more often than not provide for no payment to faculty institutions – what did they do for the client? As you might guess, institutions are not amused and typically set limits on such "opportunist" faculty.

Here's the thing. It's not just opportunists who consult. Industrialist and purist faculty do, too, but typically do less of it and with fewer potential conflicts with their institutions. But all three do engage in some sort of consulting as a normal part of an academic career. And all three types of faculty need to think about ethical issues consulting creates: conflicts of interest, erosion of institutional duties, threats to academic freedom, or potentially even civil or criminal liability that could lead to loss of tenure, termination, and/or jail time. This chapter surveys those issues and suggests practical approaches for managing them.

Why Faculty Consult: To Bridge a Gap without Falling into One

Many university faculty believe it's important to "bridge the gap" between basic and applied research – and that's okay. The two types of research are not mutually incompatible. Through our academic training and research projects, we are likely to develop a strong proficiency in some topic. Among the co-authors of this book, international business (IB) training and research projects have helped us develop expertise on issues related to, for example, transfer pricing policies among multi-national firms. It can be an exciting intellectual journey to translate basic theoretical knowledge about transfer pricing into the real world of applied situations as defined by multinationals or international tax professionals. Also, consulting work often requires a speed and efficiency that conventional academic research papers with their repeated peer-review processes typically do not permit. Add to that the satisfaction of solving a "real problem" rather than addressing it in concept only. And then there's the money as well as the kudos from the client. Both need financial and social incentives to be relevant as well as rigorous in our work, to "matter" for more than just the academic communities that we belong to first and last.

But as the public address system says at each stop on the London Underground (or "Tube" to locals), purist, industrialist, and opportunist faculty need to "mind the gap" so that they don't fall into a problematic space where their consulting work runs afoul of institutional guides limiting this work. For all three types of faculty, guides limit time that can be devoted to consulting. Often for opportunist and industrialist faculty there are also limitations related to conflicts of interest raised by consulting. Even for purist faculty there are scenarios where consulting work can raise issues threatening academic freedom. Noting and then avoiding those limitations are central to bridging rather than falling into gaps created by consulting work.

For the Opportunist: REPA What You Sow

Let's start with noting those limitations. You are not alone in that interest. Your academic institution is almost certainly quite interested in knowing what you are doing outside your day-to-day work as a faculty member. And your institution probably has a set of guidelines for reporting those activities.

At the University of Minnesota, noting such activities occurs regularly through annual submissions of a standardized form known as the Report of External Professional Activities (REPA) (2017a). Since the 2000s, it has been an electronic reporting form intended to capture key details regarding activities by university faculty and other individuals that may interfere with their day-to-day employment obligations. So REPAs are completed by faculty and other individuals with responsibility for academic research. REPAs are also completed by other individuals authorized to act on behalf of the university with its research and discovery, teaching and learning, and outreach and public service mission. Think, for example, of staff running a university technology center charged with commercializing university research by negotiating licensing agreements with local firms. Completed REPA forms are submitted for review by supervisors for the lowest-level faculty and staff member to the provost and president of the university.

Even a cursory glance at the University of Minnesota's REPA form reveals how important it is for faculty and other covered individuals to note and explain any significant consulting work. Frequently asked questions regarding REPAs begin with a list of definitions of external activities that essentially describes an externally-compensated consulting relationship (REPA, 2017b). Indeed, that first sentence defining such external activities includes a hyperlink directed to an explanation of university policies on "Outside Consulting and Other Commitments" (REPA, 2017c). And those policies start with the mandate to report all time devoted to outside consulting whether paid or unpaid. REPAs demand of faculty and other covered individuals transparency about time and type of consulting work, compensation for the consulting work, and any connection between the consulting work and university employment obligations. Failing to meet these transparency requirements is grounds for discipline, even termination.

Once noted on the REPA, what about substantive limitations, starting with time limitations on outside consulting? Institutions differ on time that faculty can devote to outside consulting. The University of Minnesota permits approximately one day each week for outside consulting consistent with the faculty member's field of expertise. An IB faculty member with expertise might devote a day each week to outside consulting work on transfer pricing problems for a local multinational firm; a faculty member in biology might not. Of course, consulting work might not occur with predictable smoothness, say on every Thursday afternoon during the academic year. More often than not, the work is done in blocks of several days in a row. With this in mind, most universities permit averaging over semesters in the academic year, or between semesters and longer vacation periods. Consulting work that exceeds the day-a-week guide is not necessarily prohibited. It just needs approval in advance from supervisors. Those conversations provide an opportunity for the faculty member to describe limits on the proposed "excess" consulting work, and to link that work to the faculty member's core commitments to university research, teaching, and service work.

Recall the three faculty types we described at the beginning of this chapter. Notification, explanation, and discussion requirements in the REPA are aimed primarily at the opportunists. They are most prone to chase after consulting work and the private gain it generates at the expense of university research, teaching, and service requirements. REPAs shine a light on outside consulting by industrialists and purists. But the light can be particularly glaring for the opportunist. And maybe that glare will give the opportunist (and her supervisor) incentives to limit such activities.

For the Industrialist: Putting the University First

REPAs do more than simply shine a light on outside consulting work. Once illuminated through REPAs, faculty then need to manage conflicts of interest (COIs), whether actual or perceived. We have discussed COIs earlier in this part of the book, so there is no need to define COIs again. It is enough here simply to assert that much of the work faculty might do for an outside client as a consultant is quite similar to the work she might do in connection with an academic presentation or publication intended for consumption by peers at other universities.

If so, then who gets the first crack at that work? This might be a particularly important question for the industrialist faculty member interested in building her career through partnerships with and grants to study applied problems in a field where the faculty member is an expert. Our IB expert on transfer pricing might develop a model for the minimization of tax liability associated with the transfer of software between multinational firm subsidiaries in two countries. She can disseminate that model to the public via academic journal publication after multiple rounds of peer review. Alternatively, she can disseminate that model piecemeal through partnership arrangements with select multinational firms agreeing to fund follow-on research as well as several doctoral students working for the industrialist faculty member. Publishing the model in an academic journal first almost certainly decreases the value of the model for individual multinational firms, which would like to have exclusive use of this innovation for a time.

It is a dilemma for the industrialist that requires some guide to resolve the actual or perceived COI. REPA guidelines at the University of Minnesota and most other universities resolve that dilemma in favor of publication in the academic journal first. The industrialist faculty member's first duty is to the university's research (and related teaching and service) mission. If the knowledge behind that model is at all related to work done as an employee of the university – using university libraries, labs, graduate students, for example – then that knowledge merits dissemination first for the benefit of the university. And that benefit is presumably greater when the knowledge appears first in academic presentations and publications available to peers in the public rather than firms in the private realm. Those firms will still find benefits after waiting in the discovery queue.

For the Purist: Protecting Academic Freedom

REPAs also shine a light on consulting issues relevant to purists. At first glance, that might seem doubtful. Purists don't necessarily seek out industrial partnerships. Purists don't engage private firms as clients in purely commercial consulting. Purists are just that – avoiding COIs whether they be actual or perceived. They do basic research for presentation and publication in conventional academic outlets. They seek financial support for it in the form of grants from other academic and government agencies devoted to supporting that basic research. And universities love purists for it.

Except purists can still fall into gaps described in REPAs. Here is how. Well-regarded academic researchers are often recruited by grant-providing, non-profit institutions such as the Robert Wood Johnson Foundation and government agencies like the US Department of Agriculture (USDA). Indeed, those same well-regarded purists built their reputation through successful competition for such grants. Some grant-providing institutions and agencies pay expenses and honoraria for the service of scholars in evaluating and recommending grant awards. This work amounts to consulting work under many REPA systems. Thus, it calls for an accounting of time devoted to that consulting work. It may also bring up COIs if the scholar evaluating a grant proposal has any connection with grant proposers who could be faculty colleagues at the same university or previous research project collaborators. Both issues are manageable via some combination of disclosure and excuse from decision-making.

But there may be another ethical dilemma facing the purist faculty member consulting for such institutions and agencies. Their aims are not necessarily those of the purist faculty member's university. The USDA may wish to allocate grants to researchers willing to study a proposed public policy priority that the purist faculty member thinks misplaced. Perhaps, the USDA grant-making program is aimed at attracting more research on bovine growth additive in feed that the purist faculty member thinks dangerous to dairy products derived from animals exposed to this additive. The issues for the purist faculty member are different from the industrialist or opportunist faculty members. The issues are about academic freedom and the obligation to speak out against the program even if the program's agency is employing you and (likely) supporting your university. Well-devised REPA systems prompt a response from the purist faculty member regarding their personal views stated with deliberate frankness, notwithstanding the response of the grant-making institution or agency. Stating a contrary view may limit the purist consulting member's work in the program, which may have negative financial implications in the short run. But academic freedom and integrity are preserved, and the reputation of the purist faculty member is likely enhanced in the medium and long term. Great universities understand and support this trade-off.

Wait for Tenure

Consulting raises many issues for faculty no matter their purist, industrialist, or opportunist profile. Sometimes those issues are subtle and the guides for resolving them less than crystal clear. But here's a situation with a crystal clear guide for resolution. Consulting by junior (untenured) faculty will attract negative attention by senior departmental peers. Junior faculty are expected to conduct their research and publish it in high-quality outlets to build their reputation in their professed scholarly field. In this context, outside consulting work for a client firm or individual will lead to the inference by senior faculty colleagues of a lack of commitment to that reputation-building process. She is using her university affiliation for personal enrichment, not career advancement benefitting the department, college, university, and related academic constituencies. It may be an unfair inference to draw, but it will be drawn.

So the right response is to defer consulting work until after tenure review is completed. Once completed, senior faculty members will find substantially increased latitude to pursue research and related teaching and service initiatives. The wait is worth it for the opportunity to build a career and bridge gaps with the right amount and type of consulting.

Discussion Questions

1. Are you aware of any REPA-like system at your university? If so, then get a copy and compare it to the REPA system at the University of Minnesota. How do they differ on, say, the definition of outside consulting and other commitments by faculty members? How do they differ on percentages of time a faculty member can devote to consulting?

2. We discussed three different faculty profiles related to consulting: purist, industrialist, and opportunist. In practice, faculty members typically exhibit a

mix of these profiles. Look around your university department. Think about what mix of profiles best describes the assistant, associate, and full professors in your department.

3.   How do you bridge the gap in your research? How do you try to render your academic research findings relevantly accessible to practitioners and public policy makers related to the field you study?

References and Additional Reading

REPA. 2017a. "Report of External Professional Activities." Minneapolis, MN: University of Minnesota. Available at: https://compliance.umn.edu/conflictAboutREPA.htm

REPA. 2017b. "REPA FAQ." Minneapolis, MN: University of Minnesota. Available at: https://policy.umn.edu/operations/conflictinterest-faq02

REPA. 2017c. "Board of Regents Policy on Outside Consulting and Other Commitments." Minneapolis, MN: University of Minnesota. Available at: http://regents.umn.edu/sites/regents.umn.edu/files/policies/Outside_Consulting.pdf

29

MEDIA ENGAGEMENT

Key insight: Media play an important role in the professional life of academics. The media contact us in connection with our research and teaching activities. They also come to us for disinterested, objective commentary on current events. Media requests raise important questions about when, how, and how much to engage. Answering these questions includes important ethical dimensions. This chapter addresses those questions and their ethical dimensions for academics at different stages in their careers.

Lost and Found in Translation

Schultz (1998) tells that it was the late 18th-century British parliamentarian and political philosopher, Edmund Burke, who first coined the term "fourth estate" to refer to the press and its influence on the other three estates: clergy, nobility, and commons. He was ruing a decision to let journalists into parliamentary sessions, thinking that written records taken in real time and published daily to the populace – voting and non-voting – would lead to less thoughtful debate, legislation, and public policy.

Burke would likely have been right at home in the 21st-century Academy. Strong traditions of academic freedom encourage faculty to research, write, present, publish, and debate often controversial issues with long-term social implications – for instance, debates in science, philosophy, and religion about when life begins or in law and business about what duties corporations owe to others. These issues also interest the media, which include the traditional print media of Burke's day as well as new forms of electronic digital media that pervade our lives.[1]

But when the media notice and write about academic research and related teaching and services activities, they tend to write for a broad community. We don't. They tend to write in brief and quickly – in a few days or maybe just a few hours. We don't. They tend to write about practical implications for current trends and events. We don't. These mismatches can lead to all sorts of "translation" challenges for academics working with the media. And those challenges have important ethical dimensions related to when and how to communicate with the media.

This chapter surveys some of those challenges and dimensions. It's important. At first glance, the media may seem to be irrelevant to work as an academic, or maybe an occasional bother to be quickly shrugged off as a diversion from a core mission centered on students and fellow scholars. We think that view is impractical. Media play an important role in academic professional life. And that role can be positive for individual faculty and their academic institutions if you keep in mind a few rules about time, place, and manner for working with them.

Why Us?

But first, let's ask why the media are so attracted to the Academy. It may be surprising how often members of the print, broadcast, and digital electronic media reach out to universities and their faculty. On any given day at the University of Minnesota's Carlson School of Management, from 10 to 20 local, national, and/ or international media inquiries will come to the dean, individual faculty, and/or into the college media relations office. The inquiries may seek background information on some current business transaction – a proposed merger of two companies, say. They may seek an opinion on the wisdom of that proposed deal.

Almost anyone is flattered to be asked for their expertise, including academics, but why do reporters often go first to academics for that expertise? Often there are working professionals with deep experience, perhaps deeper than the academic, whose emphasis is on teaching and research. But media still look to academics for insight.

Here's why: We have – or should have – a disinterested perspective. Working professionals are more likely to have some conflict of interest that may color their assessment. Even the appearance of a conflict can undermine the credibility of reporting with media consumers reading, listening, and seeing the report. The investment banker commenting on the proposed merger may represent one of the firms or compete with the bank representing one of the firms. In either case, commentary quality is undercut. Not so (or not so often) with the university academic commentator. Academic freedom gives universities and their faculty the presumption of neutrality and objectivity regarding any number of trends and events going on in the "outside" world. Unless the faculty member is also an outside consultant on such matters, there is the added advantage of no apparent financial conflicts. The professor is paid by a private college or university trust or a state college or university allocation from the legislature. Her background information and assessments avoid taints of conflict. Reporters find that attractive, especially when there are time constraints on getting the story written, the video edited, and the in-person interview recorded.

The academic advantage of disinterested perspective implies certain ethical obligations, which begin with disclosure obligations. Tell reporters immediately when contacted about any and all connections you may have financially and otherwise with the people, places, and events involved in the story. Tell reporters about any prior research funded directly or indirectly by people involved in the story. Tell reporters about any prior teaching where you had students who are now involved in the story.[2] Tell reporters about any prior consulting or other business relationships you have or had with people involved in the story.

More disclosure earlier is always better here. It lets reporters then make an informed decision about whether and how to go forward with their work involving you. It also protects you from any accusations of conflict after the story is printed, aired, or otherwise disseminated to the public.

These ethical obligations may go further if there is or was a non-disclosure agreement related to any of these business relationships. Then, your response to media inquiries is simple: "I'm sorry, but I cannot comment on this aspect of the story"; or "I'm sorry, but I cannot comment on aspects of the story involving [person X or firm Y]." You need not explain why. Indeed, the non-disclosure agreement you signed as a condition for consulting for person X or firm Y may require that you do not explain why you cannot comment. Reporters will understand and, in most cases, appreciate what you are saying. Good reporters will discern what is behind your words and appreciate the integrity it signals. And finally, all reporters will appreciate your efforts to help them find an alternate candidate to contact if you are not able to comment.

Media Time and Timing Issues

Let's assume you have been contacted by a reporter to comment on a story where you have relevant expertise and you have no actual or apparent conflicts. Do you take the call? It might seem easy to answer in the affirmative. You take the call in your office, speak for five minutes off the record, then five more on the record, spend a few additional minutes taking down some information about when and where the interview is likely to be printed, then end the phone call and return to the article you were revising. It took about 15 minutes of your time to help shape a story, raise the profile of your college, and burnish your credentials as a public intellectual. You have done a good deed.

But no good deed goes unpunished. If you are available once, then reporters will ask again. They have your address, phone number, and email. If you were particularly good at providing a concise, thoughtful comment earlier, then reporters will ask again soon and frequently. A one-time 15-minute media engagement can morph into multiple engagements on the phone, in your office, at home, or in a television studio. You can become something of a media star, at least compared to your other departmental or college faculty colleagues. Your dean will appreciate it – her board of advisors are unlikely to read your academic journal articles, but they will see and hear your media interviews.

However, becoming a media star is still not a good trend to encourage, especially if you are an untenured assistant professor. Multiple media engagements bolster a faculty member's service contributions, but teaching and research are almost always more important contributions during annual evaluations. Research contributions have paramount importance during tenure and promotion evaluations at larger universities. Multiple media engagements paired with a borderline assessment of research contributions during a tenure review can have a net negative effect on faculty votes. They can see media engagement as the root cause, thinking you were more interested in raising your profile with the public than the Academy.

In this context, it makes sense to think about when, how, and how often to engage the media. It makes sense to address these questions with two types of faculty in mind: tenure-track junior faculty at a large university; and everyone else. Tenure-track junior faculty are and should be focused on producing high-quality academic publications and teaching effectively. Service, including service assisting the media, is and should be minimal. So the "how much" question about media engagement is pretty easy to answer: Do the minimum. Indeed, it is unlikely that any senior faculty member would blink an eye if there were no records of media commentary during your tenure evaluation.

Media engagement may be included in service or research contributions, especially after their publication in those high-quality academic outlets. So it makes sense to take a reporter's call when it is about your latest journal article or book. The story is the research, now with a plausible claim of professional and/or public policy relevance as well as academic rigor. That's an answer to the "when" question. And "how" should tenure-track junior faculty engage media? Time-efficient engagement modes are preferable. It is a phone call or a short email with the reporter. However attractive it might seem when proposed, it is probably not an in-studio interview. It is almost certainly not an offer to write a separate "practitioner" version of the article or book. Let the reporter do her work. Write another academic article.

Recognizing the Public Intellectual...

Now for everyone else. We have already mentioned how deans (and provosts and presidents and their media relations staff) almost always appreciate faculty media engagements. It's not an accident. Institution builders point to media coverage of and engagement by faculty as indicators of success in community development. Our research discoveries are improving people's lives. Our teaching is educating the next generation of leaders. Both benefit the local community that hosts and often funds the institution. Both benefit the broader national and global community commercializing some of those discoveries and employing some of those future leaders. The power media have in conveying that message explains why deans and other institution builders may employ media relations staff to increase and manage such engagements, and why they typically recognize and reward faculty who are able to engage effectively with the media.

These faculty are gifted at translating academic research findings for the broader public. They are gifted at doing so on short notice and in different print, broadcast, and other digital forums. They are gifted at doing it concisely, interestingly, maybe even with a little humor. Faculty may have these gifts because they come from industry, a profession, or the public sector where the story is located. Many non-tenure track teaching specialist and adjunct faculty have that profile and those gifts. Such faculty are ideal for frequent media engagement of all types and forums. Frequent engagement related to their own research and teaching will serve them and the institution well.

Another source of such gifted faculty is the tenured, senior faculty member often holding a named professorship or chair. She can draw on a history of academically commended research and teaching achievements. She has the protection of academic tenure so that she can speak with disinterested objectivity even if those views are controversial. The terms of her professorship or chair may even include a mandate to disseminate her expertise to non-academic communities. Add to these factors an ability to translate on short notice, concisely and non-patronizingly in different media forums. She is part of a small faculty elite in a college, university, or research institute.

She serves as a public intellectual, a position with a history stretching back to the birth of universities in Western Europe during the Middle Ages and continuing today with examples like Princeton University economist and Noble Laureate Paul Krugman, Cambridge University anthropologist Caroline Humphrey, and Paris Diderot University historian Élisabeth Roudinesco. Each has outstanding research credentials to go along with a commitment to university teaching and service. But they are also prominent commentators on current issues in their respective countries. Krugman, for example, is a regular columnist on economic policy issues in the *New York Times*. Humphry in the UK and Roudinesco in France write regularly for major newspapers and appear frequently on broadcast television and radio. Public intellectuals in the 21st century are skilled at using social media (e.g., Twitter, podcasts) to share their views. They invest valuable time and attention to accomplish such engagement, but they are still active scholars. They use their record of past academic research accomplishment to step into and influence important debates in the broader public arena.

... and a Call for (More) Engaged Scholarship

Harvard historian and public intellectual Richard Pipes observed in his memoir *Vixit* (2003, ix), that "the life of an academic is not commonly of general interest since it is rather repetitious where teaching is involved and esoteric where it concerns scholarship." For most of us in the Academy, that is well known and well accepted. We do our work with little notice from outsiders.

Media engagement is one way we attract and build that outside interest. Media engagement is not for everyone in our business, nor is it for those lacking any capacity for such engagement. Think for example, of faculty who freeze up in front of an audience or at the microphone. It's possible to find such individuals who are nonetheless accomplished scholars. But it's exceptional. Most great scholars are also great storytellers. They just need a little help with the delivery of the story to a broader audience. More experienced scholars and administrators in your college can help with that.

There is something of a public intellectual in us all. The aim of this chapter has been to demonstrate how media engagement associated with that role can and should be carried out as part of a full professional life in the Academy. In the end, media engagement creates outside touchpoints of reference for our career. It helps us cultivate what Carlson School of Management Professor Andy Van de Ven (2007) calls "engaged scholarship," which is important to any academic, but especially important for academics in professional colleges such as law, business, and public policy. (Occasionally) answering a call from a reporter also answers a call for more engaged scholarship in your own life. Answer the call. And make a difference in the broader public we serve.

Discussion Questions

1. Does your college or university have a published media policy statement? If so, get a copy and compare it to the more general guidelines for media engagement proposed in this chapter. If neither your college nor university has a policy statement, there may be media relations personnel in a separate office or attached to the college dean or university president. Consult them for additional guidelines to follow.

2. We discussed the ethical obligation to disclose any conflicts of interest that might undermine the objectivity of information you provide to the media. What is "adequate" disclosure? How might the definition of adequate disclosure change depending on the kind of media request, time of that prospective engagement, or forum for that prospective engagement?

3. We also discussed ethical obligations that might compel you to decline media requests because you signed a non-disclosure agreement with a relevant individual or organization, perhaps when you were a consultant to one or the other. What about when there is no non-disclosure agreement specifying when and how you can speak about the individual or organization? If there is no non-disclosure agreement, what constraints might still limit your ability to comment?

4.   Who are the public intellectuals in your department, college, and university? What characteristics mark them as such? How are they valued by faculty colleagues, administration, and students, particularly doctoral students if applicable?
5.   How can you cultivate more engaged scholarship at your career stage?

Notes

1   A US Speaker of the House of Representatives may be as leery today of daily online commentaries about debates in the US House of Representatives as Burke was of Thomas Hansard's daily print commentaries about debates in his UK House of Commons.
2   Protection of student privacy by faculty in US universities and colleges is protected by FERPA (Family Educational Rights and Privacy Act) laws, and faculty are regularly reminded by administrators that faculty cannot share information about a student, even to their parents, without student permission.

References and Additional Reading

Pipes, R. 2003. *Vixit: Memoirs of a Non-Belonger*. London: Yale University Press.
Schultz, J. 1998. *Reviving the Fourth Estate*. Cambridge: Cambridge University Press.
Van de Ven, A. 2007. *Engaged Scholarship: A Guide for Organizational and Social Research*. Oxford: Oxford University Press.

30

THOUGHT LEADER

Andrew H. Van de Ven on Ethics and Professional Life

Key insight: It would be easy to fill a chapter in this book on Andrew Van de Ven's scholarship or teaching. This interview, however, is about Andy's experience and views on professional life, that is, how academics serve and support the growth of universities and other research institutions they call home, how they serve professional organizations to which they belong and occasionally lead, and how they serve communities related to both. Andy exemplifies a life of service to all three. An accomplished leader, mentor, and visionary for the management profession, Andy shared his experiences and opinions in summer 2016 about the business academic profession and professional life at different career stages. He summarizes his view on a fulfilling professional life in the Academy as part of a broader career of "engaged scholarship" (Van de Ven, 2007).

Andrew H. (Andy) Van de Ven: A Brief Introduction

Professor Andrew H. (Andy) Van de Ven's career in the business Academy spans more than 40 years. After receiving his PhD from the University of Wisconsin at Madison in 1972, Andy taught at the Wharton School of the University of Pennsylvania. He moved to the University of Minnesota's School of Management in 1982 and helped create the Department of Strategic Management and Organization (SMO), the predecessor to today's Department of Strategic Management and Entrepreneurship (SME). He has been in the SMO (and later SME) department ever since.

Andy's contributions to business scholarship on organizational behavior, innovation, change, and research methods are prodigious: 12 books; hundreds of scholarly articles in top-ranked outlets across disciplines such as management, psychology, and decision sciences; and dozens of other publications in scholarly volumes, reviews, and technical reports.

Andy's teaching contributions to the field are also well known. A pioneer in the study of innovation in organizations, Andy also wrote, tested, taught, and published numerous case studies for undergraduate students, masters and PhD students, and organizational executives. More recently, Andy's teaching interests have shifted to understanding trends in innovation and change in healthcare organizations. He is an award-winning teacher, and beloved by a generation of doctoral students now teaching in universities around the world.

At the University of Minnesota's School of Management, later renamed the Carlson School of Management, Andy served as the head of the SMO department, and as the head of various departmental, college, and university committees. He exemplifies the profession in balancing and creating synergies between research, teaching, and service. To that end, he founded research centers, including the SMO department's Strategic Management Research Center as a place to support early-stage work by doctoral students and faculty. Andy took leading roles in leading academic associations, including service as the President of the Academy of Management in 2000–2001. Andy served as one of the founding senior editors of *Organization Science*, and is the founding editor-in-chief of the Academy of Management's newest journal, *Academy of Management Discoveries*.

Andy has always sought to apply his research and teaching for the betterment of communities around universities and academic associations. As a graduate student at the University of Wisconsin, Andy applied his "nominal group technique" methods to local community meetings to increase feedback and debate on important public policy issues. Today, Andy sees discussion with executives in the C-suite and workers on the factory floor as essential components of engaged scholarship, a calling Andy also brought to the Academy of Management as its president.

For this conversation, we asked Andy to reflect on how he views "professional life" in the academy, and how a sense of purpose, motivation, and action orientation can come to life for academics at any career stage.

Question: Maybe we could define professional life as that part of an academic's career, aside from research and teaching, devoted to service on behalf of her home academic institution and her various academic associations. Tell us about professional life when you embarked on your career at the University of Wisconsin in the early 1970s.

I think back to the early 1970s when I was a doctoral student at the University of Wisconsin at Madison. The first thing I think about is that the National Guard was on the campus for nearly five years during my study. And there was mace being thrown in the streets. There were faculty, students in those streets, trying to protest. There were sit-ins at the university president's office. There was the Weather Underground. There were bombings, violence. The issues included the Vietnam War, civil rights, and social justice. It was a period of great passion – liberal political and social passion.

Now, nobody wants to see violence and disruption in a university, but the passionate views were exciting to hear, feel. It permeated the classroom, the library. It was motivating. I think that passion has been on the wane in the past 40 years. There are moments of isolated passion, but by and large, we lost something there, particularly in business schools where career advancement has always been important, but a deeper sense of passion for issues has been diminished.

Here's another trend that has changed. The business Academy was exploding then. Faculty to fill business school departments were in great demand. That has also waned. In the 1990s business school faculty ranks increased about 27 percent while the number of business consultants at top firms in the US grew more than 80 percent, in Europe it grew 300 percent, and personnel working in the corporate development – education and training – at *Fortune 500* firms grew more than 400 percent. We think the Academy of Management has grown substantially because it went from about 5,000 members in the late 1980s to more than 20,000 today. But what we used to call the America Association of Training and Development grew from a few to more than 100,000 members over the same time period.

Business academics and business schools have lost their "market share" to others in the last 40 years. More and more people are going to corporate training and consulting operations for their development; they used to come to universities. Universities have shed their interest in training students. They focus more inwardly on their own – navel gazing. Can you imagine a business professor not knowing managers, not knowing local businesses? And can you imagine that the same business professor expresses skepticism about anyone else on the faculty who *does* have that knowledge? I found that out first-hand in 2001 when I organized a meeting of local business executives with members of the Academy of Management during our annual meeting in Chicago. The lead representative for the executives told me after the meeting that he and his fellow executives felt irrelevant to discussions during the session. They felt rudely treated by academic attendees who assumed they knew *everything* about running a business.

It's symbolic of a growing disconnect we need to address in our professional lives. From the beginning, we need to think about the scholarship of engagement, teaching, and discovery – research. To treat engagement with our constituency, businesses, and their executives as a conflict with our discovery or our teaching is just foolish. Sure, it's important to prioritize different forms of scholarship, and that priority likely shifts with your career. But never think that they are in conflict. They aren't. All forms of an engaged scholarship are important to our professional lives.

Question: How would you advise a young doctoral student to think about how best to prioritize their time among engagement, teaching and discovery activities? And how about the newly-minted assistant professor?

Number one, the evidence shows that the best researchers tend to get high teaching evaluations, whether provided by students in the classroom or other university faculty and staff observing them in the classroom. The correlation is positive, not negative.[1] Number two, teaching and service assessment of doctoral students and assistant professors is *always* more favorable when it involves topics for which they have a competence, a passion. They love the topic, rather than have to address it as some chore.

So pick up an existing course or design a new course that you care deeply about, that you've written about, that you intend to write more about in the future. It's often hard to insist on anything when you are a doctoral student or a junior, untenured faculty member. I remember. But you are likely to get a department head or dean who will listen and try to accommodate you and your interest in teaching and service when that interest is paired with demonstrable competence and passion. That's a winner.

Question: You have given talks about your own approach to combining engagement with teaching and discovery. You have shared, for example, going on a visit to China to meet with executives at a large electronics firm. You invited your graduate students to come along to China and the meetings. Quite a field trip. That's not the first time you've done that, is it?

You're right. I've done that for years. Back when I was a graduate student at Wisconsin, I learned that technique from my PhD advisor, Andre Delbecq. He would ask me to tag along on visits to the university hospital to talk with doctors and the different wards they worked in day and night. Those meetings helped me develop new ideas about how organizational structure in those wards affected the quality of care. He would bring me to neighborhood block meetings where I would practice my nominal group technique method designed to get more people speaking out on issues. Andre knew that my research would benefit from this application in the field. When I reached a position to do the same as a faculty member, I resolved to "pass it on" to others as Andre Delbecq passed it on to me.

When you pass it on, you are giving something to the future of an individual, a group, an institution. There are givers and takers in our field. The takers do little or no service. And if they are good at research, they might slip by and carve out a career in a university. But his colleagues know he's a taker. They can only go so far in the institution. In the long run, a richer career in a department, a college, a university awaits the givers. They will have more to do administratively to be sure. But they will also find stronger faculty support when it comes time to plan teaching, research, occasional sabbatical leaves. In the long run, the university rewards givers more than takers.

Question: Talk more about how you prioritize your time between engagement in university and professional service and discovery – research.

Time has always been the great limiting factor for me, and I suspect for almost anyone in our line of work. So I make trade-offs like others do. For me, the goal is always to do a "little something" related to some interest even if time constraints don't let me do everything I want to do.

Think about the assistant professor managing a tenure clock and knowing that the first and last word of evaluation for grant of tenure will be about his or her research, not about his or her professional service activities. I know that feeling. Here is my advice.

When a department chair or dean asks you to contribute to some aspect of university service keep this question in mind. Is this service work part of the general and reasonably defined scope of my work as a professor? If it is, then do it. That's part of giving, not taking. And it's a good habit to develop. But if those requests become excessive, that is, so they substantially prevent you from other expectations related to research… and teaching, then decline and say why. It's always a defense simply to say: "Here is my situation…" Describe your current workload. Describe your best understanding of what that department chair or dean will ask of you regarding other expectations in due course. "I've got this commitment and this commitment and this commitment. Which one do you think I should drop to make time for your request?" That explanation is almost always a winner. If it isn't, then the problem is not with you, the assistant professor, but with the chair or the dean. Maybe you don't want to be a part of that institution. More often though, the chair or dean hearing that explanation will relent. Heck, she'll become your ally and friend. In any case, saying yes to some service and no with an explanation for excessive service requests is a realistic rule of thumb. It's part of engaged scholarship.

Question: How do you make service to professional associations as complementary to your scholarship?

My first reaction is to say that leading a professional association is just a box to tick – been there, done that. But it's a lot more. When I was President of the Academy of Management, I had the opportunity to try out ideas related to organizational innovation and change among my peers. I worked with them to create new types of sessions for the annual meeting, new chapters of the Academy

212 Ethics in Professional Life

in the developing world. We talk and write about organizational innovation and change. I got to do it, or at least try doing it.

You don't need to be president to make a difference, to try your hand at organizational innovation. Professional associations are nearly always in chronic need of volunteers. Try your ideas out on a division, interest group, a committee, a symposium. Remember, too, that your professional association colleagues are also your anonymous referees in the journal article submission and review process. Want to know what they are thinking? Work with them in the Academy of Management, Strategic Management Society, or Operations Research Society of America and the Institute of Management Sciences. Find out what makes members tick as people and as researchers. It's part of engaged scholarship.

Question: University service is usually done at the university, a place. Professional service can be all over the place geographically. Academic associations with global membership are omnipresent. It gives a cosmopolitan dimension to professional life. Talk about that.

Oh my gosh! The profession is wherever there are people I have come to know, respect, and enjoy. And what a number that is for me. I think primarily about the Academy of Management when I say that. It's given me a global perspective. It's an antidote for the daily grind of going to and from the university office or classroom. It gets us out in the world physically, and I think, in the world intellectually. It's a big, BIG part of engaged scholarship because it brings the academic to so many new places, people, and ideas.

I analogize engagement through professional associations to a log in a fire. On a cold Minnesota winter's eve, sitting in front of the fireplace is great. Notice the logs in the fireplace. Most are packed together, burning brightly. But maybe one or two roll away, smolder, and stop burning. To me, that's what disengagement from professional associations will do – lead to a smoldering career. Being part of those associations keeps you in the heat, the brightness – learning. We need to stay in the fire. That's part of engaged scholarship in professional associations, student associations, and community associations.

Question: Well the fire has gotten bigger. You said the Academy of Management has grown to more than 20,000 members. That's a pretty big fire. It's also become so much more international and so much less North American. Tell us how that shift has mattered in your career. How's the changing fire changed you?

That is a sensitive and difficult issue. I was President of the Academy of Management for a year, but the cycle leading up to the presidency is five years. Over that five years, my executive colleagues and I dealt with issues related to internationalization and how best to manage them. One approach to that management was to divide up the Academy of Management by geography. There would be a North American Academy of Management, and there would be EURAM for Europe, an Asian Academy of Management. The idea was that each area would be a source for nurturing excellence specific to their region. This way, we would encourage greater diversity in research, and greater diversity in the way that research and related teaching and service was delivered – universities could be different from the North American norm.

That didn't happen. And I think that was a mistake. Universities and business academics there so much wanted to imitate the North American model, but without the same resources, students, surrounding business communities. I thought it a bad goal for many of those non–North American institutions to pursue.

It's like a practice called "line breeding" in animal husbandry. The genetic line gets narrow, dangerously so. It stifles innovation in scholarship. That's why I have advocated for more decentralization in the Academy of Management and more "indigenous" scholarship based on local issues, theories, methods, and business support. The Academy of Management would become more like a loose alliance of operations around the world. Maybe it would be like a state fair where the best research, teaching, and service would be selected locally – like the county fairs that happen before the state fair – and then these local winners would gather periodically to share those best local practices. I think it's a better way to develop new ideas, to make a difference in the communities we serve, to do engaged scholarship.

But I got voted down and we have a different system based quite solidly, and I think wrongly, on the North American university model of research, teaching, and service.

Question: So there would be a more vibrant African Academy of Management with its own well-supported journals?

Yes, but it looks too much at structure and aims like the current Academy of Management. That's wrong. We see it here in North America. The regional Academy of Management associations have suffered a decline in recent years. Think of when you last attended a regional meeting. It wasn't always like that. With the right support and norms infused in doctoral programs, we could support (anew) the same more decentralized system of governance, research, teaching, and service. And then share periodically at international meetings.

Question: Let's shift the discussion again, this time to journals. You have written for, reviewed, and edited numerous leading journals in our field. Right now, you are founding a new journal as its editor-in-chief. It's *Academy of Management Discoveries* (AMD). What's it like to run a start-up journal?

You hit it right. It is to be an entrepreneur. It isn't at all like stepping into an editorial role at an established journal with a pipeline of papers to choose from, edit, and then judge, confident that the pipeline will continue. Everything has to be started anew. First, there are the administrative details: title, publisher, printer, web editors, mission statement, processes for manuscript submission and handling. Second, there is recruitment of associate editors, regular reviewers for the editorial board, a copy editor, and other administrative personnel. Third, you need papers to start that pipeline. Even if the journal belongs to the Academy of Management, there's a sell-job to make to would-be contributors. So that's about marketing.

I decided that serving as the founding editor for AMD was a five-year job. So I am serving that time and gladly. For all of that pain and hassle, I think I've also learned an incredible amount. Number one, I've learned what it's like to start a new venture, a business – that's what a journal is, a business. I can relate so much better to other entrepreneurs I analyze in my teaching and research. I'm one, too! I can talk with more confidence to entrepreneurs. I've been there and know what it's like – the pain, the glory, the frustration. Number two, it's an opportunity for me to publish content that others won't in the Academy of Management journals.

As an example, AMD is phenomenon-driven. I want papers that describe a phenomenon of interest and then bring theory to analyze and diagnose it. That's different from other more conventional journals where the papers are aimed at advancing theory, maybe with a moderator or mediator add-on. That's important, too, but it is not what we are always looking for as an engaged scholar. A recent issue of AMD includes papers addressing sexual assault in Brazil. The papers ask how and why people in the workforce and in the surrounding community deflect responsibility for this outrage. They shrug it off as part of the local institution governing relationships. There are huge issues like this not being addressed by our journals, and yet they are pressing issues in the workforce and in society more generally. That's the excitement about AMD. It provides scholars with a new outlet to analyze important issues in new ways.

Question: What would you tell a doctoral student or junior faculty member about how writing for a journal like AMD could serve their career?

I would tell them three things. Number one, it's an opportunity to read papers about analyzing and diagnosing phenomena. That's not part of doctoral education. It isn't a part of a junior faculty member's research seminar presentation. That's valuable experience to get early on in a career. It isn't a one-way street with theory pointing to phenomena. It's a two-way street. Number two, AMD provides an opportunity to get involved in journal writing early on in a career. We have an online comment box for AMD readers to enter a comment on a paper that's been published in AMD. Every comment is reviewed by the senior editors. If we think the comment advances our understanding, then we publish it. *Voilà*, publication. Number three, AMD provides an opportunity to become a reviewer early on in a career. We have a great editorial team, but we're a start-up. We can almost always use more help from others willing to put in the time with us. You can become a reviewer faster with us than with the established journals. Just make us an offer of your time.

Question: Let's conclude by returning to the university and department where young faculty begin their careers. What advice do you have for new faculty starting out?

When you choose the professorial life, you choose to contribute as a researcher, teacher, and service provider. When I see faculty in my career choosing to do just one of those three while neglecting the other two, then I see faculty unlikely to get tenured or promoted. When faculty do all three with some reasonable balance, they get tenured and promoted. Balance is a big part of success in this life. I'm even a skeptic when others tell me that success is about being good at two of the three legs. Others will tell the new faculty member to be a good researcher and teacher; don't worry about service. I don't like that advice. It leads to more takers rather than givers in our field.

And it neglects a core responsibility in the professorial life, that is, professorial governance. Faculty run their department, their college, their university. Sure, we have administrative staff, but they are administrative, not dispositive of key issues like curriculum, appointments, promotion. That's up to us as a faculty. New faculty should understand and appreciate how service contributions are governance contributions. We need them to contribute there just as we need their teaching and research contributions. Senior faculty should demonstrate that need in their own behavior. They need to be here in the office regularly, interacting with junior colleagues.

Question: In a world with digital technologies that permit us to be almost anywhere when we write, teach, or meet for service projects, it seems easier and easier to stay off campus. You're the opposite. You are in the office on campus nearly every weekday during the semester and in the summer months. Why?

We are social scientists by training. We are social animals by nature. We need to be engaged with others, to bounce off ideas, get feedback – both the words we learn from and the tacit learning from tone, expression. I want to see you nodding or shaking your head when I propose a new idea. Aristotle had it right when he discussed the rhetorical value of *logos, ethos,* and *pathos*. My Carlson School colleague, Shaker Zahra, added another need – for tacos. He meant that being together as a community of scholars, perhaps over tacos, is as much about collegial learning as the more individual and isolated aspects of scholarship are. Shaker is right.

Question: What do you find most encouraging about professional life as you move ahead in your career?

I can't believe that I get paid to do what this profession asks us to do. Being a professor in academic life is the best job in the world. I'm becoming an emeritus faculty member in retirement. I guess that means I'm in cruise control mode. But I've nearly always felt that way. I am continuously stimulated by my work, my students, my faculty colleagues, my friends in practice. I am as convinced today as I was more than 40 years ago that I'm creating and advancing knowledge, that I am making a difference in the lives of business executives and their firms, and the schools and academic associations dedicated to better understanding and serving them with new and novel discoveries. It feels awfully good to be a part of that now and into the future.

Discussion Questions

1. Consider what getting involved in your most prominent professional association could look like for you: Reviewing? Governance track? Conference track chair? How might you go about getting involved?
2. What are the tensions in your institution around relative weighting of research, teaching, and service? While Van de Ven recommends a balanced approach, pressures for scholarship are increasing. How might those tensions be resolved?
3. How might you go about creating "engaged scholarship" along the lines of what Van de Ven describes?
4. What energizes you about academic life, and how can you spend more time doing those things? Conversely, what takes away your energy, and how might you minimize your time in those activities?

Note

1 Empirical evidence on the teaching-research relationship is mixed; see, for example, Hattie and Marsh (1996), Bailey and Lewicki (2007) and Cadez, Dimovski, and Groff (2017).

References and Additional Reading

Bailey, James and Ray Lewicki. 2007. "The Scientist and the Sage." *BizEd*, July–August: 32–37.
Cadez, Simon, Vlado Dimovski, and Maja Zaman Groff. 2017. "Research, Teaching and Performance Evaluation in Academia: The Salience of Quality." *Studies in Higher Education*, 42. 8: 1455–1473.
Hattie, John and H.W. Marsh. 1996. "The Relationship between Research and Teaching: A Meta-Analysis." *Review of Educational Research*, 66. 4: 507–542.
Van de Ven, Andy. 2007. *Engaged Scholarship: A Guide for Organizational and Social Research*. Oxford: Oxford University Press.

PART IV

Conclusions

31

CONNECTING THE DOTS
Themes, Practices, and Considering What's Next

> **Key insight:** Our concluding chapter draws together the key themes that flow through this book: trust, transparency, consistency, and long-term focus. We briefly explore each in terms of research, teaching, and professional life.

Introduction

As we look back on the topics covered in this book, it might be easy to be discouraged about ethical behavior in academic jobs. Ethical dilemmas, it seems, lurk around every professional corner, and becoming skilled at the complex behaviors needed to manage them effectively may seem elusive. However, we want to return to our main goals for the book and remind readers that the value of such awareness is that you are much less likely to be caught off-guard when an ethical issue strikes. Moreover, you will have perhaps considered how you might respond *prior* to the situation ever occurring in your own professional life. And, while we have written about many of the most common and expected ethical dilemmas and complex situations, we don't know anyone who has experienced ALL of these ethically challenging situations in their career! So, please take heart. By increasing awareness and seeding discussions about ethical issues within our own professional communities of practice, and in effect practicing what our responses might be, we increase the chances we can resist pressures from others to behave unethically as well as increase our own confidence in handling ethical dilemmas.

For this last chapter, we wanted to help readers connect the dots among some macro concepts that have flowed through many of our discussions of research, teaching, and professional life issues. They may not be the only connections you make among the topics and chapters. Our aim here is to offer readers a 'shortlist' to identify key ethical issues to consider potential solutions, and to seek further guidance. Those connections include trust, transparency, consistency, and long-term focus, and it's important to note that all of them occur within relationships with others. For each theme, we'll discuss specific instances and salient examples throughout the book, and offer some considerations for reflections on practice. We start with an overview of the three main parts of the book: ethics in research, teaching, and professional life.

A Recap of the Book's Chapters

Ethical Dilemmas in Research

Part I opens with mini-cases based on real situations to which almost all doctoral students and/or junior faculty members can relate for discussion and debate. Issues such as dicey authorship questions, how research presentations should be done, dataset control and collection issues, and data analysis errors and problems that come with non-significant results are just some of the ethical topics typically faced. As Part I progresses, we offer a model for the professional development trajectory most academics move through, and point out key places where ethical issues in research may crop up, and where readers might anticipate them and be better prepared to face them.

Through our experiences as journal editors, we provide insights into research issues from multiple perspectives, such as how research manuscripts are vetted, what happens when we suspect or find plagiarism, and how the reward systems that privilege A-level publications can lead to poor ethical decision-making. Relatedly, we discuss issues of "salami publishing" or slicing a dataset into thin manuscript slices – sometimes too thin! We share norms of how datasets may be ethically used for multiple publications, and introduce readers to guidelines established by the Committee on Ethical Publishing, a non-governmental organization supporting scientific integrity through publication ethics.

Additionally, we move through issues of article retraction and offer a discussion frame about what happens when fraud or misconduct occurs in publishing. We ask about the double-blind review process in an age where identities are almost instantly searchable, and the implications of reviewing work if we know who the authors are. To facilitate more robust discussion, we share information about case-based scenarios housed on YouTube that were created within the Academy of Management as resources, highlighting real situations where ethics were challenged and offering the 'post-mortem' – what happened and how the scenario turned out in real life.

Part I ends with an interview with a thought leader in the field, Michael Hitt, who responds to questions about his own experiences and challenges with research ethics during his long-standing and incredibly productive career. Hitt discusses issues with managing research teams, authorship dilemmas, and ethical issues we may encounter when directing and mentoring doctoral students.

Ethical Dilemmas in Teaching

Part II opens with an invitation to consider very common ethical issues in teaching, making sure the reader understands that this part of the book considers ethics in teaching rather than teaching ethics as a disciplinary area.

As with Part I on research ethics, we strive in Part II to share issues and dilemmas that are likely to face doctoral students and junior faculty as teachers and educators. To that end, we include exemplar scenarios and discussions about all manner of teaching-related ethical issues, such as: what happens when we encounter cheating – and when students themselves admit to cheating; how being one instructor of many who teach the same course can prove ethically difficult when students start comparing workloads and teaching styles; our professional responsibilities around self-monitoring in the classroom when teaching controversial or polarizing subjects about which we have strong opinions; and ways to consider boundaries with students in the social media age.

We also share some heartfelt examples of the ethics of pedagogical caring, and what we might consider when students are clearly struggling. For example, what is our responsibility to engage with that student's personal issues that are affecting classroom and learning performance? In a related conversation, we note how changes in higher education per se are demanding a reimagining of the value of college, and what our ethical responsibilities are in terms of engaging with students not just on a content level, but of engaging with them in personal and mentoring relationships. There are all kinds of boundary issues that we discuss. There are chapters on student evaluations of teaching as well as potential ethical issues around writing student recommendations for students outside the "rock star" performance set.

Part II ends with a thought leader interview with Robert Giacalone. Bob is one of the most well-published and thoughtful scholarly leaders in both ethics education as well as in the management, spirituality, and religion domain. In the interview, we talk with Bob about his provocative article from 2011, "Broken When Entering: The Stigmatization of Goodness." There he challenges the assumption that students are open to learning ethical business practice as they become normed by business leadership education.

Ethical Dilemmas in Professional Life (Service)

Part III of the book begins, once again, with offering readers examples of common ethical dilemmas in professional life per se, such as how we should engage with codes of ethics, and resolve conflicts of interest. We then move through some unfortunate issues that have begun occurring with job offers in academe – or, what we think are job offers that are actually not firm offers – and what our responsibilities might be when finances impact the timing and structure of job offers. Norms of attendance and engagement while at professional meetings that our institutions have supported are another topic for discussion, and we revisit the idea of peer reviewing but from a service perspective, discussing how much reviewing work is appropriate and how to highlight its worth in the way our performance is evaluated. In a related conversation, we share insights about the ethics of disproportionate university service loads, and how to more fairly manage that work.

Part III then moves to issues of interdisciplinarity and our responsibilities to connect with other literatures and departments when declaring 'truth' in our research, as well as some of the ethical dilemmas surrounding outside or joint appointments and parsing out work requirements among sometimes competing departments, institutions, or committees. In a time when publicizing our work and making it "rigorous AND relevant" has become ever more important, we are led to engage more with external actors – media, consulting – and there are ethical considerations involved in these outside activities that also deserve our attention. We cannot only speak for ourselves, and in professional life it is important to recognize that our roles are broadened to include representing not only ourselves but our institutions, co-authors, or other organizations such as journals or publishers.

Part III ends with an interview with a thought leader, Andrew Van de Ven. Van de Ven's career in the Academy spans more than 40 years. He exemplifies the profession in balancing and creating synergies among research, teaching, and how he views contributions to professional life. To that end, he founded research centers, including the Strategic Management Research Center as a place to support early-stage work by doctoral students and faculty. Andy has taken leading roles in leading academic associations, including service as the President of the Academy of Management in 2000–2001. Andy served as one of the founding senior editors of *Organization Science*, and is the founding editor-in-chief of the Academy of Management's newest journal, *Academy of Management Discoveries*.

Overarching Themes in the Book

Trust

Trust is the glue of relationships and groups. Having trust in others allows for a much richer and wider range of experiences than would ever be possible or acceptable in its absence. Instead of considering our work as a series of one-off interactions, our lived experience in the Academy is based on global webs of collegial and relational creations. The fact that many of us consider academic life as our vocation speaks to how significantly trust is embedded in our working worldview. *Trust means having confidence in others* that they will do as they say they will, that they will act in reliable ways that have others' best interests in mind. If we trust someone, it means we believe they will act in ways that value our relationship with them, and that we are willing to experience the ebbs and flows of our work together.

Throughout the book, we've looked at the role of trust, and perhaps it's the most essentially relational construct we have in ethics – relationships are fundamentally about trust. We want to suggest here that it has three reflexive and particular expressions: assumed trust until broken; suspicion or a lack of trust until earned; and assumed then continued as earned. It's worth our reflection about where we fall among those expressions, because they soundly impact how we forge relationships with others and signal the type of behavior we are willing to accept. With our doctoral students, we probably assume trust when we take on a mentoring role, or with our colleagues we go into research projects probably assuming trust. We have to re-evaluate those relationships, however, when trust has been broken, such as when data are manipulated or falsified. Students in the classroom will allow us much more latitude in pushing them to learn difficult topics when they believe we have their best interests in mind – something perhaps we have to earn from them before they are willing to go along with engaged learning practices. They'll be much more likely to come to our offices and share difficulties they are experiencing outside the classroom when they believe we'll act on their behalf. Or, they'll be willing to provide evaluations of our courses in ways that signal engagement with helping us improve our teaching rather than having a critical last word. None of those scenarios is possible without trust that we earn or maintain.

Conversely, the practice of rescinding job offers once they have been offered, the subject of Chapter 22, represents broken trust. It's hard to imagine fostering a working relationship with those who let us down in such a dramatic and impactful way. Similarly, whether peer review works as intended is largely up to a consideration of trust: Does the reviewer have improving our work as the primary goal, or is there some other agenda, like "strongly recommending" that we cite specific authors' work before our manuscript may move forward toward publication? Trusting that editors' acceptance and rejection decisions are based on serving their journal's readership instead of enacting personal and self-enriching plans is one of the reasons that journal publication itself is flourishing.

Trust in academic relationships is a non-negotiable behavior, particularly as our world globally connects in ways we could not have anticipated when we joined the Academy. Many of us, for example, have co-authored work with people we have never actually met face to face, instead relying on the ease of collaborative online tools and electronic communication media. Building and maintaining trust does not have to happen face to face, or even synchronously, but it does have to be a concerted effort based on holding others in a space of respect and mutual accountability. Closely related is the idea of consistency in ethics, which we'll also discuss in this chapter.

Transparency

Being transparent in academic work has many manifestations among all three of the essential work components of research, teaching, and professional life. Transparency in ethical behaviors means *a proactive willingness to share what may not be obvious or visually apparent*. This can include being open about our motives for doing something (or not), such as how we are determining author order on a publication, or signaling in a cover letter for a journal submission exactly how one manuscript differs from another when they are based on the same dataset. Transparency can mean that we share important process-based information, such as with students being told precisely how they are being evaluated and how their work is marked at the beginning of the term. Being transparent can mean that we include both critical comments from our teaching evaluations as well as the complimentary ones in our annual faculty report. Reporting on and maintaining boundaries about conflicts of interest (or even the appearance of one) or our role with another institution in a dual appointment represents transparency that helps others gain confidence that what we're doing has integrity. The practice of "disclosure +" from Chapter 21 is a helpful and actionable way of making transparency a behavioral norm.

A key aspect of transparency is the proactivity of sharing what we've done, or are about to do, and sharing with others the 'why' of our actions. Transparency does not 'work' the same way when something we've done is discovered; excuses on an *ex post* basis do not serve to build confidence in others that we have *a priori* considered ethical implications of our position, work, or decision, and have been willing to share them. Thus, transparency has the added requirement of being on the front end of our academic practices, in the form of disclosure, rather than on the back end, in the form of explanation.

Transparency in relationships and workplace responsibilities has a helpful way of being assessed, quickly and relatively accurately, in the "Billboard Principle" – considering how others might perceive your actions if they were advertised on a billboard, or in the newspaper headlines. (Katz and Green, 2013) If what you're considering doing, or not doing, could be viewed negatively by those around you if they knew about it, such action or inaction deserves more thought and energy.

Consistency

In some ways, consistency can be an antecedent of trust; it's quite difficult to trust someone when their behavior varies widely, unpredictably, or even wildly. Throughout the book, *consistency* has taken on important forms that ultimately serve the purpose of *allowing those around us to be reasonably certain that we will behave in ways they can count on*. Consistency in behavior is an ethical issue because it's a disciplined approach to interactions, and it allows others to consider our practices within a frame they can understand and anticipate.

Consistency in research practice can mean our work is verifiable and replicable, allowing others to confirm and build on our findings. Consistent practices in data analysis, too, can keep 'analysis' from becoming 'snooping' as shown in Chapter 9, Scenario 4, where episodic and self-serving variable or construct 'edits' may render research results difficult to justify.

Retraction Watch, the leading and independent site that tracks and reports on research improprieties that result in articles being removed from publications, could be seen as an arbiter of consistency. It's consistency, in many ways, that is a factor weighing in on whether a scholar and their work appear on Retraction Watch's Leaderboard. A mistake, of course, is not the same as systematic manipulation or outright falsification of data, and at least some of that consideration falls on whether that scholar's research consistently exhibits questionable attributes.

Consistency takes the form of reliability when it comes to teaching evaluations, and the comments students make over time about our teaching practices. Just as with research outcomes, reliability in student evaluations has real and lasting impact on our careers. If we have bad evaluations for a section of a course or even all courses in one semester, but those evaluations represent an outlier picture of how students over time have experienced us as teachers, we would expect repercussions to take a very different form than if poor evaluations were consistently delivered by our students. Ethical consistency would require more discussion about what happened – what might have been unique or different that term? – rather than encountering a knee-jerk reaction of sanctions or a salary hit by administrators. The same could be true for students' work and the way it's evaluated. If a student routinely turns in outstanding work, but for one or two assignments we receive dismal quality work from her, the ethical discipline of consistency may lead us to reach out to her to explore what might be going on, instead of simply recording failing marks.

In professional life, consistently looking beyond our disciplinary silos builds confidence that we're examining as a topic holistically and that we're willing to learn from others before us and around us. Such engagement makes it easier for our colleagues, for example, to know our recommendations on committees or evaluations for promotion and tenure are grounded in best practices from different academic traditions. Peer review, too, benefits from editors being able to call on us as careful judges of submitted manuscripts where we have only commented on those areas in which we have expertise.

Kelley's Covariation Model of attribution theory relies on consistency as a key yardstick of whether someone is responsible for actions others perceive, and it's helpful here: if we're consistent in responding to our work and our colleagues in particular ways, and others can rely on us because of that consistency, we're more likely to get some understanding and a second chance when something goes awry. The flexibility afforded to us in relationships when our behavior is built on ethical consistency can be a make-or-break factor in a geographically distributed Academy, when we may not have the benefit of calling a colleague to clear up a misunderstanding, or we may not fully understand the context in which our collaborator is working. Consistency affords us a second look, and if our behavior falls out of that consistent pattern, we earn the right to being given the benefit of the doubt.

Long-Term Focus

Finally, the time-frame within which we do our work is a theme running throughout the book. The type of academic career trajectories in which the ethical issues we described can occur is a traditional, tenure-track to (hopefully) tenured position, and as such is predicated on a long-term model. Being aware of the *long-term focus of our work means understanding the iterative nature of working in the Academy* among colleagues we will encounter many times, in many different contexts, over our careers. The process of earning tenure and moving through to the rank of professor may itself run 15–20 years. There may be colleagues with whom we co-author for more than one paper or project; sometimes, there are career-long collaborations that result in enormous productivity and professional gratification. Although our student rosters change each term, much about our teaching practice requires evolution over time: our foundational teaching philosophy, our reputations as instructors, our teaching material troves. Professional service and engagement work, too, tends to ramp up over time, moving from our being participants on committees to chairing them, or moving from ad hoc peer reviewing to editorial board membership.

Throughout the book we've shared instances of and reflections on where trade-offs between short- and long-term outcomes are evident. Sacrificing data gathering or analysis integrity for the sake of a hit in a sparklingly high-profile journal will, in an age of Google and repositories like Research Gate, eventually lead to difficult questions being asked, a spot on Retraction Watch, or even an entire career derailed. If that scenario seems dire and unlikely, we need only to point to the poor research ethics choices made by Michael LaCour, and his now infamous canvassing study retracted from *Science*, as an example. Encouraging doctoral students or junior faculty to cut research corners, or modeling poor research ethics ourselves, is an unfortunately powerful norming practice that can have a decades-long effect on others.

In Chapter 16, we shared incidences of student struggles and despair, where engaging in an emotionally complex relational role became an ethical issue. Such struggles in college have the chance to become embedded aspects of students' selves and have a potentially long-range impact on their identity as adult learners. Chapter 19 shares stories and examples of how student letters of recommendation could be decisive pieces of an opportunity they may otherwise not be able to access. And, in the professional ethics part of the book, Chapter 23 notes the strong precedential effect on others that failing to show up for professional meetings for which we have had work accepted and appearing on the program – others, particularly less seasoned faculty, take their behavioral cues from more senior people in terms of what's acceptable. It's transparency in a different way: We are more visible than we think in our community-based behaviors, and others are watching to see how we behave. Those engaged in ethics as a disciplinary research or teaching field, too, are perhaps held at a higher standard for 'walking the talk.'

It's tempting, in our busy and multifaceted academic work lives, to consider these issues as one-off instances of decisions. Should we write the letter for that slightly below-average student? Should we data 'snoop' this one time for significant results? Should we vote against promotion for that annoying (yet deserving) colleague with whom we had an authorship disagreement five years ago? Should we take a walk on the beach instead of attend the conference session for which we are chair? Our work, as a long-term-oriented endeavor, offers so many benefits of deepened and richly iterative and developmental outcomes that those in industry, perhaps, do not get to experience. The other side, however, is recognizing those long-term implications of our decisions – there may be few places to hide, waiting for our colleagues to forget, when there has been an ethical breach. By considering both the immediate context of a dilemma as well as the implications for what the likely outcomes might be down the road, we can employ a fuller choice set of potential resolutions to a situation we're experiencing as potentially unethical.

A Final Note

In this book, we have asked you to consider situations, issues, and scenarios for your own reflection while weighing in with our normative responses to them. If we have one final piece of advice it is that when faced with an ethical dilemma, seek counsel on what to do. You do not have to do this alone.

As its co-authors, we are aware of the prescriptive nature of our book. Throughout the book, we have included a variety of normative ethical reasoning tools to assist you in evaluating complex situations, such as professional ethical codes (Chapter 3, Chapter 21), the Committee on Publishing Ethics Guidelines (Chapter 5), institutional academic honesty or honor codes (Chapter 12), Hosmer's ethical framework (Chapter 19), and reporting designed for transparency (Chapter 28). There are many other frameworks, some of which we have listed below in Additional Resources, but we wanted to broaden the frameworks in value-added ways to share those we found immediately helpful in difficult situations we have faced.

It has been a balancing act to write from both a descriptive as well as a normative space. We are also present to the intentionality of action included in our topics and examples, leaving the unintentional but very powerful reasons why people behave unethically to our colleagues (please see, for example, Bazerman and Tenbrunsel's work in blind spots (2012), or Harvard's Project Implicit). Our hope is to have provided food for thought and some structured ways of considering the ethical dilemmas that are commonly encountered in our profession, and ways to respond that preserve integrity and reputation over the long term. We would be delighted to hear from you – what worked, what did not, what your experiences have been, and how such situations were ultimately resolved. We invite you to continue the conversation!

References

Joseph Badaracco (2016) invites those facing ethical dilemmas to consider their options through five key questions:

1. What are the net consequences of all my options?
2. What are my core obligations?
3. What will work in the world as it is?
4. Who are we?
5. What can I live with?

Badaracco, Joseph L. 2016. "How to Tackle Your Toughest Decisions." *Harvard Business Review*, 94.9: 104–107.

Bazerman and Tenbrunsel: These authors offer robust conversations about why we persist in making unethical decisions, made more complex because we think we are being ethical! Using experiments and examples, Bazerman and Tenbrunsel offer ways of recognizing our own blind spots and working to lessen the negative impact. Bazerman, Max H. and Ann E. Tenbrunsel. 2012. *Blind Spots: Why We Fail to Do What's Right and What to Do about It*. Princeton, NJ: Princeton University Press.

Harvard University has housed the Implicit Association Test within Project Implicit since 1998. Project Implicit, a non-profit organization that explores links between intention and action, offers research as well as powerful self-assessments testing one's own implicit biases among many different demographics such as gender and race. Materials available at: https://implicit.harvard.edu/implicit/

The Billboard Principle can be a very helpful first-stop 'test' of something we are considering doing, saying, or conversely leaving out. A one-minute video demonstration of this is from Katz and Green. Videos available at: https://katzesb.wordpress.com/part-1-chapters-1-2-3-4/chapter-2-the-billboard-principle-in-action/Katz, J. and R. Green. 2013. *Entrepreneurial Small Business*. New York: McGraw-Hill Irwin.

Kelley's Covariation Model of attribution theory, which helps us understand from where a behavioral reaction might be coming in an ethical dilemma. It may help us understand how context matters in ethical decision making by particularly considering consistency in behavior. Kelley, H.H. 1971. *Attribution in Social Interaction*. New York: General Learning Press.

Kelley, H.H. 1973. "The Process of Causal Attribution." *American Psychologist*, 28: 107–128.

Kelley, H.H. and J.L. Michela. 1980. "Attribution Theory and Research." *Annual Review of Psychology*, 31: 457–501.

McGuire's Inoculation Theory, which offers an empirically grounded process by which we may resist pressures from others to engage in behaviors or accept values that we do not want to do or accept. McGuire, W.J. 1961. "The Effectiveness of Supportive and

Refutational Defenses in Immunizing and Restoring Beliefs against Persuasion." *Sociometry*, 24: 184–197.

McGuire, W.J. 1964. "Inducing Resistance to Persuasion." In L. Berkowitz (ed.), *Advances in Experimental Social Psychology* (Vol. 1, pp. 191–229). New York: Academic Press.

Retraction Watch (retractionwatch.com) is an independently funded site that collates and lists major research project and article retractions across any discipline. The goal of Retraction Watch is "Tracking retractions as a window into the scientific process" to increase both transparency of unethical behavior and call out those who consistently violate ethical research practices.

Retraction Watch Leader Board (http://retractionwatch.com/the-retraction-watch-lea derboard/) shows what its name implies: The dishonorable list of researchers with the most articles retracted from published sources.

Linda Treviño and Katherine Nelson crafted an eight-step decision-making process that supplies a structured reasoning method many find helpful.

1. Gather the facts.
2. Define the ethical issue.
3. Identify the affected parties.
4. Identify the consequences.
5. Identify the obligations.
6. Consider your character and identity.
7. Think creatively about potential actions.
8. Check your intuition.

Linda Treviño and Katherine Nelson. 1995. *Managing Business Ethics: Straight Talk about How to Do It Right*. New York: Wiley.

INDEX

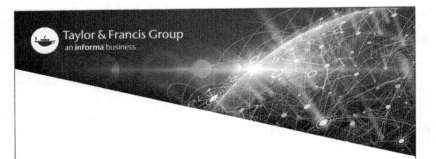